Authors

Dr. Gordon Gore
BIG Little Science Centre (Kamloops)

Lionel Sandner
Edvantage Interactive

EDVANTAGE
INTERACTIVE

COPIES OF THIS BOOK MAY BE OBTAINED BY CONTACTING:

Edvantage Interactive

E-MAIL:
info@edvantageinteractive.com

TOLL-FREE FAX:
866.275.0564

TOLL-FREE CALL:
866.422.7310

ISBN 978-1-77430-038-1

Vice-President of Marketing: *Don Franklin*
Director of Publishing: *Yvonne Van Ruskenveld*
Design/Illustration/Production: *Donna Lindenberg*
Photos: *p. 10, K. Jung; p. 11, Bureau international des poids et mesures (BIPM)*
Chapter 9 Illustrations: *Syed Abdul Qadir*

ACKNOWLEDGEMENT

The Edvantage Interactive author and editorial team would like to thank Asma-na-hi Antoine, Toquaht Nation, Nuu-chah-nulth, Manager of Indigenous Education & Student Services, Royal Roads University and the Heron People Circle at Royal Roads University for their guidance and support in the ongoing development of resources to align to the Physics 11 curriculum.

QR Code — What Is This?
The image to the right is called a QR code. It's similar to bar codes on various products and contains information that can be useful to you. Each QR code in this book provides you with online support to help you learn the course material. For example, find a question with a QR code beside it. If you scan that code, you'll see the answer to the question explained in a video created by an author of this book.
You can scan a QR code using an Internet-enabled mobile device. The program to scan QR codes is free and available at your phone's app store. Scanning the QR code above will give you a short overview of how to use the codes in the book to help you study.
Note: We recommend that you scan QR codes only when your phone is connected to a WiFi network. Depending on your mobile data plan, charges may apply if you access the information over the cellular network. If you are not sure how to do this, please contact your phone provider or us at info@edvantageinteractive.com

Welcome to the ____________________ traditional lands.

We would like to acknowledge the traditional territory of the ____________________ people and extend our appreciation for the opportunity to learn on this land.

Understanding the Welcome and the Land Acknowledgments

At the beginning of each day, students and teachers are encouraged to start with a welcome or land acknowledgement. The traditional teachings for this practice are to understand the history of these lands as well as the history of indigenous people to the present day. A welcome to the traditional land can only be done by members from the Nation(s) and are approved by an Elder and/or Chief and Council. Guests and visitors who live, work, learn and play within the traditional lands conduct a Land Acknowledgement. On the previous page both examples are included for use in your classroom. Your teacher will provide guidance on the practice to be used in your class.

Reflection on Terminology

The Ministry of Education in British Columbia defines the follows terms:

Aboriginal

Aboriginal is a term defined in the Constitution Act of 1982 that refers to all indigenous people in Canada (status and non-status), Métis, and Inuit people. More than one million people in Canada identified themselves as Aboriginal on the 2006 Census, and are the fastest growing population in Canada.

First Nations

A First Nation is the self-determined political and organizational unit of the Aboriginal community that has the power to negotiate, on a government-to government basis, with BC and Canada. Currently, there are 615 First Nation communities in Canada, which represent more than 50 nations or cultural groups and about 60 Aboriginal languages.

First Peoples

First Peoples refers to First Nations, Métis, and Inuit peoples in Canada, as well as indigenous peoples around the world.

Indigenous

Indigenous has become more used recently provincially, federally, and internationally to replace "Aboriginal," but the terms are frequently used interchangeably.

Inuit

Inuit are Aboriginal peoples whose origins are different from people known as "North American Indians." The Inuit generally live in northern Canada and Alaska.

Métis

Métis is a person of French and Aboriginal ancestry belonging to or descended from the people who established themselves in the Red, Assiniboine, and Saskatchewan River valleys during the 19th century, forming a cultural group distinct from both European and Aboriginal peoples. The Métis were originally based around fur trade culture, when French and Scottish traders married First Nations women in the communities they traded with. The Métis created their own communities and cultural ways distinct from those of the First Nations. This term has also come to mean anyone of First Nations mixed ancestry who self-identifies as Métis.

In respect to traditional teachings from Elders, it is best to ask what terminology or title, individual or families would prefer when being acknowledged.

Written by Indigenous Consultants:

Asma-na-hi Antoine, Toquaht Nation, Nuu-chah-nulth, Manager of Indigenous Education & Student Services, Royal Roads University

Shirley Alphonse, Cowichan Tribes, resides in T'Sou-ke Nation, member of the Heron People Circle at Royal Roads University

Reference

BC Ministry of Education (2019) Retrieved from https://curriculum.gov.bc.ca/sites/curriculum.gov.bc.ca/files/pdf/glossary.pdf

For more information:
edvantagescience.com

Contents

1 Introduction to the Skills of Physics

Using the skills developed in this chapter, you should be able to do the following:

- Describe the nature of physics
- Apply the skills and methods of physics including:
  - conduct appropriate experiments
  - systematically gather and organize data from experiments
  - produce and interpret graphs
  - verify relationships (e.g., linear, inverse, square, and inverse square) between variables
  - use models (e.g., physics formulae, diagrams, graphs) to solve a variety of problems
  - use appropriate units and metric prefixes
  - perform vector analysis in one or two dimensions

By the end of this chapter, you should know the meaning to these key terms:

- accuracy
- dependent variable
- experimental error
- independent variable
- law
- linear function
- model
- precision
- scientific method
- slope
- uncertainty
- *y*-intercept

In this chapter, you'll learn about the tools, skills, and techniques you'll be using as you study physics and about the nature of physics itself.

1.1 What is Physics?

Warm Up

This is probably your first formal physics course. In the space below, describe your definition of physics.

____

____

____

Physics Explains the World

We live in an amazing place in our universe. In what scientists call the Goldilocks principle, we live on a planet that is just the right distance from the Sun, with just the right amount of water and just the right amount of atmosphere. Like Goldilocks in the fairy tale eating, sitting, and sleeping in the three little bears' home, Earth is just right to support life.

Yet there is much that we don't know about our planet. To study science is to be part of the enterprise of observing and collecting evidence of the world around us. The study of physics is part of this global activity. In fact, from the time you were a baby, you have been a physicist. Dropping food or a spoon from your baby chair was one of your first attempts to understand gravity. You probably also figured out how to get attention from an adult when you did this too, but let's focus on you being a little scientist. Now that you are a teenager you are beginning the process of formalizing your understanding of the world. Hopefully, this learning will never stop as there are many questions we do not have answers to and the wonder of discovering why things happen the way they do never gets boring. That is part of the excitement of physics — you are always asking why things happen.

Physics will give you many opportunities to ask, "Why did that happen?" To find the answers to this and other questions, you will learn skills and processes to help you better understand concepts such as acceleration, force, waves, and special relativity. You will learn how to apply what you have learned in math class to solve problems or write clear, coherent explanations using the skills from English class. In physics class, you can apply the skills and concepts you have learned in other classes. Let's begin by looking at one method used to investigate and explain natural phenomena: the scientific method.

The Scientific Method

How do you approach the problems you encounter in everyday life? Think about beginning a new class at the start of the school year, for example. The first few days you make observations and collect data. You might not think of it this way, but when you observe your classmates, the classroom, and your teachers, you are making observations and collecting data. This process will inevitably lead you to make some decisions as you consider the best way to interact with this new environment. Who would you like for a partner in this class? Where do you want to sit? Are you likely to interact well with this particular teacher? You are drawing conclusions. This method of solving problems is called the **scientific method**. In future courses you may have an opportunity to discuss how the scientific method varies depending on the situation and the type of research being undertaken. For this course, an introduction to the scientific method is provided to give you a foundation to develop habits of thinking scientifically as you explore our world.

Figure 1.1.1 *Galileo (top) and Newton*

Four hundred years ago, scientists were very interested in understanding the world around them. There were hypotheses about why the Sun came up each day or why objects fell to the ground, but they were not based on evidence. Two physicists who used the scientific method to support their hypotheses were the Italian Galileo Galilei (1564–1642) and the Englishman Sir Isaac Newton (1642–1727).

Both Galileo and Newton provided insights into how our universe works on some fundamental principles. Galileo used evidence from his observations of planetary movement to support the idea that Earth revolved around the Sun. However, he was forced to deny this conclusion when put on trial. Eventually, his evidence was accepted as correct and we now consider Galileo one of the fathers of modern physics. Sir Isaac Newton, also considered one of the fathers of modern physics, was the first to describe motion and gravity. In this course, you will be introduced to his three laws of motion and the universal law of gravitation. Both ideas form a foundation for classical physics. Like many others that followed, both Galileo and Newton made their discoveries through careful observation, the collection of evidence, and interpretations based on that evidence.

Different groups of scientists outline the parts of the scientific method in different ways. Here is one example, illustrating its steps.

Steps of the Scientific Method

1. **Observation**: Collection of data. **Quantitative** observation has numbers or quantities associated with it. **Qualitative** observation describes qualities or changes in the quality of matter including, for example, a substance's color, odor, or physical state.
2. **Statement of a hypothesis**: Formulation of a statement in an "if…then…" format that explains the observations.
3. **Experimentation**: Design and carry out a procedure to determine whether the hypothesis accurately explains the observations. After making a set of observations and formulating a hypothesis, scientists devise an experiment. During the experiment they carefully record additional observations. Depending on the results of the experiment, the hypothesis may be adjusted and experiments repeated to collect new observations many times.

   Sometimes the results of an experiment differ from what was expected. There are a variety of reasons this might happen. Things that contribute to such differences are called **sources of error**. They can include random errors over which the experimenter has no control and processes or equipment that can be adjusted, such as inaccurate measuring instruments.

4. **Statement of a Theory**: Statement of an explanation for the hypotheses being investigated. Once enough information has been collected from a series of experiments, a reasoned and coherent explanation called a theory may be deduced. This theory may lead to a **model** that helps us understand the theory. A model is usually a simplified description or representation of a theory or phenomenon that can help us study it. Sometimes the scientific method leads to a **law**, which is a general statement of fact, without an accompanying set of explanations.

Quick Check

1. What is the difference between a law and a theory?

2. What are the fundamental steps of the scientific method?

3. Classify the following observations as quantitative or qualitative by placing a checkmark in the correct column. **Hint:** Look at each syllable of those words: quantitative and qualitative. What do they seem to mean?

Observation	Quantitative	Qualitative
Acceleration due to gravity is 9.8 m/s^2.		
A rocket travels faster than fighter jet.		
The density of scandium metal is 2.989 g/cm^3.		
Copper metal can be used for wire to conduct electricity.		
Mass and velocity determine the momentum in an object.		
Zinc has a specific heat capacity of 388 J/(kg·K).		
The force applied to the soccer ball was 50 N.		

4. Use the steps of the scientific method to design a test for the following hypotheses:
   (a) If cardboard is used to insulate a cup, it will keep a hot drink warmer.

   (b) If vegetable oil is used to grease a wheel, the wheel will turn faster.

   (c) If hot water is placed in ice cube trays, the water will freeze faster.

The Many Faces of Physics

There are many different areas of study in the field of physics. Figure 1.1.2 gives an overview of the four main areas. Notice how the areas of study can be classified by two factors: size and speed. These two factors loosely describe the general themes studied in each field. For example, this course focusses mainly classical mechanics, which involves relatively large objects and slow speeds.

A quick Internet search will show you many different ways to classify the areas of study within physics. The search will also show a new trend in the study of sciences, a trend that can have an impact on your future. Rather than working in one area of study or even within one discipline such as physics, biology, or chemistry, inter-disciplinary studies are becoming common. For example, an understanding of physics and biology might allow you to work in the area of biomechanics, which is the study of how the human muscles and bones work. Or maybe you will combine biology and physics to study exobiology, the study of life beyond the Earth's atmosphere and on other planets.

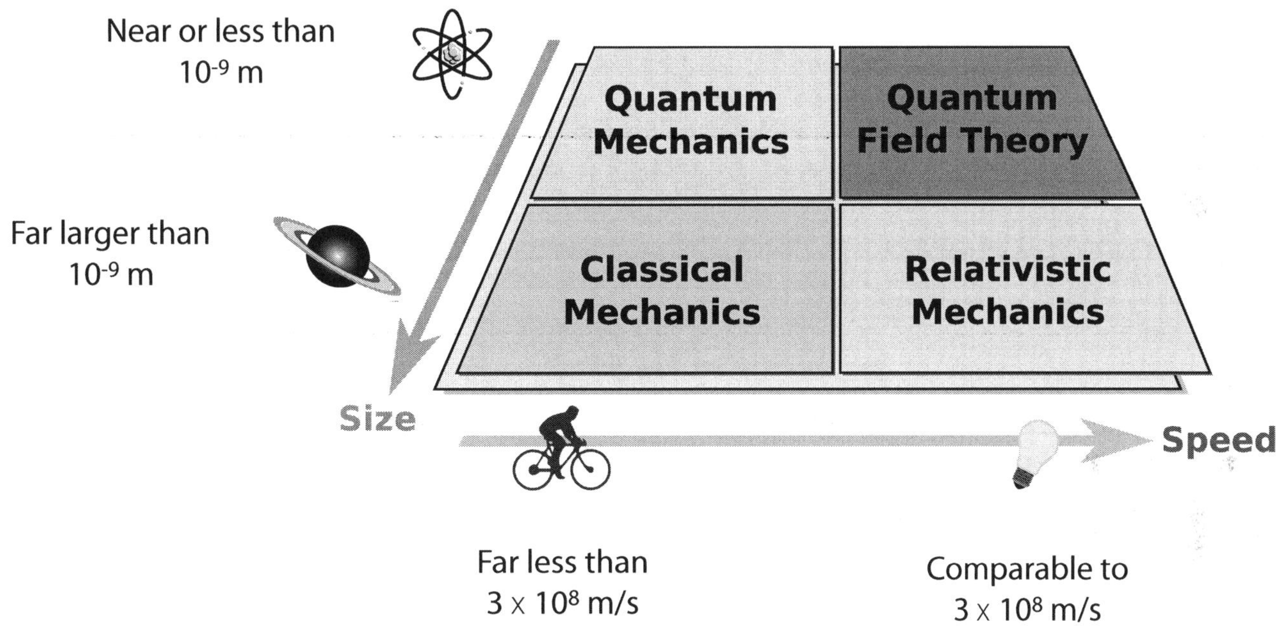

Figure 1.1.2 *The four main areas of physics. (Credit: Yassine Mrabet)*

1.2 Essential Skills

Warm Up

Your teacher will give you a pendulum made from some string and a washer. One swing of the pendulum back and forth is called a period and measured in seconds. Work with a partner to determine the period of your pendulum. Outline your procedure and results below. When you are done, identify one thing you would change in your procedure to improve your answer.

Using a Calculator

A calculator is a tool that helps you perform calculations during investigations and solving problems. You'll have your calculator with you for every class. At the same time, however, you are not to rely on it exclusively. You need to understand what the question is asking and what formula or calculation you need to use before you use your calculator. If you find yourself just pushing buttons to find an answer without understanding the question, you need to talk to your teacher or a classmate to figure it out. Many times you'll just need one concept clarified and then you can solve the problem.

Every calculator is different in terms of what order of buttons you need to push to find your answer. Use the Quick Check below to ensure you can find trigonometric functions and enter and manipulate exponents. If you cannot find the answers for these questions, check with your teacher immediately.

Quick Check

Using your calculator, what are the answers to the following mathematical statements?

1. sin 30° ____________________
2. $\tan^{-1}$ .345 ____________________
3. 34^2 ____________________
4. $(3.2 \times 10^{-4}) \times (2.5 \times 10^{6})$ ____________________
5. pi – cos 60° ____________________

Measuring Time

For objects that have a regularly repeated motion, each complete movement is called a **cycle**. The time during which the cycle is completed is called the **period** of the cycle. The number of cycles completed in one unit of time is called the **frequency** (*f*) of the moving object. You may be familiar with the frequencies of several everyday objects. For example, a car engine may have a frequency of several thousand rpm (revolutions per minute).

The turntable of an old phonograph record player may have frequencies of 33 rpm, 45 rpm, or 78 rpm. A pendulum 24.85 cm long has a frequency of one cycle per second. Tuning forks may have frequencies such as 256 vibrations per second, 510 vibrations per second, and so on.

Any measurement of time involves some sort of event that repeats itself at regular intervals. For example, a year is the time it takes Earth to revolve around the Sun; a day is the time it takes Earth to rotate on its axis; a month is approximately the time it takes the Moon to revolve around Earth. Perhaps *moonth* would be a better name for this time interval.

All devices used to measure time contain some sort of regularly vibrating object such as a pendulum, a quartz crystal, a tuning fork, a metronome, or even vibrating electrons. With a pendulum you can experiment with the properties to make it a useful timing device. When a pendulum undergoes regularly repeated movements, each complete movement is called a cycle, and the time required for each cycle is called its period.

A frequency of one cycle per second is called a **hertz** (**Hz**). Higher frequencies (such as radio signal frequencies) may be expressed in kilohertz (kHz) or even megahertz (MHz), where 1 kHz is 1000 Hz, and 1 MHz is 1 000 000 Hz.

The Recording Timer

In Investigation 1.2.1, you will use a device called a recording timer like the one in Figure 1.2.1. The timer is a modified electric buzzer. A moving arm driven by an electromagnet vibrates with a constant frequency, and each time it vibrates, it strikes a piece of carbon paper. The carbon paper makes a small dot on a moving piece of ticker tape. The small dots are a record of both time and distance. If you know the frequency of vibration of the timer, you can figure out the period of time between the dots, because period (T) and frequency (f) are reciprocals of one another.

Figure 1.2.1 *A recording timer that uses ticker tape to record time and distance*

$$T = 1/f, \text{ and } f = 1/T$$

If you measure the distance between the dots, this will tell you how far the object attached to the tape has moved. Knowing both distance and time, you can also calculate speed, since the speed of an object is the distance travelled divided by the time.

Using a Motion Probe

Another method for recording motion is a motion probe. There are several different models that can be used, but they all follow the same basic principles. Using a computer or graphing calculator, the probe is plugged in and run via a software program. The software program collects data on the motion you are studying and represents them as a graph on your computer screen.

Using the data collected, you can analyze the motion. Your teacher will demonstrate how to use the motion probe in your lab.

Accuracy and Precision

Measured values are determined using a variety of different measuring devices. There are devices designed to measure all sorts of different quantities. The collection pictured in Figure 1.2.2 measures temperature, length, and volume. In addition, there are a variety of precisions (exactnesses) associated with different devices. The micrometer (also called a caliper) is more precise than the ruler while the burette and pipette are more precise than the graduated cylinder.

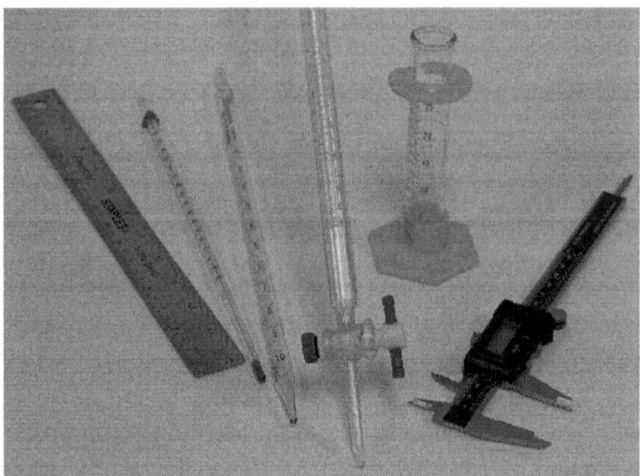

Figure 1.2.2 *A selection of measuring devices with different levels of precision*

Despite the fact that some measuring devices are more precise than others, it is impossible to design a measuring device that gives perfectly exact measurements. All measuring devices have some degree of **uncertainty** associated with them.

The 1-kg mass shown in Figure 1.2.3 is kept in a helium-filled bell jar at the BIPM in Sèvres France. It is the only exact mass on the planet. All other masses are measured relative to this and therefore have some degree of uncertainty associated with them.

In May 2019 the definition of the kilogram was changed. Rather than a physical object as the standard, the new definition is based on Planck's constant - a tiny, but unvarying number. While the change will have no direct impact on your daily life, it does make life a bit easier for any scientist neeing ultra-precise measurements of mass.

> **Accuracy** refers to the agreement of a particular value with the *true value.*

Accurate measurements depend on careful design and calibration to ensure a measuring device is in proper working order. The term **precision** can actually have two different meanings.

> *Precision* refers to the reproducibility of a measurement or the agreement among several measurements of the same quantity.
>
> – *or* –
>
> *Precision* refers to the exactness of a measurement. This relates to uncertainty: the lower the uncertainty of a measurement, the higher the precision.

A measurement can be very precise, yet very inaccurate. In 1895, a scientist estimated the time it takes planet Venus to rotate on its axis to be 23 h, 57 min, 36.2396 s. This is a very precise measurement! Unfortunately, it was found out later that the period of rotation of Venus is closer to 243 days! The latter measurement is much less precise, but probably a good deal more accurate!

Figure 1.2.3 *This kilogram mass was made in the 1880s. In 1889, it was accepted as the international prototype of the kilogram. (©BIPM — Reproduced with permission)*

Experimental Error

There is no such thing as a perfectly accurate measurement. Measurements are always subject to some uncertainty. Consider the following sources of experimental error.

Systematic Errors

Systematic errors may result from using an instrument that is in some way inaccurate. For example, if a wooden metre stick is worn at one end and you measure from this end, every reading will be too high. If an ammeter needle is not properly "zeroed," all the readings taken with the meter will be too high or too low. Thermometers must be regularly checked for accuracy and corrections made to eliminate systematic errors in temperature readings.

Random Errors

Random errors occur in almost any measurement. For example, imagine you make five different readings of the length of a laboratory bench. You might obtain results such as: 1.626 m, 1.628 m, 1.624 m, 1.626 m, and 1.625 m. You might average these measurements and express the length of the bench in this way: 1.626 ± 0.002 m. This is a way of saying that your average measurement was 1.626 m, but the measurements, due to random errors, range between 1.624 m and 1.628 m.

Quick Check

Four groups of Earth Science students use their global positioning systems (GPS) to do some geocaching. The diagrams below show the students' results relative to where the actual caches were located.

1. Comment on the precision of the students in each of the groups. (In this case, we are using the "reproducibility" definition of precision.)

   ____

2. What about the accuracy of each group?

   ____

3. Which groups were making systematic errors?

   ____

4. Which groups made errors that were more random?

   ____

Other Errors

Regardless of the accuracy and precision of the measuring instrument, errors may arise when you, the experimenter, interact with the instrument. For example, if you measure the thickness of a piece of plastic using a micrometre caliper, your reading will be very precise but inaccurate if you tighten the caliper so much that you crush the plastic with the caliper!

A common personal error made by inexperienced experimenters is failing to read scales with eye(s) in the proper position. In Figure 1.2.4, for example, only observer B will obtain the correct measurement for the length of the block.

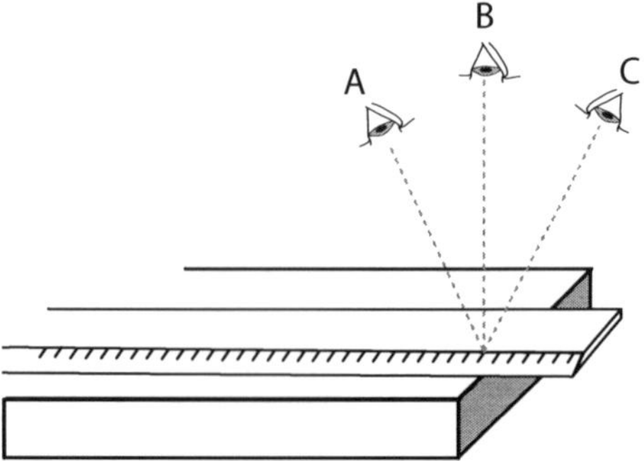

Figure i.2.4 *Observers A and C will make incorrect readings because of their positions relative to the ruler.*

Graphing

In Figure 1.2.5, a variable y is plotted against a variable x. Variable y is the **dependent** variable and variable x is the **independent** variable. In this particular situation, the graph is a straight line. (You might say that variable y is a **linear function** of the variable x.)

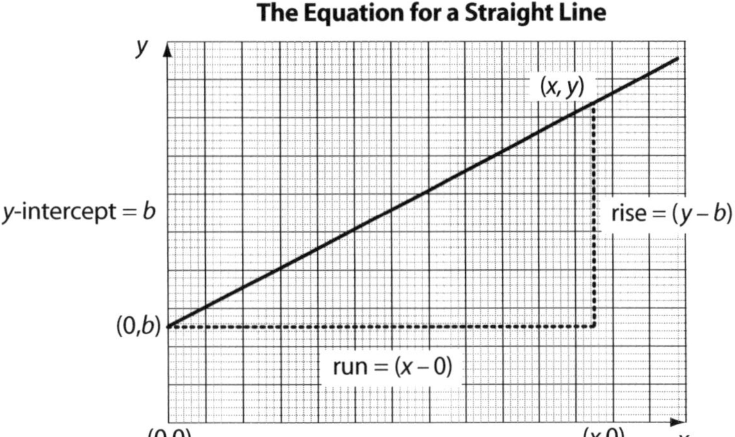

Figure 1.2.5 *In a straight line graph like this one, the variable y is a linear function of the variable x*

The **slope** of the graph is given the symbol m, where $m = \frac{\text{rise}}{\text{run}}$.

To find the value of the slope, the two points with coordinates $(0,b)$ and (x, y) will be used. The value of y where the graph intercepts the y-axis is called the **y-intercept**, and it is given the symbol b.

$$\text{Since } m = \frac{\text{rise}}{\text{run}} = \frac{(y - b)}{(x - 0)},$$

Therefore, $mx = y - b$, or

$$y = mx + b$$

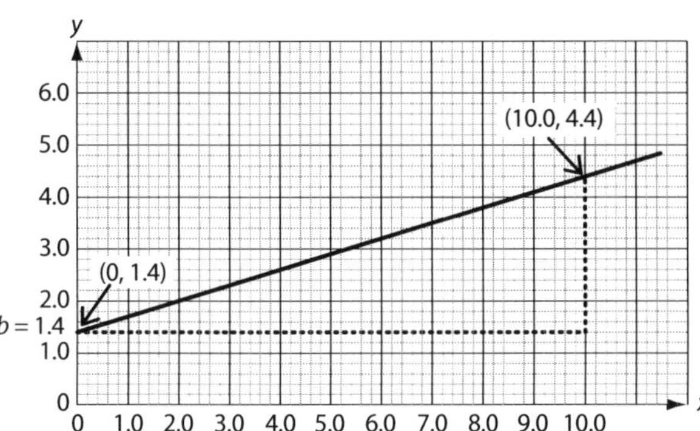

Figure 1.2.6 *The slope of a line can be calculated using just two points.*

This is a general equation for any straight line. The slope of the line is m and the y-intercept is b.

To write an equation for any straight-line graph, you need only determine the value of the y-intercept by inspection and the slope by calculation. You can then substitute these values into the general equation.

For the linear graph in Figure 1.2.6, the y-intercept, by inspection, is 1.4. ($b = 1.4$) The **slope** is calculated using the two points with coordinates (0, 1.4) and (10.0, 4.4).

$$m = \frac{(4.4 - 1.4)}{(10.0 - 0)} = \frac{3.0}{10.0} = 0.30$$

The equation for this straight line is therefore: $y = 0.30\,x + 1.4$

In these examples, the units of measure of the variables have not been included, in order to simplify the explanation. In experiments, the observations you make are frequently summarized in graphical form. When graphing experimental data, always include the measuring units and the specific symbols of the variables being graphed.

The three most common types of graphic relationships are shown in Figure 1.2.7.

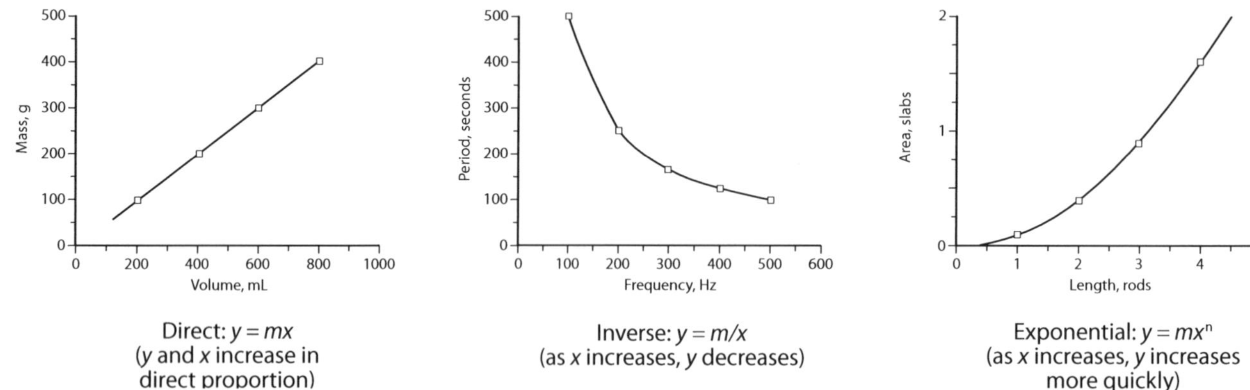

Figure 1.2.7 *Three common types of graphic relationships*

Sample Problem — Determination of a Relationship from Data

Find the relationship for the graphed data below:

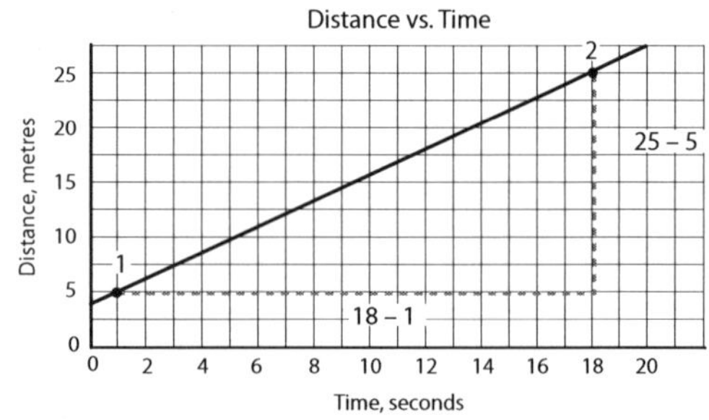

What to Think About	How to Do It
1. Determine the slope for the straight line. To do this, select two points on the line of best fit. These should be points whose values are easy to determine on both axes. *Do not use data points* to determine the constant. Determine the change in y (Δy) and the change in x (Δx) including the units. The constant is $\Delta y / \Delta x$.	Δy is 25-5 = 20 m Δx is 18 - 1 = 17 s $\frac{20 \text{ m}}{17 \text{ s}} = 1.18 \text{ m/s}$
2. Determine the relationship by subbing the *variable names* and the constant into the general equation, $y = mx + b$. Often, a straight line graph passes through the origin, in which case, $y = mx$.	distance = (1.18 m/s)time + 4.0 m.

Practice Problems — Determination of a Relationship from Data

1. Examine the following graphs. What type of relationship does each represent? Give the full relationship described by graph (c).

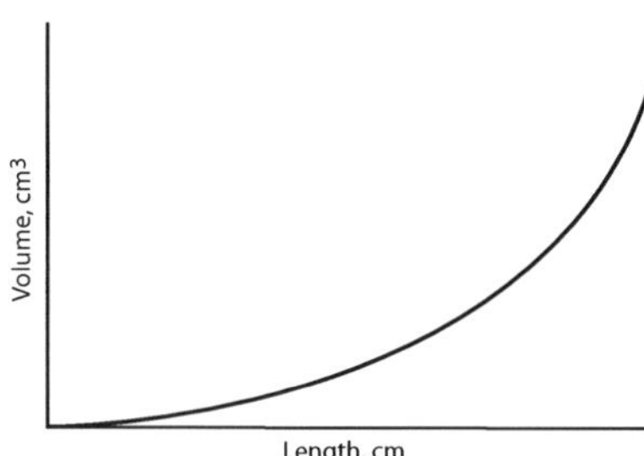

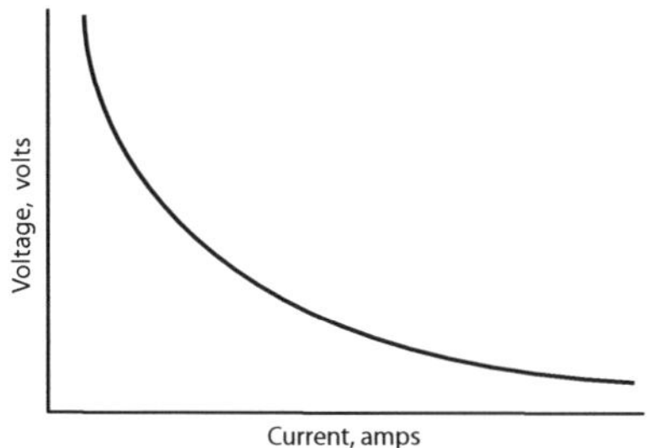

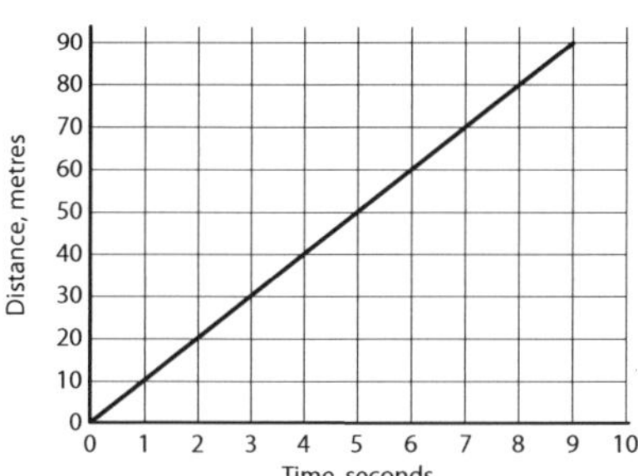

2. A beaker full of water is placed on a hotplate and heated over a period of time. The temperature is recorded at regular intervals. The following data was collected. Use the following grid to plot a graph of temperature against time. (Time goes on the *x*-axis.)

Temperature (°C)	Time (min)
22	0
30	2
38	4
46	6
54	8
62	10
70	12

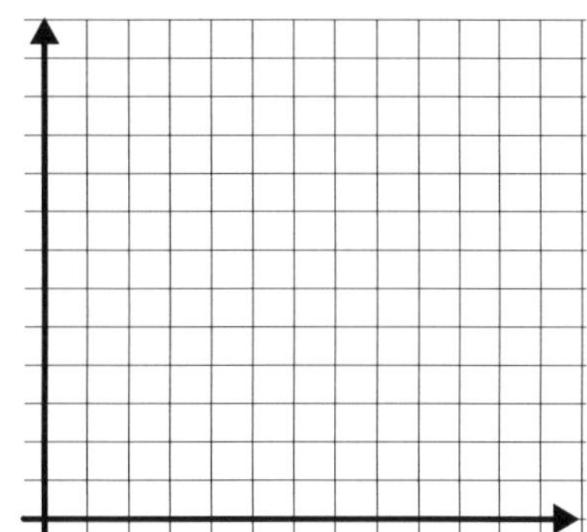

Continued on the next page

Practice Problems — Determination of a Relationship from Data (Continued)

(a) What type of relationship was studied during this investigation?

(b) What is the constant (be sure to include the units)?

(c) What temperature was reached at 5 min?

(d) Use the graph to determine the relationship between temperature and time.

(e) How long would it take the temperature to reach 80°C?

(f) What does the *y*-intercept represent?

(g) Give a source of error that might cause your graph to vary from that expected.

Investigation 1.2.1 Measuring the Frequency of a Recording Timer

Purpose

To measure the frequency of a recording timer and calculate its period

Procedure

1. Load the recording timer with a fresh piece of carbon paper. Pass a piece of ticker tape through the guiding staples, so that the carbon side of the paper faces the ticker tape. When the timer arm vibrates, it should leave a black mark on the tape.
2. To measure the frequency of the recording timer, you must determine how many times the arm swings in 1 s. Since it is difficult to time 1 s with any reasonable accuracy, let the timer run for 5 s, as precisely as you can measure it, then count the number of carbon dots made on the tape and divide by 5. Practise moving the tape through the timer until you find a suitable speed that will spread the dots out for easy counting, but do not waste ticker tape.
3. When you are ready, start the tape moving through the timer. Have your partner start the timer and the stopwatch simultaneously. Stop the timer when 5 s have elapsed. Count the number of dots made in 5 s and then calculate the frequency of your timer in hertz (Hz).

Concluding Questions

1. What was the frequency of your recording timer in Hz?
2. Estimate the possible error in the timing of your experiment. (It might be 0.10 s, 0.20 s, or whatever you think is likely.) Calculate the percent possible error in your timing. To do this, simply divide your estimate of the possible error in timing by 5.0 s and then multiply by 100.

   Example: If you estimate your timing error to be 0.50 s, then

   $$\text{percent possible error in timing} = \frac{0.50\text{ s}}{5.0\text{ s}} \times 100\% = 10\%$$

3. Your calculated frequency will have the same percent possible error as you calculated for your timing error. Calculate the range within which your timer's frequency probably falls.

   Example: If you calculate the frequency to be 57 Hz, and the possible error is 10%, then the range is 57 Hz $\pm$ 5.7 Hz, or between 51.3 Hz and 62.7 Hz. Rounded off, the range is between 51 Hz and 63 Hz. You might therefore conclude that the frequency of your timer is 57 $\pm$ 6 Hz.

4. If your timer operates on household voltage, its frequency (in North America) should be 60 Hz. Is 60 Hz within your estimated range for your timer?
5. (a) What is the period of your timer?
   (b) How many dots on the ticker tape represent
   (i) 1.0 s?
   (ii) 0.10 s?

Investigation 1.2.2 Making a Pendulum Clock

Purpose

To learn how a pendulum can be used as a clock

Procedure

1. Prepare a simple pendulum by tying a string to a pendulum bob, either a large washer, as in the image below or a drilled metal ball. Feed the string through the opening of the pendulum support. Avoid winding the string around the support rod. If you do this, the length of the pendulum changes during a swing.

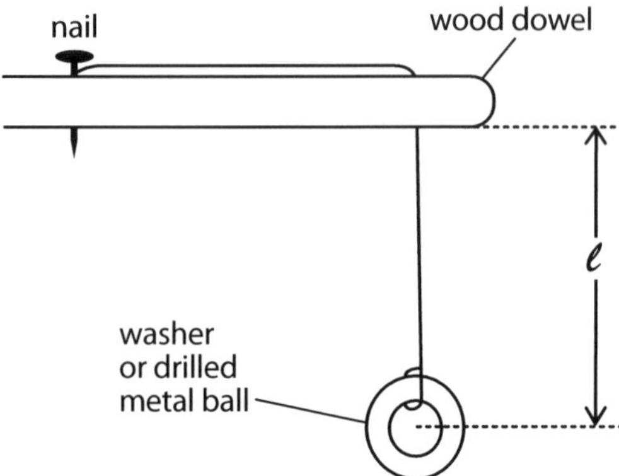

Setup for Investigation 1.2.2

2. Start by adjusting the length l of the pendulum so that it is as close to being 10.00 cm as you can make it. Measure l from the bottom of the pendulum clamp to the centre of the bob, as shown in the image above.
3. Push the bob a small distance, about 2 cm, to one side and let it swing freely. To get a rough idea of how long the pendulum takes to make one swing, use a stopwatch to measure the time it takes for the bob to swing from the highest point on one side of the swing to the highest point on the other side, then back to its starting position. The time it takes the pendulum bob to complete a full swing like this is called the period (T) of the pendulum. Try measuring the period of one swing several times with your stopwatch. Why do you think your measurements are so inconsistent?
4. To obtain a more reliable measurement of the period of the pendulum, you will now measure the time for a large number of swings (50) and find the average time for one swing by dividing by 50. Set your 10.00 cm pendulum swinging through a small arc, as before. Start counting backward (3, 2, 1, <u>0</u>, 1, 2, 3, 4, etc.) and start your stopwatch at 0. Stop your watch after 50 swings and record the time your pendulum took to complete 50 swings.
5. To figure out the period of the pendulum, divide the time for 50 swings by 50.0. Record the period, T, in your table similar to the Table on the next page. Check your result by repeating the measurement. If necessary, repeat a third time.

6. Measure the period of your pendulum for each of the lengths and record them in the Table below.
7. Prepare a graph with headings and labels like those in graph below. In this experiment, the period of the pendulum depends on its length, so the period is called the **dependent variable.** The dependent variable goes on the *y*-axis. Length is the **independent variable.** We chose what its values would be. Length is on the *x*-axis. Plot period against length using all your data from the Table below. Use a small dot with a circle around it to make each position more visible. See graph below for a sample point. When you have plotted all the points, draw one smooth curve through as many of the points as possible. If one or two points are obvious errors, ignore them when drawing your curve.
8. Make pendulums with the lengths you obtain from your graph for pendulums with periods of 1.0 s and 2.0 s. See if the lengths predicted by the graph actually do produce 1.0 s and 2.0 s "clocks."

Data Table

Length of Pendulum, ℓ (cm)	Time for 50 Swings (s)	Time for 1 Swing, Period, *T* (s)
10.00		
15.00		
20.00		
25.00		
30.00		
40.00		
50.00		
60.00		
70.00		
80.00		
90.00		
100.0		

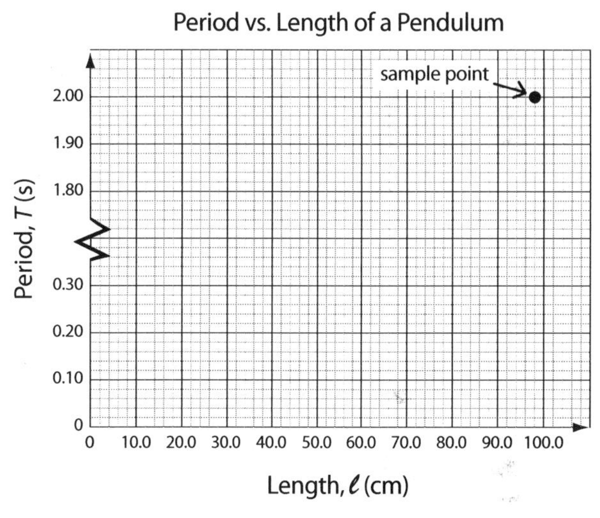

Concluding Questions

1. According to your graph of period vs. length, how long must your pendulum be if it is to be used as (a) a "one-second clock"? (b) a "two-second clock"? (Such a pendulum takes 1s to swing one way, and one second to swing back.)
2. To increase the period of your pendulum from 1 s to 2 s, by how many times (to the nearest whole number) must you increase its length?

Challenges

1. Predict what length a 3.0 s pendulum clock would have to be. Test your prediction by experiment.
2. Predict what will happen to the period of a pendulum if you double the mass of the pendulum bob. Test your prediction.

2 Kinematics

In this chapter the focus will be on the Big Idea:

An objects motion can be predicted, analyzed and described.

The content learning standards will include:

- horizontal uniform and accelerated motion
- projectile motion

By the end of this chapter, you should know the meaning to these **key terms**:

- acceleration
- average velocity
- constant acceleration
- displacement
- distance
- final velocity
- initial velocity
- instantaneous velocity
- projectile motion
- scalar quantity
- speed
- vector quantity
- velocity

By the end of the chapter, you should be able to use and know when to use the following formulae:

$v = \frac{\Delta d}{\Delta t}$ $a = \frac{\Delta v}{\Delta t}$ $d = \bar{v}t$ $v = v_0 + at$

$\bar{v} = \frac{v + v_0}{2}$ $d = v_0 t + \frac{1}{2}at^2$ $v^2 = v_0^2 + 2ad$

A roller coaster is an exciting example of kinematics in action.

2.1 Speed and Velocity

Warm Up

Imagine you are on a hike from a parking lot to a waterfall 2 km away. Is there a way you could describe to someone that the hike was 4 km long and 0 km long? Explain your answer.

___

___

___

___

The Study of Motion

How far did it travel? How long did it take? How fast did it move? Did it speed up or slow down? These are typical questions one might ask about any object that moves, whether it is a car, a planet, an electron, or a molecule. All of these questions fall under the heading of **kinematics:** the study of the motion of objects, without reference to the cause of the motion. In kinematics, we learn how to describe the motion of objects in terms of measurable variables such as time, distance, speed, and acceleration.

Distance and Displacement

When you take a trip a road sign will tell you the distance you have to travel to reach your destination. This distance is usually measured in kilometres. Other distances you are familiar with include metres, centimeters, and millimetres. Each of these measurement units tells you how far two points are apart. Because magnitude, or amount of distance covered, and not direction is stated, distance is a scalar quantity. The symbol for distance is d.

In the vector section, two methods for determining direction were described. The first method involved the use of positive (+) and negative (–) signs to indicate direction. Any motion right or up is usually considered positive. Any motion left or down is usually considered negative. The second method uses compass points. North and east are usually considered positive, and west and south are negative. Sometimes this can change depending on the question. For example if all the motion is downward, you may consider using down as positive so the math calculations do not involve negative signs.

When a direction is added to a distance, the position of an object or person is described. For example, if you are 5 km [east] of your home you are describing your position. **Position** is the shortest distance between the origin and where the person or object is located. Position is a vector quantity and includes magnitude and direction. The symbol for position is $\vec{d}$.

If you change your position by moving another position 5 km [east] of your original position, then you have a displacement. **Displacement** is a change in position and is a straight line between initial and final positions. It includes magnitude and direction. The symbol for displacement is $\Delta\vec{d}$. It is calculated by determining the change from one position to another. Or put mathematically:

$$\Delta\vec{d} = \vec{d}_f - \vec{d}_0$$

The Δ sign is important because it indicates a change. In this situation, displacement is defined as the change between the initial position and final position, not the displacement from the origin, which is your home.

Sample Problem — Calculating Displacement

A person is 2.0 m to the left of a viewpoint sign enjoying the view. She moves 4.5 m to the right of the sign to get a better view. What is the person's displacement?

What to Think About	How to Do It
1. Assume right is positive and identify the positions.	$\vec{d}_o = 2.0\text{ m [left]} = -2.0\text{ m}$ $\vec{d}_f = 4.5\text{ m [right]} = 4.5\text{ m}$
2. Find the displacement.	$\Delta\vec{d} = \vec{d}_f - \vec{d}_o$ $\Delta\vec{d} = 4.5\text{ m} - (-2.0\text{ m})$ $= 6.5\text{ m}$ The person's displacement is 6.5 m [right]

Practice Problems — Calculating Displacement

1. A woman walking her dog travels 200 m north, then 400 m west, then 500 m south.
   (a) What was the total distance she travelled?

   (b) What was the magnitude of her displacement for the entire trip?

Continued on the next page

Practice Problems — Calculating Displacement (Continued)

2. The diagram below shows the displacements of a golf ball caused by a rookie golfer attempting to reach hole number 7 on Ocean View Golf and Country Club. The golfer requires six shots to put the ball in the hole. The diagram shows the six displacements of the ball.

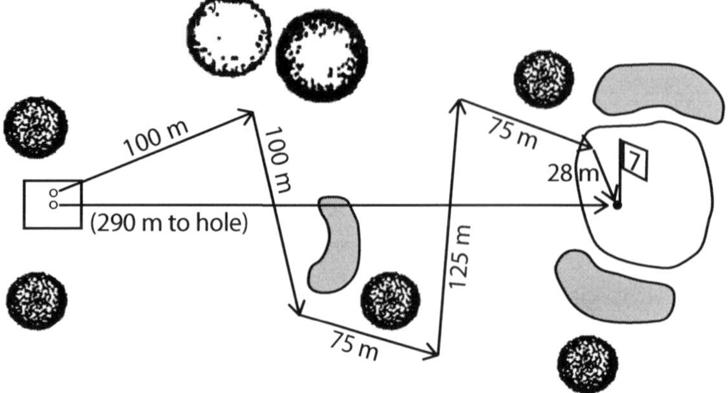

(a) What is the total distance the golf ball travelled while the golfer was playing the seventh hole?

(b) What is the resultant displacement of the ball?

3. What is the total distance and displacement the dog (*aka Buddy*) takes after it leaves the front porch?

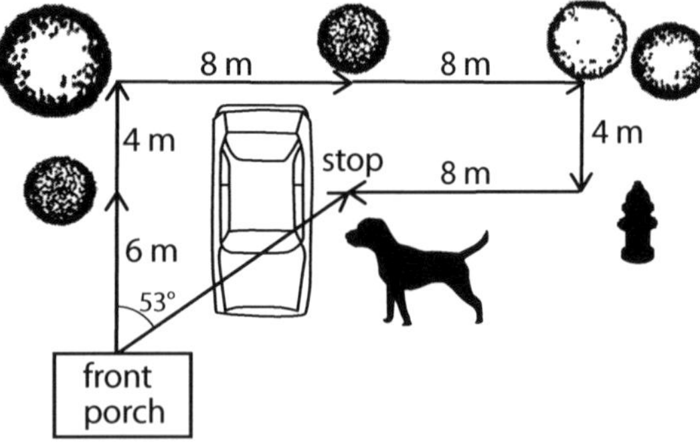

Speed

The **speed** of an object such as a car is defined as the distance it travels in a unit of time. For highway traffic, speeds are measured in kilometres per hour (km/h). Typical highway speed limits are 80 km/h, 100 km/h, and 120 km/h. Within city limits, speed limits may be 60 km/h, 50 km/h, or 30 km/h (school zone or playground). The average speed of an athlete in a 100 m dash might be approximately 9.0 m/s. The speed of sound is 330 m/s, while the speed of light is approximately 300 000 000 m/s or 300 000 km/s.

If you make a long journey by car, you might be interested in calculating your **average speed** for the trip. For example, if you travel a distance of 450 km in a time of 6.0 h, you would calculate your average speed by dividing the total distance by the total time.

$$\text{average speed} = \frac{\text{total distance}}{\text{total time}} = \frac{450 \text{ km}}{6.0 \text{ h}} = 75 \text{ km/h}$$

The symbol used for speed is *v*, and for average speed, $\bar{v}$. Note that it is a line above the *v* is not an arrow. The formula for calculating average speed from distance (*d*) and time (*t*) is therefore:

$$\bar{v} = \frac{d}{t}$$

If you are driving along the highway and spot a police car parked beside the road with its radar aimed at your car, you will be less interested in your average speed and more concerned with your **instantaneous speed**. That is how fast your car is going at this instant in time! Your speedometer will indicate what your instantaneous speed is.

Quick Check

1. (a) What is the difference between average speed and instantaneous speed?

   (b) Under what condition may average speed and instantaneous speed be the same?

2. A tourist travels 320 km in 3.6 h. What is her average speed for the trip?

3. A trucker travels 65 km at an average speed of 85 km/h. How long does the trip take?

4. If your car averages 92 km/h for a 5.0 h trip, how far will you go?

The Difference Between Speed and Velocity

You learned that speed is distance travelled in a unit of time. Average speed is total distance divided by time, and instantaneous speed is the speed of an object at a particular instant. If an object moves along at the same speed over an extended period of time, we say its speed is uniform or constant.

Uniform speed is uncommon, but it is possible to achieve nearly uniform speed in some situations. For example, a car with "cruise control" may maintain fairly constant speed on the highway. Usually, however, a vehicle is making small changes in speed and direction all the time.

If an object is not travelling in a straight line all the time, then its direction becomes important and must be specified. When both the size and the direction of a speed are specified, we call the two properties (speed and direction) the **velocity** of the object. The symbol for velocity is $\vec{v}$. If you say your car is moving 80 km/h, then you are describing your car's speed. If you say your car is travelling 80 km/h in a northerly direction, then you are describing your car's velocity. The difference between speed and velocity becomes important in situations where direction changes during a trip. For example, when a ball is thrown into the air, both its speed and its direction change throughout its trajectory, therefore velocity is specified in this situation. Velocity is calculated by finding the displacement of an object over a period of time. Mathematically this is represented by:

$$\vec{v} = \frac{\Delta\vec{d}}{\Delta t} = \frac{\vec{d}_f - \vec{d}_0}{\Delta t}$$

Position-Time Graphs

Speed and velocity can be graphically represented. The slope of a position-time graph gives the velocity of the moving object. A positive slope indicates positive velocity. A negative slope indicates negative velocity. When an object is not moving, the position does not change, so the slope is zero. That is, the line is horizontal.

Sometimes it can be confusing to determine the direction and the sign to use. It is important to remember what point of view or frame of reference you are using to observe the action. For example, if you are riding a bike toward your friend at a velocity of 10 km/h [west], your friend sees you coming at 10 km/h [east]. Both of you observe the same situation, it's just the direction that is different. That is why it is important to know which direction is positive and which direction is negative before you start. Usually, if all the motion is in one direction, positive values will be used unless indicated. That will be the case in this book.

The next sample problem describes how the motion of a skateboarder can be solved mathematically and graphically and the velocity of the skateboarder determined.

Sample Problem — Solving Motion Problems Mathematically

You are on a skateboard and moving to the right covering 0.5 m each second for 10 s. What is your velocity?

What to Think About	How to Do It
1. Motion is uniform so the velocity is the same for each time interval. Right will be positive.	$\Delta \vec{d}_o = 0.0\text{ m}$ $\Delta \vec{d}_f = 0.5\text{ m}$ $\Delta t = 1.0\text{ s}$
2. Solve for velocity.	$\vec{v} = \frac{\Delta \vec{d}}{\Delta t} = \frac{\vec{d}_f - \vec{d}_o}{\Delta t}$ $= \frac{0.5\text{ m} - 0.0\text{ m}}{1.0\text{s}}$ $= 0.5\text{ m/s}$
3. Include direction in the answer, which is right since the answer is positive.	$\vec{v} = 0.5\text{ m/s [right]}$

Sample Problem —Solving Motion Problems Graphically

You are on a skateboard and moving to the right covering 0.5 m each second for 10 s. What is your velocity?

What to Think About

1. Collect data and record in table. Moving right will be considered positive.

How to Do It

d (m)	0	0.5	1.0	1.5	2.0	2.5	3.0	3.5	4.0	4.5	5.0
t (s)	0	1.0	2.0	3.0	4.0	5.0	6.0	7.0	8.0	9.0	10

2. Graph data and draw best fit line.

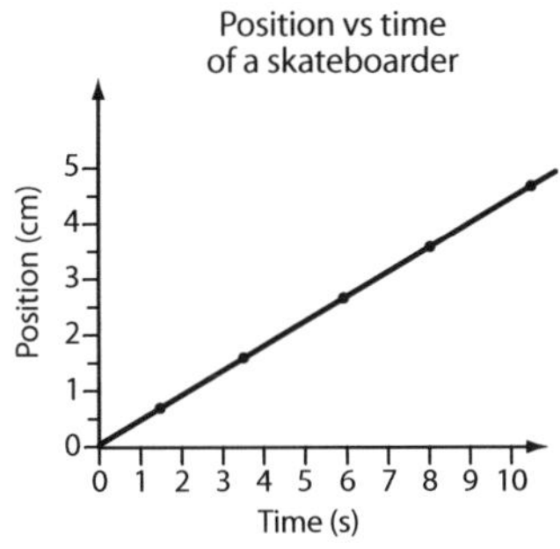

3. Find slope as it is equal to the velocity of the skateboarder.

$$\text{slope} = \frac{\Delta \vec{d}}{\Delta t} = \frac{\vec{d}_f - \vec{d}_o}{\Delta t} = \vec{v}$$

$$\vec{v} = \frac{5.0\text{ m} - 0.0\text{ m}}{10\text{ s}}$$

$$= 0.5\text{ m/s}$$

4. The slope is positive, so the direction is to the right.

$$\vec{v} = 0.5\text{ m/s [right]}$$

Practice Problems —Solving Motion Problems Graphically

1. Describe the motion represented in each of the following position-time graphs.

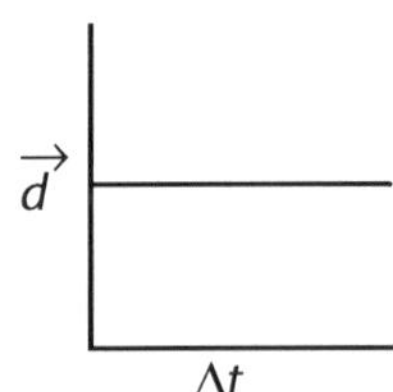

(a)

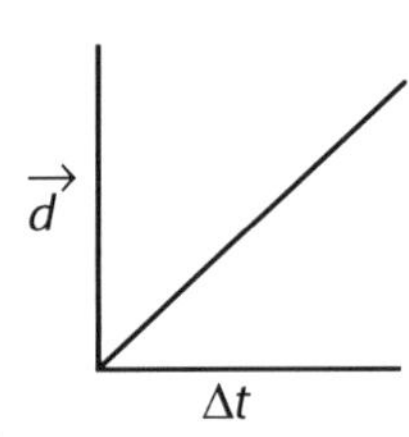

(b)

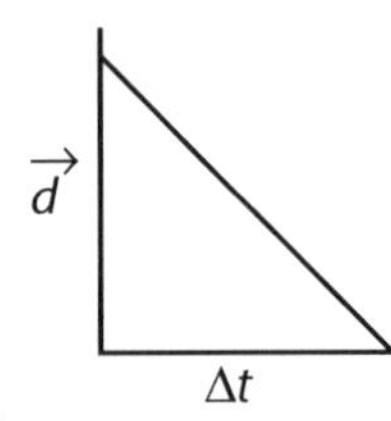

(c)

2. (a) Fill in the data table if a car is traveling at 30 km/h through a school zone.

Time (s)	1.0	2.0	3.0	4.0	5.0	6.0	7.0	8.0
Distance (m)								

(b) Graph this data on a distance vs. time graph.

Investigation 2.1.1 Measuring the Speed of a Model Car

Purpose

To measure the speed of a model car, such as a radio-controlled vehicle

Procedure

1. Remove a 5.0 m length of ticker tape from a roll. Pass one end of it through a recording timer, and then tape it to a battery-powered toy car. (Figure 2.1.1)

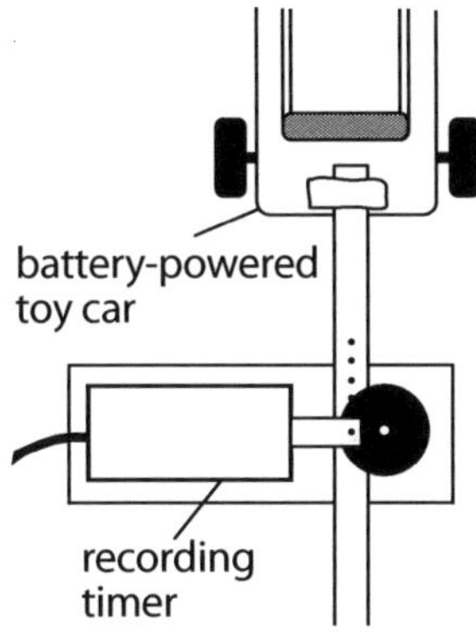

Figure 2.1.1 *Step 1*

2. Turn on the timer and let the car travel at its full speed until all the tape has passed through the timer.
3. Every six dots is one-tenth of a second. Mark off the time intervals in one-tenth of a second on your tape
4. Measure the distance traveled in each tenth of a second. Record your data in a table similar to Table 2.1.1.

Table 2.1.1 *Data Table for Investigation 2.1.1*

Time (s)	0.0	0.1	0.2	0.3	0.4	0.5	0.6	0.7	0.8	0.9	1.0	1.0	1.1	...
Distance per interval (cm)														...
Total distance (cm)														...

5. Create a distance vs. time graph. On the *y*-axis, use total distance and on the *x*-axis, use time. Draw a best-fit line on your graph.
6. Find the slope of your graph and record it along with the appropriate units.

Concluding Questions

1. What does the slope of a distance-time graph represent?
2. Find the average speed of the toy car over five 1 s intervals of the trip.
3. Compare your slope of the distance-time graph with your average speed over the five 1 s intervals.

2.1 Review Questions

1. Can objects with the same speed have different velocities? Why or why not?

2. What are two ways of describing the direction of an object's motion?

3. If you run with an average speed of 12.0 km/h, how far will you go in 3.2 min?

4. If the average speed of your private jet is 8.0×10^2 km/h, how long will it take you to travel a distance of 1.8×10^3 km?

5. A red ant travels across a driveway, which is 3.5 m wide, at an average speed of 2.6 cm/s. How long will the ant take to cross the driveway? Express your answer (a) in seconds and (b) in minutes.

6. If your car moves with a steady speed of 122 km/h for 20.0 min, then at a steady speed of 108 km/h for 30.0 min, what is the average speed of your car for the entire trip?

7. A car moves with a steady speed of 84 km/h for 45 min, then 96 km/h for 20 min.
   (a) What was the total distance travelled during the whole trip?

   (b) What is its average speed for the whole trip?

8. After a soccer practice, Gareth and Owen are heading home. They reach the corner, where they go separate ways. Gareth heads south to the bus stop. Owen walks north to his house. After 5.0 min, Gareth is 600 m [S] and Owen is 450 m [N].
   (a) On the same graph (below), graph the position of each boy after 5.0 min and find the velocity of each boy.

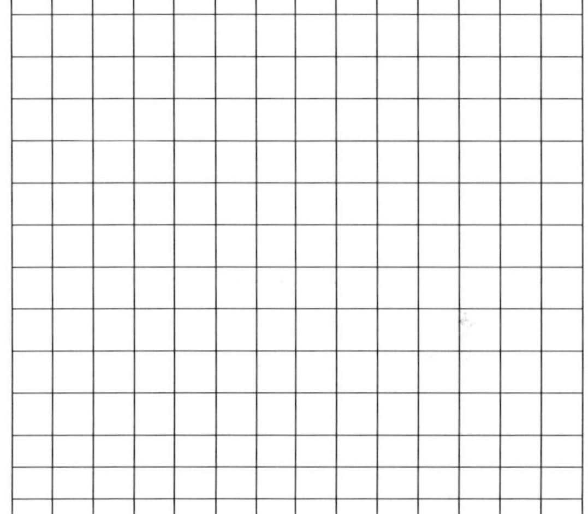

(b) Find the velocity of each boy using algebra.

2.2 Acceleration

Warm Up

Below are two blank speed-time graphs.
On graph (a), sketch the slope that represents a sports car traveling at constant speed.
On graph (b), sketch the slope of the same car starting from rest and speeding up at a constant rate.

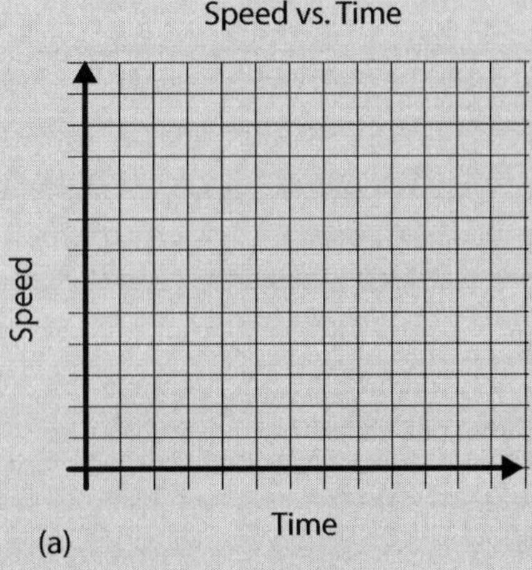

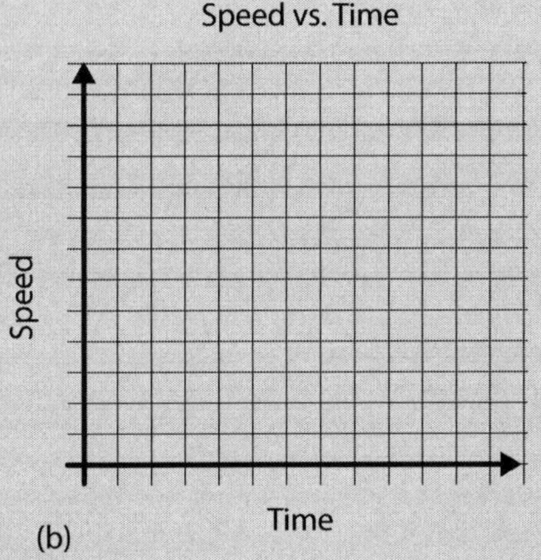

Changing Velocity

Whenever the velocity of an object changes, the object experiences **acceleration.** Acceleration is a change in velocity over a period of time:

$$\textbf{acceleration} = \frac{\textbf{change in velocity}}{\textbf{change in time}}$$

The symbol for acceleration is *a*. Velocity has the same symbol as speed, which is *v*. If the velocity at the start of the time interval is v_0, and at the end of the time interval is v_f, then the change in velocity will be $v_f - v_0$. If the time at the beginning of the time interval is t_0, and the time at the end of the time interval is t_f, then the change in time, the time interval, is $t_f - t_0$. Using these symbols, acceleration can be defined as:

$$a = \frac{v_f - v_0}{t_f - t_0} \text{ or } a = \frac{\Delta v}{\Delta t}$$

where the Δ symbol is shorthand for "change in" or "interval."

Since velocity has two aspects to it, both speed and direction, acceleration can occur under three conditions:

(a) if speed changes,
(b) if direction changes or
(c) if both speed and direction change.

The standard unit for expressing acceleration is m/s^2. An object is accelerating at a rate of 1 m/s^2 if its speed is increasing at a rate of 1 m/s each second.

Sample Problem — Calculating Acceleration

A runner racing in a 100 m dash accelerates from rest to a speed of 9.0 m/s in 4.5 s. What was his average acceleration during this time interval?

What to Think About	How to Do It
1. Determine the correct formula.	$a = \frac{\Delta v}{\Delta t} = \frac{v_f - v_o}{t_f - t_o}$
2. Solve for acceleration. Note that runner's average acceleration was 2.0 m/s/s, which is usually written 2.0 m/s^2	$= \frac{9.0 \text{ m/s} - 0 \text{ m/s}}{4.5 \text{ s} - 0 \text{ s}}$ $a = 2.0 \text{ m/s}^2$ The runner's average acceleration was 2.0 m/s^2.

Practice Problems — Calculating Acceleration

1. What is the average acceleration for the following?
   (a) A car speeds up from 0 km/h to 60.0 km/h in 3.00 s.

   (b) A runner accelerates from rest to 9.00 m/s in 3.00 s.

2. What is the average acceleration of a truck that accelerates from 45.0 km/h to 60.0 km/h in 7.50 s?

3. A car travelling 120 km/h brakes hard to avoid hitting a deer on the road, slowing to 60 km/h in 4.0 s. What is its acceleration? Why is it negative?

Negative Acceleration

Sometimes you will find a situation where the acceleration is negative. You may think this implies that an object is slowing down, but that is not always the case. Consider the situations shown in Figure 2.2.1.

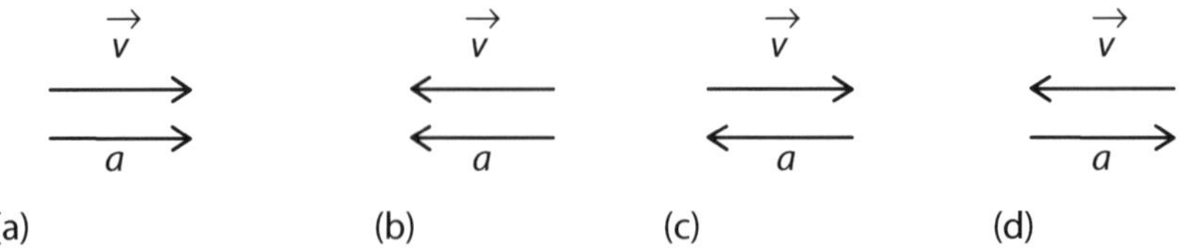

Figure 2.2.1 *The vectors represent the velocity and acceleration of a car in different situations.*

In (a) and (b) the velocity of the car and the acceleration are in the same direction. This means the car is speeding up, even though the acceleration is negative in (b). In (c) and (d) the velocity and acceleration are in opposite directions and the car is slowing down. We can summarize that this way:

When the velocity and acceleration are in the same direction, the object is speeding up, even if the acceleration is negative. When the velocity and acceleration are in opposite directions, the object is slowing down.

Graphing Acceleration

In Figure 2.2.2, fictitious data is used to show how your results from Investigation 2.1.1 might have been graphed. In this figure, the average speed of the cart is plotted on the *y*-axis, since it is the dependent variable. Time is on the *x*-axis, because it is the independent variable.

Notice that in Figure 2.2.2 the speeds are plotted halfway through each time interval. For example, the average speed of 11 cm/s, which occurs in the first time interval of the sample tape, would be plotted at 0.05 s, not at 0.10 s. This is because the average speed during the interval will occur halfway through it, not at the end of the interval. This assumes, of course, that the speed is increasing at a constant rate and therefore acceleration is constant. The average speed for each interval is the same as the instantaneous speed half way through the interval, if acceleration is constant.

The graph you see in Figure 2.2.2 is, in fact, a graph of the instantaneous speed of the cart vs. time, although average speeds were used to obtain it. To write an equation describing the line in this graph, you need to know the *y*-intercept and the slope.

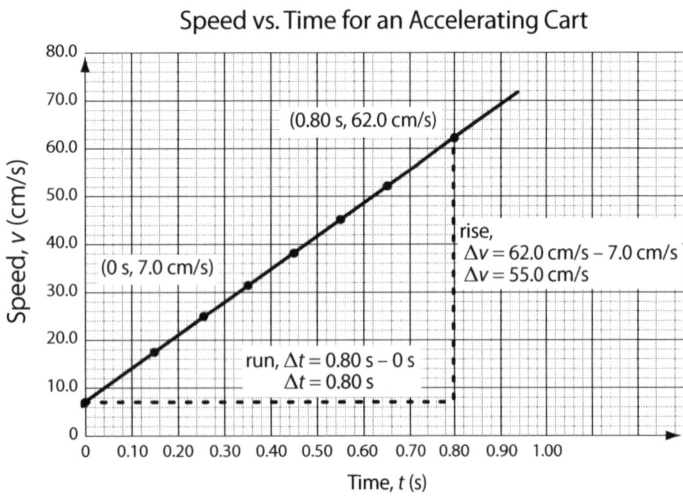

Figure 2.2.2 *An example of a graph showing acceleration*

By inspection, the *y*-intercept, *b*, equals 7.0 cm/s. The slope *m* is found by using the points (0 s, 7.0 cm/s) and (0.80 s, 62 cm/s). Notice that the "rise" of the line is equal to the change in the speed of the cart, Δv, and $\Delta v = v_f - v_0$. The "run" of the graph is the change in time Δt, and $\Delta t = t_f - t_0$.

$$\text{slope} = m = \frac{\Delta v}{\Delta t} = \frac{v_f - v_0}{t_f - t_0} = \frac{62.0\ \text{cm/s} - 7.0\ \text{cm/s}}{0.80\ \text{s} - 0\ \text{s}} = \frac{55.0\ \text{cm/s}}{0.80\ \text{s}} = 69\ \text{cm/s}^2$$

Notice that the slope has units of acceleration. This is because the slope of the speed-time graph *is* acceleration! Remember that acceleration is equal to the change in speed of the cart per second. The slope $m = \Delta v/\Delta t$, which is the acceleration of the cart.

The equation for the line in Figure 2.2.2 will have the same form as the general equation for a straight line, which is $y = mx + b$. When describing experimental results from a graph, however, we substitute the specific symbols for the variables used in the experiment. We also use the numerical values for the *y*-intercept and slope, complete with their measuring units. The equation for the line in Figure 2.2.2 is therefore

$$v = (69\ \text{cm/s}^2)t + 7.0\ \text{cm/s}$$

where *v* is the speed of the cart at any time *t*.

2.2 Review Questions

1. A policeman travelling 60 km/h spots a speeder ahead, so he accelerates his vehicle at a steady rate of 2.22 m/s^2 for 4.00 s, at which time he catches up with the speeder.
   (a) How fast was the policeman travelling in m/s?

   (b) How fast is the police car travelling after 4.00 s? Give your answer in both m/s and km/h.

2. A motorbike accelerates at a constant rate from a standing start. After 1.2 s, it is travelling 6.0 m/s. How much time will have elapsed (starting from rest) before the bike is moving with a speed of 15.0 m/s?

3. The graph below shows lines representing speed vs. time for an accelerating aircraft, prepared by observers at two different locations on the runway.

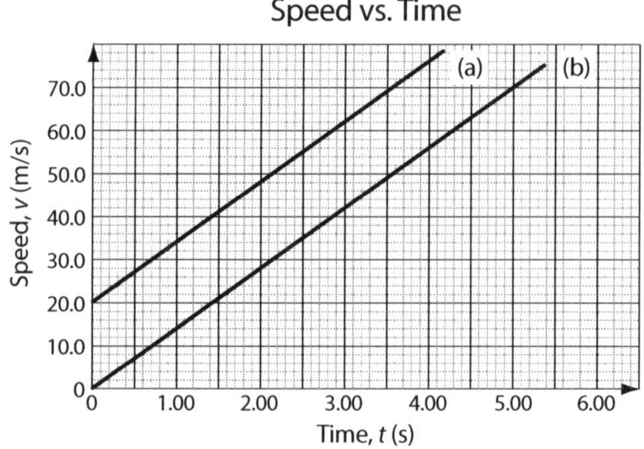

   (a) What is the equation for line (a)?

   (b) What is the equation for line (b)?

   (c) What is the acceleration of the aircraft according to line (a)?

   (d) What is the acceleration of the aircraft according to line (b)?

   (e) Explain why the y-intercept for line (b) is different than the intercept for line (a).

4. A racing motorbike's final velocity is 38 m/s in 5.5 s with an acceleration of 6.0 m/s^2. What was the initial velocity of the motorbike?

5. While starting your car, which is a standard gearshift, you coast downhill getting to a speed of 2.0 m/s before the engine starts. This takes a total of 3.0 s. If downhill is the positive direction, what is the average acceleration of your car?

6. The graph below describes the motion of a vehicle whose acceleration changes twice. Find the acceleration of the vehicle for the parts of the graph labeled (a), (b) and (c), by finding the slope of each part of the graph.

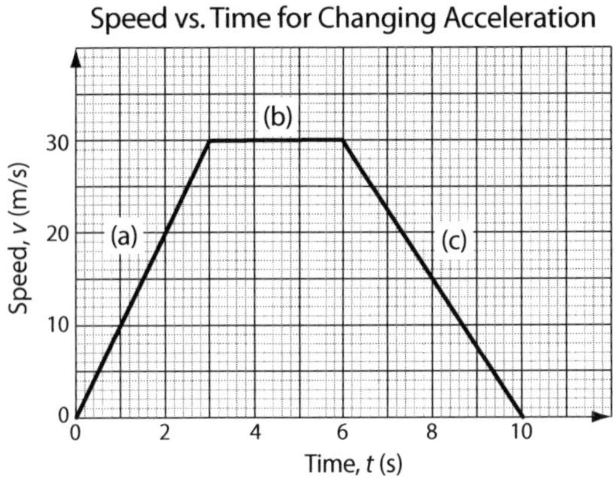

Speed vs. Time for Changing Acceleration

(a)

(b)

(c)

2.3 Uniform Acceleration

Warm Up

In your own words, describe the difference between average velocity, initial velocity, final velocity, and a change in velocity.

___

___

___

___

Graphing Acceleration

In a situation where the speed of a moving body increases or decreases at a uniform rate the acceleration is considered uniform. This motion can be graphed on a speed vs. time and will be linear (Figure 2.3.1). Since speed is the dependent variable, it is plotted on the *y*-axis. Time, the independent variable, will be on the *x*-axis.

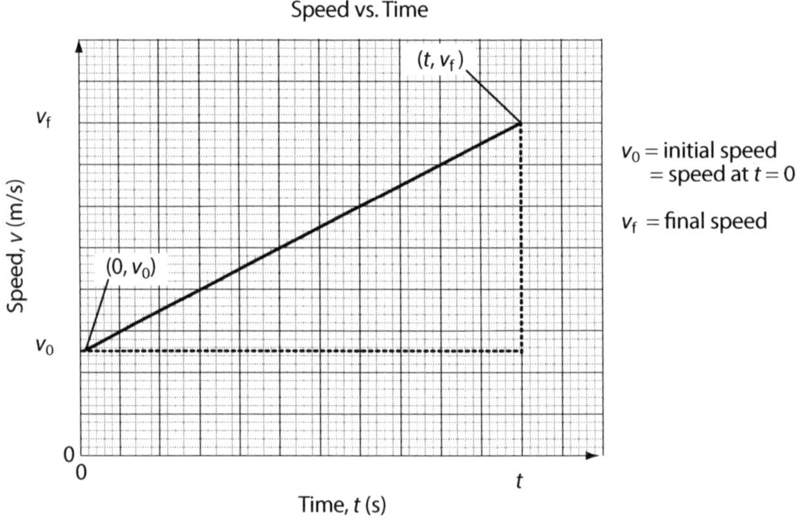

Figure 2.3.1 *This graph shows speed changing at a uniform rate.*

The *y*-intercept for the speed-time graph is $b = v_0$, where v_0 is the speed of the object at time $t = 0$. In Figure 2.3.1, the initial time is zero and the final time is t, so the time interval is simply $\Delta t = t - 0 = t$.

The slope of the graph is $m = \dfrac{\Delta v}{\Delta t} = a$, since acceleration is change in speed divided by change in time.

$$\text{If } a = \frac{v_f - v_0}{t}$$

$$\text{Then } at = v_f - v_0 \text{ and}$$

$$\boldsymbol{v_f = v_0 + at} \qquad \textbf{(1)}$$

This is a general equation for any object that accelerates at a uniform rate. It says that the final speed of the accelerating object equals the initial speed plus the change in speed (*at*).

Sample Problem — Determining Uniform Acceleration

The graph below shows the uniform acceleration of an object, as it was allowed to drop off a cliff.

(a) What was the acceleration of the object?

(b) Write an equation for the graph.

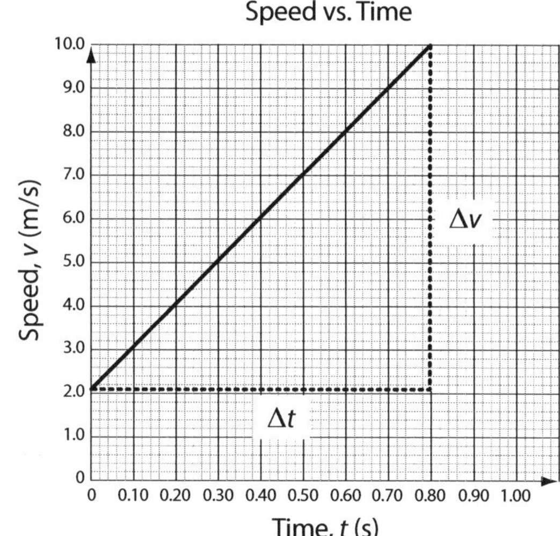

$\Delta v = v_f - v_0$

$\Delta t = t_f - 0$

What to Think About	How to Do It
(a)	
1. The acceleration is determined by finding the slope of the speed-time graph.	$a = \frac{\Delta v}{\Delta t} = \frac{v_f - v_0}{t_f - t_0}$ $= \frac{10.0\ \text{m/s} - 2.0\ \text{m/s}}{0.80\ \text{s} - 0\ \text{s}} = \frac{8.0\ \text{m/s}}{0.80\ \text{s}}$ $a = 1.0 \times 10^1\ \text{m/s}^2$
(b)	
1. Determine the general equation for any straight line.	$y = b + mx$
2. For this line, the slope *m* is the acceleration. Inspection of the graph reveals that the *y*-intercept, *b*, is 2.0 m/s.	$m = 1.0 \times 10^1\ \text{m/s}^2$ $b = 2.0\ \text{m/s}$ $x = t$ $y = v_f$
3. Derive the specific equation for this line. Note that the final, specific equation for this graph includes the actual numerical values of the *y*-intercept and slope, complete with their measuring units. Once this equation is established, it can be used in place of the graph, since it describes every point on the graph.	$v_f = 2.0\ \text{m/s} + (1.0 \times 10^1\ \text{m/s}^2) \cdot t$

Practice Problems — Determining Uniform Acceleration

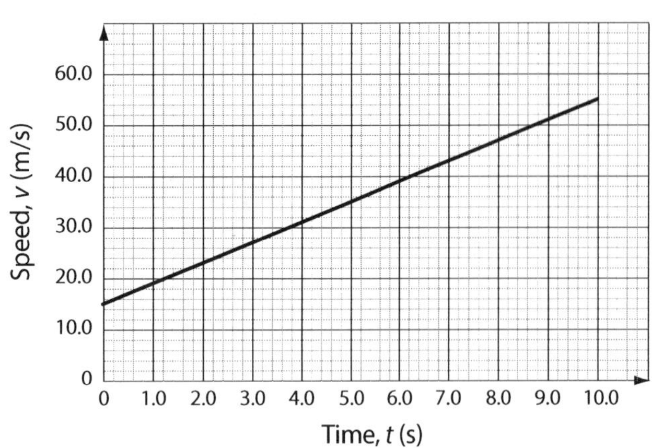

1. (a) What is the *y*-intercept (v_0) for the graph shown above?

   (b) What is the slope of the graph?

   (c) What property of the moving object does this slope measure?

   (d) Write the specific equation for the graph, using symbols *v* for speed and *t* for time.

2. The following equation describes the motion of a ball thrown straight down, by someone leaning out of the window of a tall building:

$$v_f = 5.0 \text{ m/s} + (9.8 \text{ m/s}^2)\cdot t$$

   (a) At what speed was the ball initially thrown out of the window?

   (b) What was the acceleration of the ball?

   (c) How fast was the ball moving after 1.2 s?

Calculating Distance from Uniform Acceleration

Consider an object that is accelerating uniformly from initial speed v_0 to a final speed v_f in time *t*. as shown in Figure 2.3.2. How would you calculate the distance travelled by the object during this time?

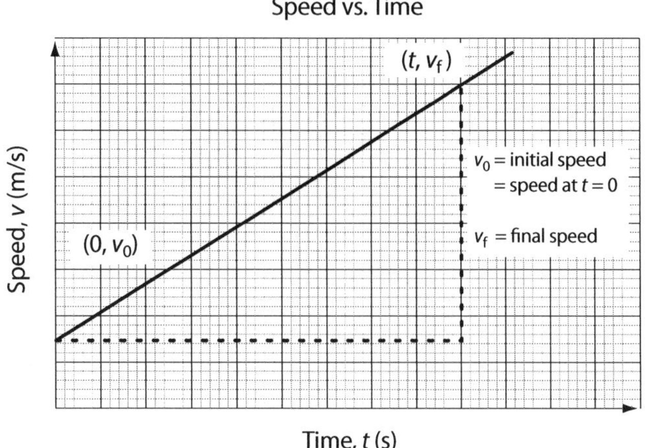

Figure 2.3.2 *This graph represents an object accelerating at a uniform rate.*

The total distance *d* travelled in time *t* will equal the average speed $\bar{v}$ multiplied by time *t*. The average speed $\bar{v}$ is just the average of the initial speed v_0 and the final speed v_f, which is:

$$\bar{v} = \frac{v_0 + v_f}{2}$$

Distance travelled is $d = \bar{v} \times t$ or $$d = \frac{v_0 + v_f}{2} \cdot t \qquad \textbf{(2)}$$

However, it has already been shown that $$v_f = v_0 + at \qquad \textbf{(1)}$$

Therefore, $$d = \frac{v_0 + v_0 + at}{2} \cdot t$$

and $$d = \frac{2v_0 + at}{2} \cdot t = \frac{2v_0 + at^2}{2}$$

Finally, $$\boldsymbol{d = v_0 t + \frac{1}{2} at^2} \qquad \textbf{(3)}$$

Sometimes you encounter situations involving uniform acceleration where you have no information about the time interval, *t*, during which the motion occurred. If you know the initial speed v_0 and the final speed v_f, you can still calculate the distance travelled if you know at what rate the object is accelerating.

For uniform acceleration, $$d = \frac{v_0 + v_f}{2} \cdot t, \text{ and } v_f = v_0 + at$$

Therefore, $$t = \frac{v_f - v_0}{a}$$

Substituting for *t* in the first equation, $$d = \frac{v_0 + v_f}{2} \cdot \frac{v_f - v_0}{a}$$

Thus, $$2ad = v_f^2 - v_0^2$$

Therefore, $$\boldsymbol{v_f^2 = v_0^2 + 2ad} \qquad \textbf{(4)}$$

The Four Uniform Acceleration Equations

Four equations describing uniform acceleration were introduced above. These four equations are extremely useful in this course and in future courses you might take in physics. For your convenience, they are summarized here:

$$(1)\quad v_f = v_0 + at$$

$$(2)\quad d = \frac{v_0 + v_f}{2} \cdot t$$

$$(3)\quad d = v_0 t + \frac{1}{2}at^2$$

$$(4)\quad v_f^2 = v_0^2 + 2ad$$

Quick Check

1. What is the initial velocity of a car accelerating east at 3.0 m/s^2 for 5.0 s and reaching a final velocity of 25.0 m/s east?

2. If we assume acceleration is uniform, how far does a plane travel when it lands at 16.0 m/s west and comes to rest in 8.00 s?

3. What is the stopping distance of a car if it accelerates at –9.29 m/s^2 and has an initial velocity of 100 km/h.

Investigation 2.3.1 Measuring Acceleration

Purpose

To measure the uniform acceleration of an object

Part 1

Procedure

1. Figure 2.3.a shows one way to produce uniformly accelerated motion. (Your teacher may have a different method and will explain it to you.) Remove a 1-m piece of ticker tape from a roll. Pass the tape through a recording timer and tape it to a laboratory cart, as shown in the diagram. A 500 g mass is attached to the cart by a 1 m string that passes over a pulley. The force of gravity on the mass accelerates both the mass and the cart.
2. For best results in this experiment, there should be no slack in the ticker tape before the cart is released. One partner should place the hanging mass over the pulley, and hold onto the cart so that it does not accelerate prematurely. When all is ready, simultaneously turn on the timer and release the cart.

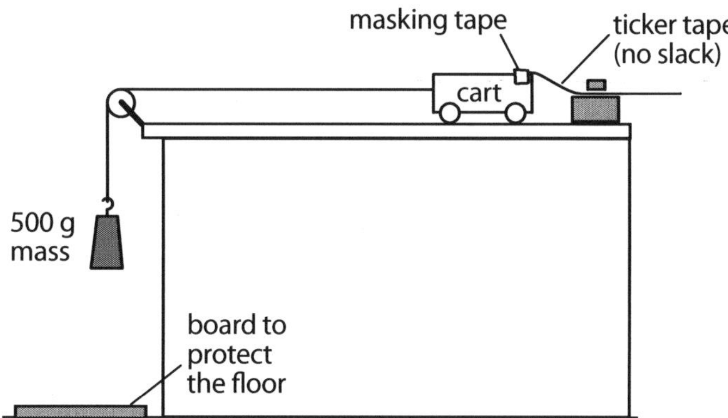

Figure 2.3.a *Apparatus setup for Part 1*

3. Your finished ticker tape record will look something like the one in Figure 2.3.b. Often there is a smudged grouping of dots at the start, so choose the first clear dot and label it the "0th" dot. On your tape, mark clearly the 0th dot, 6th dot, 12th dot, 18th dot, 24th dot, and so on until you have at least six time intervals. The timer has a frequency of 60 Hz. This means it makes 60 vibrations each second. The time interval between dots on your tape is 1/60 s. If you use a time interval of six dots, this is 6/60 s or 1/10 s. In other words, an interval of six dots is the same as 0.10 s.

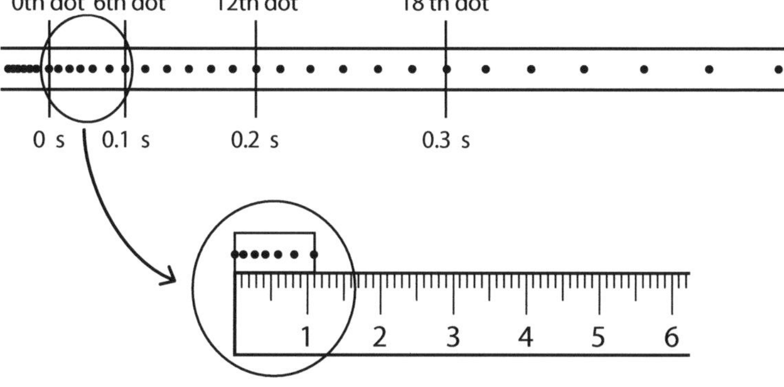

Figure 2.3.b *The beginning of the tape may have a smudged group of dots.*

4. Carefully measure the distance the cart travelled during each successive 0.10 s time interval. For example, in the sample tape in Figure 2.3.b, the distance travelled during the interval between 0 and 0.10 s was 1.1 cm. Figure 2.3.c shows how to measure the distance travelled during the second 0.10 s interval between 0.10 s and 0.20 s. In the sample tape, the distance is 2.8 cm. Prepare a table like Table 2.3.1. Record the distances travelled in each of the recorded intervals in your table.

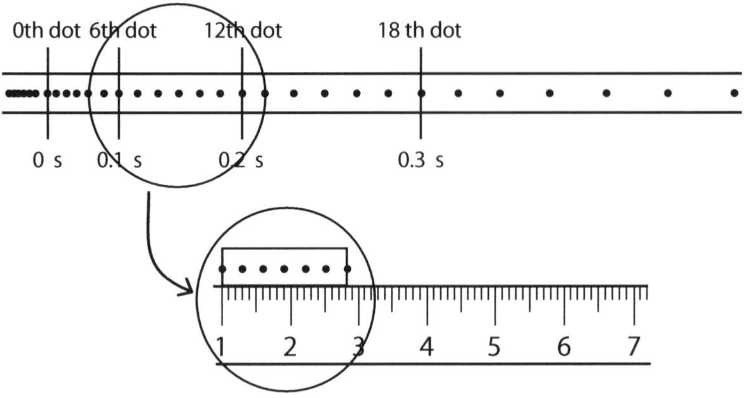

Figure 2.3.c *How to measure the distance between 0.10 s and 0.20 s*

Table 2.3.1 *Data for an Accelerating Cart*

Time Interval (s)	Distance Travelled (cm)	Average Speed for the Interval (cm/s)
0 to 0.10		
0.10 to 0.20		
0.20 to 0.30		
0.30 to 0.40		
0.40 to 0.50		
0.50 to 0.60		

5. Your next task is to figure out the average speed of the cart during each of the 0.10 s time intervals. Since average speed is just the distance travelled during the time interval divided by the time interval, all you have to do is divide each measured distance by the time interval (0.10 s). During the first time interval on the sample tape, the cart moved a distance of 1.1 cm. The average speed of the cart during the first 0.10 s was therefore

$$\bar{v} = \frac{1.1 \text{ cm}}{0.10 \text{ s}} = 11 \text{ cm/s}$$

During the second time interval (between 0.10 s and 0.20 s), the cart moved a distance of 1.8 cm. Its average speed during the second interval was therefore

$$\bar{v} = \frac{1.8 \text{ cm}}{0.10 \text{ s}} = 18 \text{ cm/s}$$

6. Using your own tape data, calculate the average speed of the cart during each of the time intervals and complete Table 2.3.1.

Concluding Questions

1. (a) What was the average speed of the cart during the first 0.10 s time interval?
   (b) What was the average speed of the cart during the second 0.10 s interval?
   (c) By how much did the average speed of the cart increase between the first interval and the second interval?
   (d) Calculate the acceleration of the cart between the first interval and the second interval by dividing the increase in average speed by the time interval, which was 0.10 s.

   Example: On the sample tape, the average speed increased from 11 cm/s to 18 cm/s between the first and second time intervals. Therefore, the acceleration was:

$$a = \frac{18 \text{ cm/s} - 11 \text{ cm/s}}{0.10 \text{ s}} = \frac{7.0 \text{ cm/s}}{0.10 \text{ s}} = 70 \text{ cm/s}^2$$

2. Calculate the acceleration of the cart between the second and third intervals, third and fourth intervals, fourth and fifth intervals, and fifth and sixth intervals. Allowing for slight variations due to experimental errors, is there any pattern to your results?

Part 2

Procedure

1. Using your data table from Investigation 2.3.1 (Table 2.3.1), plot a graph of speed vs. time for the accelerating cart, like the example shown below in Figure 2.3.d. Remember that the speeds in the table are average speeds for each interval and should be plotted midway through each time interval.

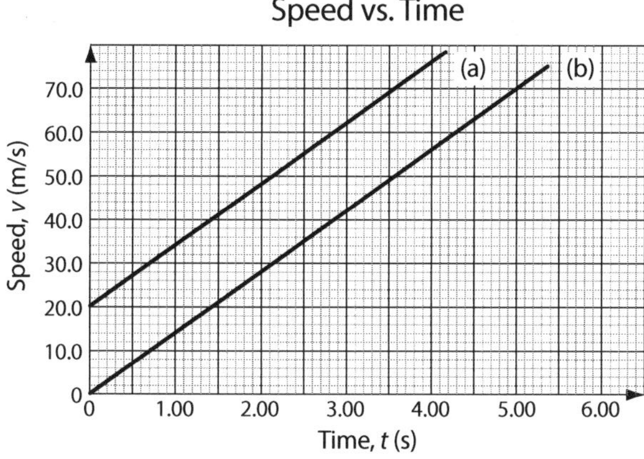

Figure 2.3.d *This is an example of a speed-time graph like the one you will draw.*

2. Draw a single straight line through all the plotted points. If there are stray points due to experimental error, try to draw a line that leaves as many strays on one side of it as on the other. If a point is an obvious gross error, ignore it when drawing your "best-fit line." If in doubt, ask your teacher for advice.
3. Determine the *y*-intercept of your line. Also, determine the slope of the line

Concluding Questions

1. What was the acceleration of your cart according to the slope of your graph?
2. What is the equation for the speed-time graph you plotted for the cart?
3. In Investigation 2.3.1, you figured out the acceleration of your cart simply by comparing average speeds of the cart in successive time intervals. Compare the acceleration you calculated in Investigation 2.3.1 with the acceleration you just obtained using the slope of your speed-time graph. Which method of finding the acceleration "averages out" the experimental errors better? Explain.

2.3 Review Questions

1. Use the following graph to answer the questions below.

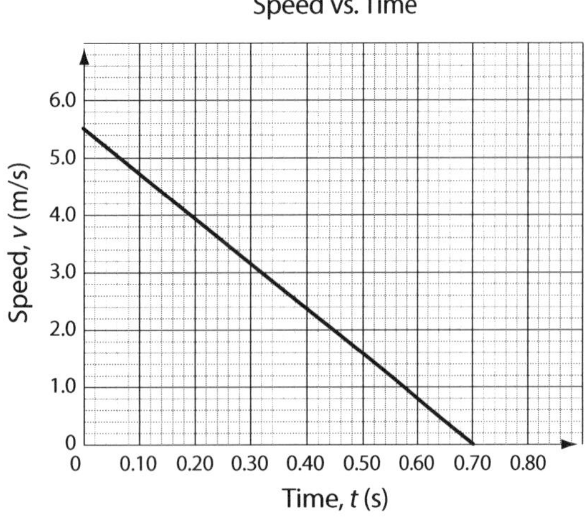

   (a) What is the y-intercept (v_0) of the speed-time graph shown above?

   (b) What is the acceleration of the moving object?

   (c) What is the specific equation for this graph?

2. A cyclist coasting along a road allows her bike to come to rest with the help of a slight upslope in the road. The motion of the bike is described by the equation:

$$v_f = 6.6 \text{ m/s} - (2.2 \text{ m/s}^2) \cdot t$$

   (a) What was the initial speed of the bike?

   (b) At what rate did the bike accelerate while coming to rest?

   (c) How long did the bike take to come to rest?

3. What is the rate of acceleration of a mountain bike, if it slows down from 12.0 m/s to 8.0 m/s in a time of 3.25 s?

4. A truck parked on a down slope slips its brakes and starts to coast downhill, accelerating from rest at a constant rate of 0.80 m/s^2.

   (a) How fast will the truck be moving after 5.0 s?

   (b) How far will the truck coast during the 5.0 s?

5. An aircraft starts from rest and accelerates at a constant rate down the runway.
   (a) After 12.0 s, its speed is 36.0 m/s. What is its acceleration?

   (b) How fast is the plane moving after 15.0 s?

   (c) How far down the runway will the plane be after 15.0 s?

6. A truck is moving along at 80.0 km/h when it hits a gravel patch, which causes it to accelerate at –5.0 km/h/s. How far will the truck travel before it slows to 20.0 km/h?

7. A very frustrated physics student drops a physics textbook off the top of a tower. If the tower is 5.3×10^2 m high, how long will the book take to reach the ground, assuming there is no air resistance?

8. If an electron accelerates in a space of 5.0 cm from rest to 1/10 *c*, (where *c* is the speed of light, 3.0×10^8 m/s), what is its acceleration?

2.4 Acceleration of Bodies Due to Gravity

Warm Up

Take a piece of paper and book in each hand and raise them to about the height of your shoulder. Predict which one will hit the ground first if they are both dropped at the same time. Drop both and record results. Now crumple the same piece of paper and repeat. Describe and suggest reasons for any differences between the two events.

____

____

____

____

Free Fall

One of the most common situations involving uniform acceleration is the phenomenon known as **free fall**. For example, if a coin drops out of your pocket, it accelerates toward the ground. If the effects of air resistance are ignored, the acceleration of the coin toward the ground is uniform. The coin starts its downward fall with zero speed, but gains speed as it falls toward Earth. Since gravity is the cause of the acceleration, we call the acceleration during free fall the **acceleration of gravity.** The acceleration of gravity is given a special symbol, g.

The magnitude of g depends on your location. At Earth's surface, g is approximately 9.81 m/s^2. At higher altitudes, g decreases. For our present purposes, g is assumed to be constant at Earth's surface and to be 9.81 m/s^2. On the Moon, the magnitude of g is approximately 1/6 of what it is here on Earth's surface. A body in free fall near the Moon's surface has an acceleration of gravity of only 1.60 m/s^2.

Of course, the four equations for uniform acceleration apply to free fall as well as other uniform acceleration situations. The symbol g may be substituted for a in those equations.

Figure 2.4.1 *These sky divers are in free fall until they open their parachutes to slow their descent.*

Sample Problem — Free Fall

A golf ball is dropped from the top of a tower. Assuming that the ball is in true free fall (negligible air resistance), answer these questions:

(a) How fast will the ball be falling after 1.0 s?

(b) How far down will the ball have fallen after 1.0 s?

What to Think About	How to Do It
(a)	
1. Determine initial conditions in the problem so you can choose the correct formula.	The ball starts from rest, so $v_o = 0.0$ m/s The rate of acceleration is $g = 9.8$ m/s^2 The time of fall is $t = 1.0$ s
2. Determine which formula to use.	The first uniform acceleration equation (1) applies to this question.
3. Solve.	$v_f = v_o + at$ $v_f = 0 \text{ m/s} + (9.8 \text{ m/s}^2)(1.0 \text{ s})$ $v_f = 9.8 \text{ m/s}$ The ball will be falling 9.8 m/s after 1 s.
(b)	
1. Determine which formula to use.	The third uniform acceleration equation (3) applies to this question.
2. Solve.	$d = v_o t + \frac{1}{2} at^2$ $d = (0 \text{ m/s})(1.0 \text{ s}) + \frac{1}{2}(9.8 \text{ m/s}^2)(1.0 \text{ s})(1.0 \text{ s})$ $d = 4.9 \text{ m}$ The ball will have fallen 4.9 m after 1 s.

Practice Problems — Free Fall

1. (a) How fast will the golf ball in the Sample Problem be moving after it has fallen a distance of 530 m, which is the height of the tower? (Assume free fall.)

   (b) Why does the ball not reach this speed when it hits the ground?

Practice Problems — Free Fall

2. How high is the cliff if you toss a small rock off of it with an initial speed of 5.0 m/s and the rock takes 3.1 s to reach the water?

3. (a) At the Pacific National Exhibition in Vancouver, one of the amusement park rides drops a person in free fall for 1.9 s. What will be the final velocity of the rider at the end of this ride?

   (b) What is the height of this ride?

4. At an air show, a jet car accelerates from rest at a rate of $3g$, where g is 9.81 m/s^2. How far does the jet car travel down the runway in a time of 4.0 s?

Projectiles

There are different types of projectile motion. From throwing a ball up and having it land on your hand to a golf ball being hit off a tee to throwing a rock off a cliff. The golf ball and rock examples require analysis of motion using two dimensions and will be studied in later courses. The example of throwing a ball up in the air and having it land back in your hand is an example of projectile motion in one dimension. This type of projectile motion will be studied next.

Recall that acceleration is a vector quantity with both magnitude and direction. In situations where the acceleration is caused by the force of gravity, the direction of acceleration is downward. This is a negative direction. In gravitational acceleration problems, therefore, you use $a = -9.81$ m/s^2.

If a body is thrown into the air, it accelerates downward ($a = -9.81$ m/s^2) at all times during the trajectory, whether the velocity is upward (+), zero, or downward (–).

You throw a baseball straight up. It leaves your hand with an initial velocity of 10.0 m/s. Figure 2.4.2 is a graph showing how the velocity of the ball varies with time, starting when you begin to throw the ball and ending when you finish catching it. At A, the ball has just left your hand. At C, the ball has just reached the glove in which you will catch the ball. Notice that between A and C, the velocity is changing at a uniform rate. If you take the slope of this graph, you will obtain the acceleration of the ball due to gravity alone.

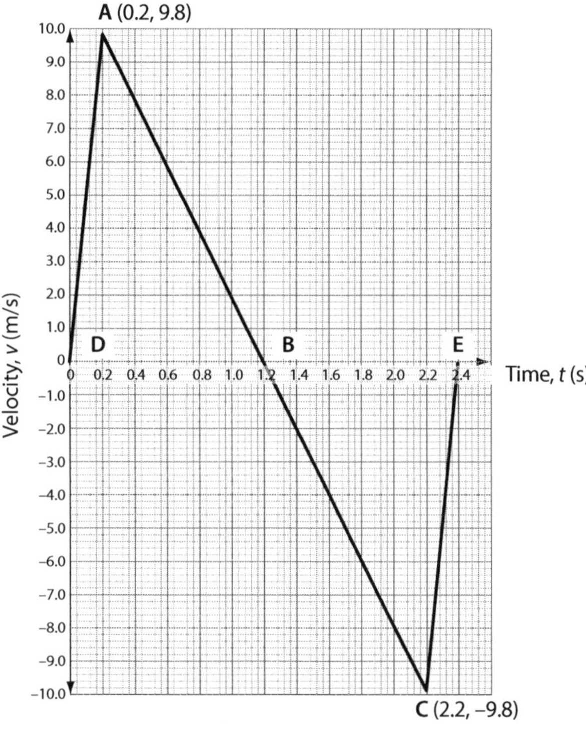

Figure 2.4.2 *This graph represents the velocity of a ball as a function of time, when you throw a ball straight up in the air.*

Quick Check

1. In Figure 2.4.2, what was the acceleration of the ball
   (a) while it was being thrown?

   (b) while it was in free fall?

   (c) while it was being caught?

2. What point on the graph corresponds with the instant when the ball reached the "peak" of its flight? Explain how you know this.

3. What altitude did the ball reach? **Hint:** The distance the ball travels equals the average speed multiplied by the time elapsed when it reaches its "peak" altitude. What property of the graph would give you $d = \bar{v} \cdot t$?

2.4 Review Questions

1. On a certain asteroid, a steel ball drops a distance of 0.80 m in 2.00 s from rest. Assuming uniform acceleration due to gravity on this asteroid, what is the value of g on the asteroid?

2. The graph below represents the velocity of a ball thrown straight up by a strong pitcher as a function of time. In the first part of the graph ending at A, the ball is accelerated to 39.2 m/s in a time of 0.20 s. After the ball leaves the pitcher's hand, it experiences only the acceleration due to gravity until it is caught in a glove and brought to rest in the hand of the catcher.

Velocity vs. Time for a Ball Thrown Straight up

A (0.2 s, 39.2 m/s)
B (4.20 s, 0 m/s)
D (8.40 s, 0 m/s)
C (8.20 s, – 39.2 m/s)
Velocity, v (m/s)
40 30 20 10 0 −10 −20 −30 −40
0 1.0 2.0 3.0 4.0 5.0 6.0 7.0 8.0 9.0 10.0
Time, t (s)

(a) What is the acceleration of the ball while it is being thrown?

(b) What is the acceleration of the ball after it leaves the pitcher's hand? (ABC)

(c) What is the acceleration of the ball while it is being caught? (CD)

(d) What point on the graph (A, B, C, or D) corresponds with the instant when the ball is at the peak of its flight? Explain your answer.

(e) Why is the slope of the graph negative as soon as the ball leaves the pitcher's hand?

(f) Why is the graph labelled velocity rather than speed?

(g) How far up did the ball travel?

(h) How far down did the ball fall?

(i) What is the average velocity of the ball for the whole trip from pitcher's hand to catcher's hand?

3. A body in free fall accelerates at a rate of 9.81 m/s^2 at your latitude. How far does the body fall during (a) the first second? (b) the second second? (Think first!)

Chapter 2 Conceptual Review Questions

1. Give an example in which there are clear distinctions among distance traveled, displacement, and magnitude of displacement. Specifically identify each quantity in your example.

2. Under what circumstances does distance traveled equal magnitude of displacement? What is the only case in which magnitude of displacement and displacement are exactly the same?

3. There is a distinction between average speed and the magnitude of average velocity. Give an example that illustrates the difference between these two quantities

4. If you divide the total distance traveled on a car trip (as determined by the odometer) by the time for the trip, are you calculating the average speed or the magnitude of the average velocity? Under what circumstances are these two quantities the same?

5. Is it possible for speed to be constant while acceleration is not zero? Give an example of such a situation.

6. Is it possible for velocity to be constant while acceleration is not zero? Explain.

Chapter 2 Review Questions

1. What is the difference between velocity and speed?

2. A traveller drives 568 km in 7.2 h. What is the average speed for the trip?

3. The following distances and times, for consecutive parts of a trip made by a red ant, were recorded by different observers. There is considerable variation in the precision of their measurements.

   A. 4.56 m in 12 s B. 3.4 m in 6.89 s
   C. 12.8 m in 36.235 s

   (a) What total distance did the ant travel?

   (b) What was the total time for the trip?

   (c) What was the average speed of the ant?

4. Light travels with a speed of 3.00×10^5 km/s. How long will it take light from a laser to travel to the Moon (where it is reflected by a mirror) and back to Earth? The Moon is 3.84×10^5 km from Earth.

5. Under what condition can acceleration be calculated simply by dividing change in speed by change in time?

6. A high-powered racing car accelerates from rest at a rate of 7.0 m/s^2. How fast will it be moving after 10.0 s? Convert this speed to km/h.

7. The graph below is a speed-time graph for a vehicle.

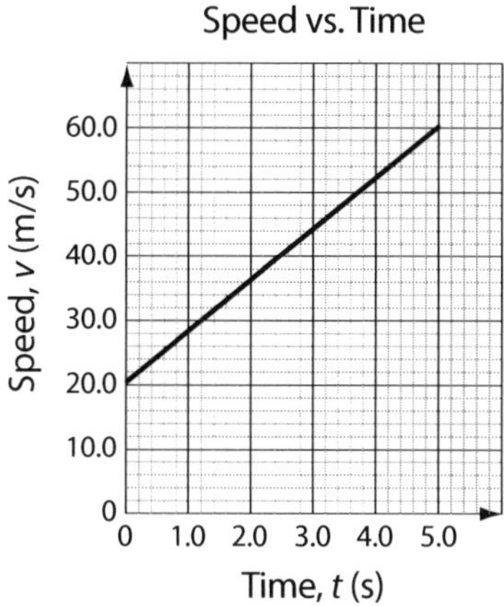

(a) What was the acceleration of the vehicle?

(b) What was the average speed of the vehicle during its 5.00 s trip?

(c) What distance did the vehicle travel during the 5.00 s?

(d) Write a specific equation for this graph.

8. A child on a toboggan slides down a snowy hill, accelerating uniformly at 2.8 m/s^2. When the toboggan passes the first observer, it is travelling with a speed of 1.4 m/s. How fast will it be moving when it passes a second observer, who is 2.5 m downhill from the first observer?

9. A space vehicle is orbiting the Earth at a speed of 7.58×10^3 m/s. In preparation for a return to Earth, it fires retrorockets, which provide a negative acceleration of 78.4 m/s^2. Ignoring any change in altitude that might occur, how long will it take the vehicle to slow down to 1.52×10^3 m/s?

10. Snoopy is taking off in his World War I biplane. He coasts down the runway at a speed of 40.0 m/s, then accelerates for 5.2 s at a rate of 1/2 g, where g is the acceleration due to gravity (9.81 m/s^2). How fast is the plane moving after 5.2 s?

11. A woman biker (leader of the local chapter of *Heck's Angels*) is driving along the highway at 80.0 km/h, in a 60.0 km/h speed zone. She sees a police car ahead, so she brakes and her bike accelerates at –8.0 km/h/s. How far along the road will she travel before she is at the legal speed limit?

12. Spiderman is crawling up a building at the rate of 0.50 m/s. Seeing Spiderwoman 56 m ahead of him, he accelerates at the rate of 2.3 m/s^2.
   (a) How fast will he be moving when he reaches Spiderwoman?

   (b) How much time will he take to reach Spiderwoman?

   (c) When he reaches Spiderwoman, Spiderman discovers that she is a Black Widow and, as you know, Black Widows consume their mates! He is 200.00 m from the road below. How long will it take him to fall to the safety of the road, if he drops with an acceleration of $g = 9.81$ m/s^2?

13. A stone is dropped from the top of a tall building. It accelerates at a rate of 9.81 m/s^2. How long will the stone take to pass a window that is 2.0 m high, if the top of the window is 20.0 m below the point from which the stone was dropped?

14. An aircraft, preparing for take-off, accelerates uniformly from 0 m/s to 20.0 m/s in a time of 5.00 s.
   (a) What is the acceleration of the aircraft?

   (b) How long will the plane take to reach its take-off speed of 36.0 m/s?

15. At an air show, a jet car accelerates from rest at a rate of $3g$, where g is 9.81 m/s^2. How fast is the jet travelling after 0.25 km?

16. To start a soccer game, the referee flips a coin that travels 50 cm into the air.
    (a) What was the coin's initial speed?

    (b) How long was the coin in the air before landing back in the hand of the referee?

17. A glider on an air track is made to accelerate uniformly by tilting the track at a slight angle. The distance travelled by the glider was measured at the end of each 0.10 s interval, resulting in the following data:

DISTANCE	d (cm)	0	0.025	0.100	0.225	0.400	0.625
TIME	t (s)	0	0.100	0.200	0.300	0.400	0.500

    (a) Plot a graph with distance d on the y-axis and time t on the x-axis.
    (b) Plot a second graph with distance d on the y-axis and t^2 on the x-axis.
    (c) Use the slope of your second graph to figure out the acceleration of the glider on the air track. HINT: Think about the third equation for uniform acceleration.

18. Assuming no air resistance, how far must a small steel ball fall from rest before it reaches a speed of 100.0 km/h?

19. How far does a freely falling body travel during the fourth second of its fall?

20. A small, free-falling pebble takes 0.25 s to pass by a window 1.8 m high. From what height above the window was the pebble dropped?

21. A disgruntled physics student sees the front end of his teacher's car directly below him at the base of a cliff. See the drawing below. If the student is 5.00 m above the car, which is 3.00 m long and travelling only 3.00 m/s to the right, will the apple the student drops hit the teacher's car? (Will physics be a "core" subject?) Show all details of your argument.

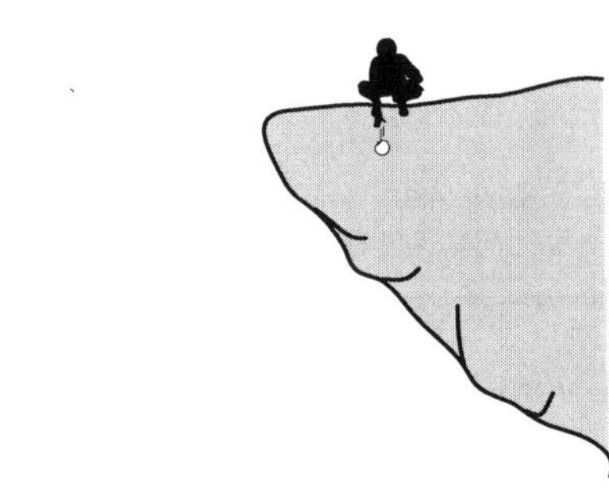

3 Forces

In this chapter the focus will be on the Big Idea:

Forces influence the motion of an object.

The content learning standards will include:

- contact forces and the factors that affect magnitude and direction
- mass, force of gravity and apparent weight.

By the end of this chapter, you should know the meaning to these **key terms**:

- coefficient of friction
- force
- force due to gravity
- gravitational field strength
- gravity
- Hooke's law
- inverse square law
- kinetic friction
- Newton's law of universal gravitation
- normal force
- spring constant
- static friction
- universal gravitational constant
- weight

By the end of the chapter, you should be able to use and know when to use the following formulae:

$F_g = mg$

$F_g = G\frac{m_1 m_2}{r^2}$

$F_{fr} = \mu F_N$

$F = k\Delta x$

This bungee jumper experiences both the force of gravity and elastic force during her jump.

3.1 Force of Gravity

Warm Up

Take a sheet of paper and a book in each hand. Hold at shoulder level. If you release them at the same time, which will hit the ground first? Now place the sheet of paper on top of the book. The paper should not extend over the edges of the book. Will the paper fall at the same rate as the book, faster or slower? Test your prediction. Can you create a rule for falling objects that explains how different masses fall to Earth?

____

____

____

Force

Every time you push, pull, twist or squeeze something you exert a force on it. Almost every time you exert a force on an object, you change something about that object: its speed, its direction, or its shape. A **force** is a push or a pull.

When a soccer player "heads" the ball the speed of the ball changes, and sometimes its direction does too. When a hockey player is given a solid body check, the force changes his direction and speed. When a golf ball is struck by a golf club, the force of the impact changes the ball's shape during the collision. The force due to air friction alters the shape of a raindrop, from a perfect sphere to something more like a teardrop.

Forces are measured in a unit called the **newton (N)**, named after Sir Isaac Newton.

Gravitational Force

The force of gravity pulls on you all the time. The force of attraction between planet Earth and you keeps you from floating aimlessly off into space! Any two bodies in the universe exert a gravitational force on each other. The amount of force they exert depends upon how massive the bodies are and how far apart they are. Two unique facts about the force of gravity are: (1) it cannot be "shut off"; and (2) it is always an attractive force, never repulsive.

Gravitational force is an example of a force that acts on objects without touching them. This classifies gravity as an action-at-a-distance force. Gravitational force creates a gravitational field around a body. Think of a field as an area where a force is exerted. For example, magnets have a field around them created by the attraction and repulsion between magnetic poles. A gravitational field depends on the mass of an object. The bigger the mass, the bigger the gravitational field. For Earth, this means a small mass like a person is attracted to the centre of Earth because Earth is the larger mass. The gravitational force experienced by the person results mainly from the Earth's gravitational field. The force within the gravitational field is referred to as the gravitational field strength. It is measured as the gravitational force per unit mass or $g = \frac{F_g}{m}$. The symbol for gravitational field strength is g. At Earth's surface, g is approximately 9.81 N/kg.

Weight

Regardless of where you are on Earth, near the surface, objects will fall with the same acceleration regardless of their mass. Other forces such as air resistance may slow an object down, but the acceleration due to gravity remains constant. Gravitational force is equal to the product of an object's mass and the acceleration due to gravity.

$$F_g = mg$$

When we calculate the gravitational force acting on an object, we are calculating its **weight**. This is an example of a term that has a specific meaning in science, but has other everyday uses. Many times people use the term *weight* to refer to mass. For example, when someone asks you how much you weigh, they are actually asking you what your mass is. The difference between weight and mass is that weight in measured in newtons and mass is measured in metric units such as grams or kilograms.

Quick Check

1. What is the force of gravity on a 90 kg person? What is the weight of this person?

2. If a person experiences a 637 N force of gravity on Earth's surface, what is the person's mass?

3. A 75 kg person would experience a force of gravity of 127.5 N on the Moon. What is the gravitational field strength on the Moon?

Measuring the Force of Gravity

Gravity causes unsupported objects to fall toward Earth. The usual way to measure the force of gravity is to balance it with another force acting upward. For example, when you stand on a bathroom scale, gravity pulls you downward. A coiled spring inside the scale pushes upward and balances the force of gravity.

The common laboratory spring balance uses a spring that is stretched by the force of gravity acting on the object that is being "weighed" (Figure 3.1.1). If the spring is of good quality, the amount it stretches will depend directly on the force of gravity. That is, if the force of gravity doubles, the stretch will double. If the force of gravity triples, the stretch will triple. In other words, the amount of stretch is directly proportional to the force of gravity on the object.

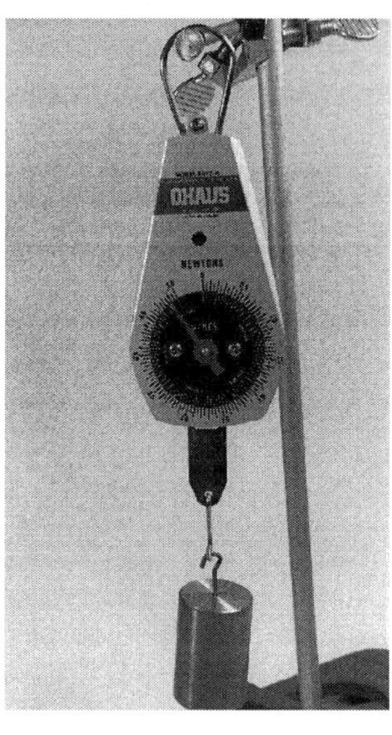

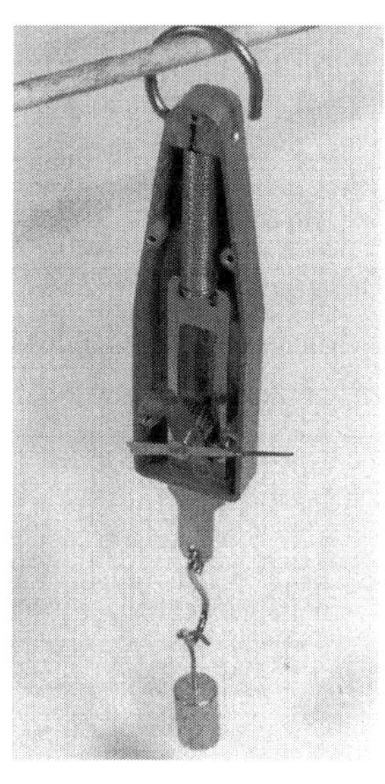

(a) (b)

Figure 3.1.1 *An example of a laboratory spring balance showing the gauge (a) and the spring (b)*

Newton's Law of Universal Gravitation

One of Sir Isaac Newton's many valuable contributions to science is his law of universal gravitation. Newton (1642–1727) realized that the force of gravity, which affects you and everything around you, is a universal force. Any two masses in the universe exert a gravitational force on each other. The force that keeps planets in orbit is the same force that makes an apple fall to the ground. How strong the force is depends on how massive the bodies are. It also depends on the distance between the two bodies.

Like all other forces, gravity is a mutual force. That is, the force with which the Earth pulls on a falling apple is equal to the force with which the apple pulls on the Earth, but in the opposite direction. The Earth pulls on your body with a force of gravity that is commonly referred to as your "weight." Simultaneously, your body exerts a force on planet Earth of the same magnitude but in the opposite direction.

Newton was able to use Kepler's laws of planetary motion as a starting point for developing his own ideas about gravity. Johannes Kepler (1571–1630) was a German astronomer who described the motion of the planets around the Sun now called Kepler's Laws. You will study these laws in future courses. Using Kepler's laws, Newton showed that the force of gravity between the Sun and the planets varied as the inverse of the square of the distance between the Sun and the planets. He was convinced that the inverse square relation would apply to everyday objects near Earth's surface as well. He produced arguments suggesting that the force would depend on the product of the masses of the two bodies attracted to one another. The result was his law of universal gravitation.

Newton's law of universal gravitation can be summarized as follows:

Every body in the universe attracts every other body with a force that (a) is directly proportional to the product of the masses of the two bodies, and (b) is inversely proportional to the square of the distance between the centres of mass of the two bodies.

The equation for Newton's law of universal gravitation is:

$$F_g = G\frac{m_1 m_2}{r^2}$$

where G is the **universal gravitation constant**, m_1 and m_2 are the masses of the bodies attracting each other, and r is the distance between the centres of the two bodies.

Isaac Newton was unable to measure *G*, but Henry Cavendish (1731–1810) measured it later in experiments. The modern value for *G* is 6.67×10^{-11} N•m²/kg².

Cavendish's Experiment to Measure *G*

You can imagine how difficult it is to measure the gravitational force between two ordinary objects. In 1797, Henry Cavendish performed a very sensitive experiment that was the first Earth-bound confirmation of the law of universal gravitation. Cavendish used two lead spheres mounted at the ends of a rod 2.0 m long. The rod was suspended horizontally from a wire that would *twist* an amount proportional to the gravitational force between the suspended masses and two larger fixed spherical masses placed near each of the suspended spheres. (See Figure 3.1.2.)

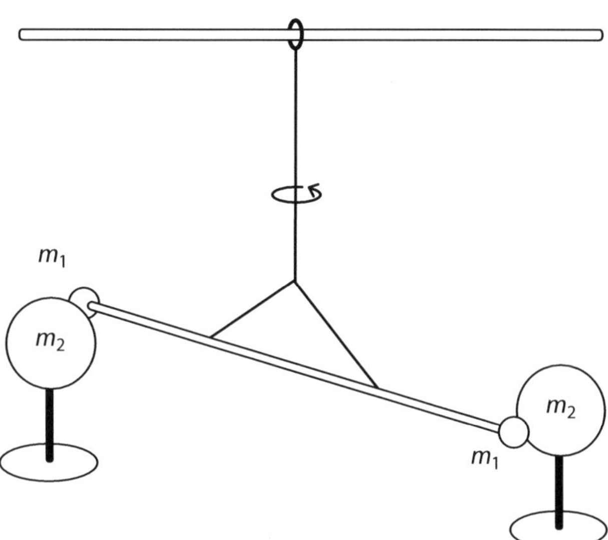

Figure 3.1.2 *Cavendish's apparatus*

The forces involved in this experiment were extremely small (of the order 10^{-6} N), so great care had to be taken to eliminate errors due to air currents and static electricity. Cavendish did manage to provide confirmation of the law of universal gravitation, and he arrived at the first measured value of *G*.

Earth's Gravitational Field Strength

To calculate the force of gravity on a mass m, you could simply multiply the mass by the gravitational field strength, g ($F = mg$). You could also use the law of universal gravitation:

$$F_g = G\frac{Mm}{r^2}, \text{ where } M \text{ is the mass of Earth.}$$

This means that $mg = G\frac{Mm}{r^2}$, and therefore,

$$g = G\frac{M}{r^2}$$

Thus, the gravitational field strength of Earth depends only on the mass of Earth and the distance, r, from the centre of Earth to the centre of mass of the object that has mass m.

Quick Check

1. Given two small, chocolate-centred candies of masses M and m, what will happen to the force of gravity F_g between them in the following situations?
   (a) r is doubled.

   (b) r is tripled.

   (c) r is reduced to 1/2 r.

   (d) r is reduced to 1/3 r.

2. The constant G in the law of universal gravitation has a value of 6.67×10^{-11} N•m²/kg². Calculate the force of gravity between the following objects:
   (a) a 100.0 kg person and Earth. Earth's mass is 5.98×10^{24} kg, and its radius is 6.38×10^{6} m.

   (b) a 100.0 kg person and the Moon. The Moon's mass is 7.35×10^{22} kg, and its radius is 1.74×10^{6} m.

   (c) two 46 g golf balls whose centres of mass are 10 cm apart.

Investigation 3.1.1– The Force of Gravity (Demonstration)

Purpose

To observe some interesting facts about falling bodies

Procedure

1. Two steel balls, one more massive than the other, will be dropped from the same height at the same time. Predict which of the two balls will reach the floor first. Give a reason for your prediction. Now listen when the two balls are dropped to the floor.
2. A piece of tissue paper and a steel ball will be dropped to the floor from the same height at the same time. Predict what will happen and explain your prediction. Observe what happens when the two objects are dropped.
3. Figure 3.1.3 shows a long glass tube from which most of the air can be removed with a vacuum pump. Inside it are two objects: a coin and a feather. Before pumping the air out, let the coin and feather drop the length of the tube and observe which falls faster. Explain. Predict what will happen when the air is removed from the tube. Which will fall faster this time? Now test your prediction.
4. Figure 3.1.4 illustrates an apparatus that can release two identical steel balls at the same time. One ball is projected straight out, while at precisely the same time an identical steel ball is dropped straight down. Predict which ball will hit the floor first. Give a reason for your prediction. Now test your prediction. Listen for the sounds of the balls hitting the floor.

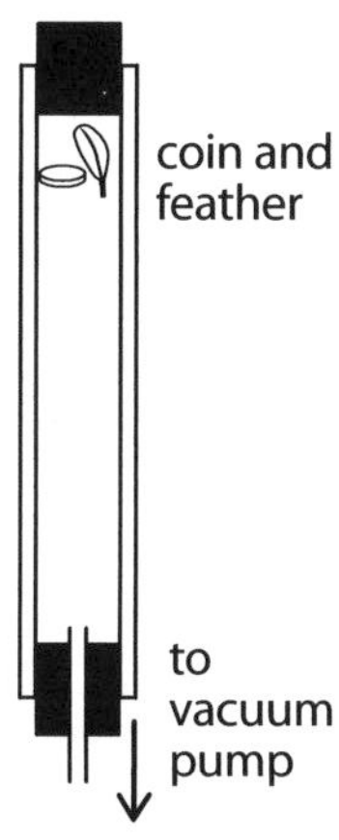

Figure 3.1.3 *Force of Gravitation — Step 3*

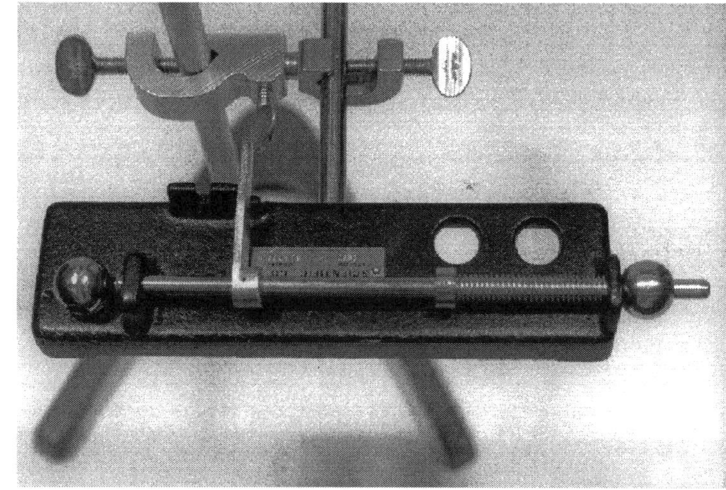

Figure 3.1.4 *Force of Gravitation — Step 4*

Concluding Questions

1. Describe what happened when you dropped two steel balls of different mass simultaneously. Does the mass of the balls affect their rate of fall?
2. (a) Describe what happened when you dropped a piece of tissue paper and a steel ball simultaneously. Explain.
   (b) What would happen if you did this experiment in a vacuum? Explain.
3. What happened when you fired a steel ball straight out horizontally while simultaneously dropping an identical ball? Does horizontal motion affect the rate of vertical fall of a ball?
4. On the Moon, the force of gravity on a given mass is only about 1/6 of what it is on Earth. As a result, there is no atmosphere around the Moon. Explain what you would expect to observe if you did Procedure steps 1 to 4 on the Moon.

Investigation 3.1.2– How Gravitational Force Depends on Distance

Purpose

To use data to discover the nature of the relationship between gravitational force and distance

Procedure

1. In an imaginary experiment, Superman was hired to measure the force of gravity on a 1 kg mass at different distances from the centre of Earth. He used a precise spring balance to obtain the data in Table 3.1.1. Make a graph with the force of gravity (F_g) on the *y*-axis and the distance from the centre of Earth (*r*) on the *x*-axis.
2. Your first graph will not be a straight line, because the relationship between F_g and *r* is not linear ($y \neq mx + b$) and is not a direct proportion ($y \neq mx$). The relationship is a **power law** ($y = m{\cdot}x^n$) where the power *n* is neither 1 nor 0. How can you find out what the value of *n* is? If you look at Figure 3.1.a, you will see the shapes of the graphs of several power law relationships. Which of these graphs does your graph most resemble? To find out if your graph is a particular type of relationship, plot force of gravity (F_g) on the *y*-axis, as before, and your chosen r^n on the *x*-axis. Plot the following graphs and see which one gives a straight line: (a) F_g vs. r^{-1} (b) F_g vs. r^{-2}

Table 3.1.1 *The Force of Gravity on a Kilogram Mass*

Force of Gravity (N)	Distance from Centre of Earth (Mm*)
9.81	6.37
2.45	12.74
1.09	19.11
0.61	25.48
0.39	31.85

*1 Mm = 1 megametre = 10^6 m

Concluding Questions

1. (a) What variables must you plot to obtain a straight line (through the origin)?
   (b) What is the specific equation for your final straight line?
2. From your equation, calculate the following:
   (a) the distance at which the force of gravity on the kilogram mass is half of what it is at Earth's surface
   (b) the force of gravity on the 1 kg mass at a distance of 10 Earth radii (63.7 Mm)

Graphs of various power law relations

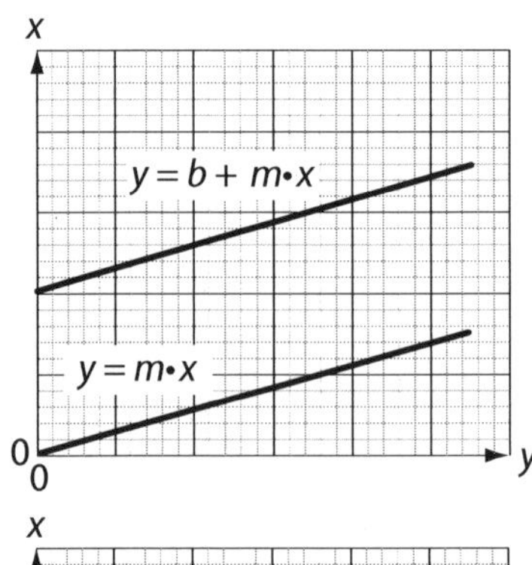

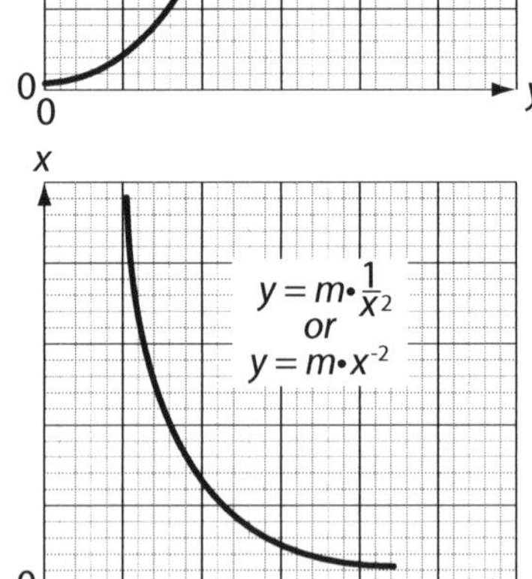

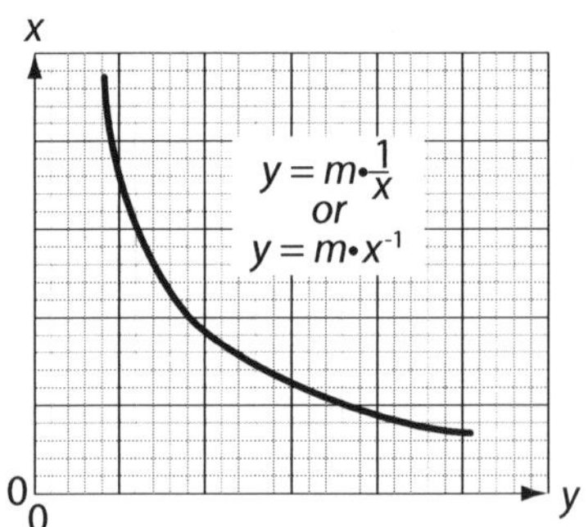

Figure 3.1.a *Power law graphs*

3.1 Review Questions

$G = 6.67 \times 10^{-11}$ N•m²/kg² $g = 9.81$ N/kg
Earth's mass $= 5.98 \times 10^{24}$ kg Earth's radius $= 6.38 \times 10^{6}$ m

1. What is the force of gravity on a 600 N person standing on Earth's surface?

2. How would the force of gravity between the Sun and Earth change if the mass of the Sun was three times greater than it is?

3. (a) What is the weight of an 80 kg person?

   (b) What is the weight of an 80 kg astronaut on the Moon where $g = 1.7$ m/s^2?

4. Given two candies with masses M and m a distance d apart, what will the force of gravity F_g between them become in the following situations?
   (a) Only M is doubled.

   (b) Only m is doubled.

   (c) Both M and m are doubled.

   (d) M, m, and d are *all* doubled.

5. What is the force of gravity on a 70.0 kg man standing on Earth's surface, according to the law of universal gravitation? Check your answer using $F = mg$.

6. What is the force of gravitational attraction between a 75 kg boy and a 60.0 kg girl in the following situations?
   (a) when they are 2.0 m apart

   (b) when they are only 1.0 m apart

7. What is the force of gravity exerted on you when standing on the Moon, if your mass is 70.0 kg and the Moon's mass is 7.34×10^{22} kg? The Moon's radius is 1.74×10^{6} m.

8. What is the force of gravity exerted on you on Mars, if your mass is 70.0 kg and the mass of Mars is 6.37×10^{23} kg? The radius of Mars is 3.43×10^{6} m, and you are standing on its surface, searching for Mars bars.

9. What is the force of gravity exerted on a 70.0 kg person on Jupiter (assuming the person could find a place to stand)? Jupiter has a mass of 1.90×10^{27} kg and a radius of 7.18×10^{7} m.

3.2 Friction

Warm Up

Fill a narrow-neck jar to the brim with rice. Poke a pencil into the jar and push the pencil until it can't go any farther. Repeat the poking until you can lift the jar with the pencil in the rice. Why does this happen?

____

____

____

Why We Need Friction

When a body moves, there is almost always a resisting force exerted on it by materials in contact with it. An aircraft moving through the air must overcome the resistance of the air. A submarine encounters resistance from the water. A car experiences resistance from the road surface and from the air. In all cases like this, the force opposing the motion of the body is called **friction**. Engineers attempt to design aircraft, ships, and automobiles so that friction is minimized.

Friction is not always a "bad" thing, of course. You need friction to bring your bike, car, or yourself to a stop. Walking on a frictionless floor would be a major challenge. Friction is desirable when you wish to strike a match or write with a pencil. If you ever have to use a parachute, you will appreciate the resisting force of the air on your parachute.

If you want to push a book along your bench, you know that you have to keep on pushing to keep it moving. This is true in many everyday situations. A skateboarder cannot coast along a level road indefinitely without some force being applied to counter the friction force. Friction is such a normal phenomenon, that for centuries it was believed impossible for an object to keep moving without a constant force being applied. About 400 years ago, Galileo Galilei (1546–1642) suggested that a body, once moving, would continue moving at the same speed and in the same direction indefinitely if friction were eliminated and no other unbalanced forces were present. It is difficult to verify this idea experimentally, and it seems to contradict everyday experiences. For some time, it was a hard concept for people to accept.

Static and Kinetic Friction

Even the smoothest-looking piece of metal, if viewed under a microscope, will have irregular bumps and hollows. Where the bumps come in contact, the electrical attraction between the atoms of the two surfaces produces a small-scale "welding" of the materials at the points of contact (Figure 3.2.1). When one surface is moved over the other, the welded regions must be broken apart. Friction arises from the breaking of these welded regions and from the "plowing" effect as the harder surface moves through the softer one.

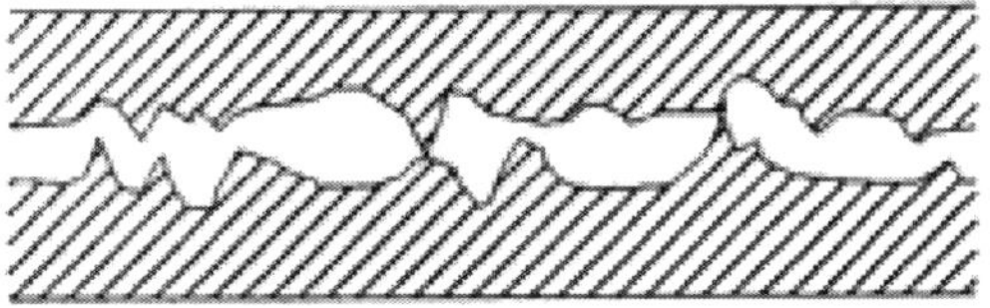

Figure 3.2.1 *An artist's impression of two metal surfaces magnified*

Static friction acts when you have two objects at rest relative to one another. Static friction, for example, keeps a car with its parking brakes on from sliding down a hill. A block of wood will remain stationary on a sloped table until you increase the angle sufficiently that it begins to slide. The force required to overcome static friction is always greater than the force needed to balance **kinetic friction**. Kinetic friction is the friction force between two flat surfaces that exists when one surface slides over the other.

To overcome static friction, you have to break the "welds" before the objects can move relative to one another. When you push a a heavy object, you have probably noticed that the force needed to get the object moving was slightly greater than the force needed to keep it moving at steady speed.

The force of friction F_{fr} is proportional to the force of gravity F_g on the object sliding over a smooth surface. A more general fact about kinetic friction is that the force of friction is proportional to the **normal force** F_N, which is the force acting perpendicular to the surfaces.

If a block slides horizontally across a table as in Figure 3.2.2 (a), the force of gravity is equal in magnitude to the normal force, but if the surfaces are at an angle to the horizontal as in Figure 3.2.2 (b), the normal force does not equal the force of gravity. You will encounter situations like this in future physics courses.

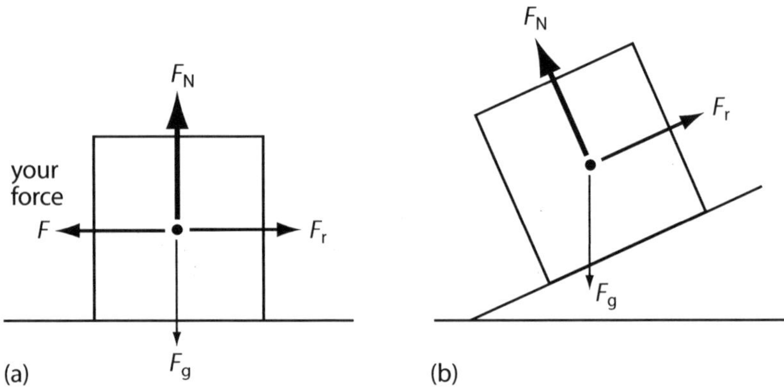

Figure 3.2.2 (a) *For a block sliding horizontally, the force of gravity and the normal force are equal.* **(b)** *For block sliding on a slope, these two forces are not equal.*

Coefficients of Friction

In general, for two objects with smooth flat surfaces sliding over one another, the force of friction is proportional to the normal force. The constant of proportionality is called the **coefficient of kinetic friction**. It is given the special symbol μ, which is the Greek letter *mu*.

$$\boldsymbol{F_{fr} = \mu F_N}$$

Table 3.2.1 lists some coefficients of kinetic friction.

Table 3.2.1 *Coefficients of Kinetic Friction**

Surfaces in Contact	Coefficient μ*
wood on wood	0.25
steel on steel	0.50
steel on steel (lubricated)	0.10
rubber on dry asphalt	0.40
rubber on wet asphalt	0.20
rubber on ice	0.005
steel on ice	0.01

* All values are approximate. Precise values vary with conditions such as degree of smoothness.

Surface area does not affect the force of friction appreciably. For example, it will require the same force to slide a building brick on its edge, as it will on its broad side. The two factors that have the greatest effect on friction are:

1. the normal force pushing the surfaces together, and
2. the nature of the surfaces.

Sample Problem — Kinetic Friction

The coefficient of kinetic friction between a wooden box and a concrete floor is 0.30. With what force must you push to slide the box across the floor at steady speed if the force of gravity on the box is 450 N?

What to Think About	How to Do It
1. If the box is moving at a constant speed, the forces acting on it are balanced. This means the force need top push the box is equal and opposite to the force of friction. Find the force of friction.	$F_{fr} = \mu F_N$
2. The box is on a flat surface. This means the force of gravity equals the normal force. Find the normal force	$F_N = F_g$ $F_N = 450\ \text{N}$
3. Solve.	$F_{fr} = \mu F_g$ $= (0.30)(450\ \text{N})$ $= 135\ \text{N}$ $= 1.4 \times 10^2\ \text{N}$ You have to push the box with a force of 1.4×10^2 N.

Practice Problems — Kinetic Friction

1. What is the total force of friction on a wagon's wheels if it takes 30 N to move it at a constant speed across a bumpy path?

2. (a) A 10 kg box of candy rests on a floor with a coefficient of static friction of 0.30. What force is needed to move the box?

   (b) If the coefficient of kinetic friction is 0.25, what force is needed to keep the box moving at a constant speed?

3. What is the coefficient of kinetic friction between a rubber tire and the road if a 2000 kg car needs 1.57×10^4 N to keep the car moving at a constant speed?

Investigation 3.2.1– Friction Can Be a Real Drag!

Part 1

Purpose

To determine how does the force of friction (F_{fr}) depends on the force of gravity (F_g) on an object when the object slides over a "smooth" horizontal surface

Procedure

1. Use a spring balance to measure the force of gravity on each of four nearly identical wood blocks provided. Write their weights, in N, in pencil on each block.
2. Prepare a data table like Table 3.2.2.

Table 3.2.2 *Data For Investigation*

Number of Blocks	Total Force of Gravity (N)	Force of Friction (N)
1		
2		
3		
4		

3. Adjust your spring balance so that it reads 0 N when it is held in a horizontal position or parallel to the bench top. Attach it to the hook on one of the four blocks. See Figure 3.2.a. Set the wide side of the block on a smooth, clean bench top. To measure the force of sliding friction, measure the smallest force needed to keep the block sliding at a slow, steady speed along the bench top. You will have to give the block a small extra nudge to get it moving. Once it is moving, however, a steady force equal to the force of kinetic friction should keep it moving at a steady speed. Do several trials until you are satisfied you have a meaningful average friction force. Record the

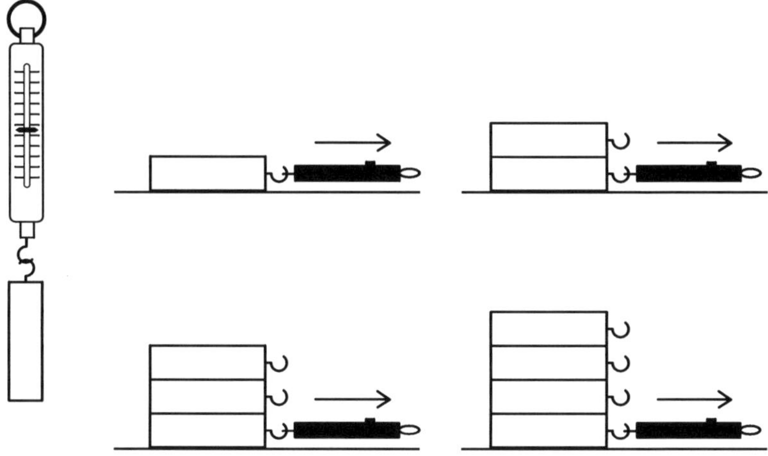

Figure 3.2.a *Friction — Part 1*

force of gravity and the force of sliding friction in your copy of Table 3.2.2.

4. Place a second block on top of the first. The total force of gravity will now be the sum of the weights of the two blocks. Measure the force of friction with two blocks.
5. Repeat with three, then four blocks. Record the total force of gravity and force of friction each time in Table 3.2.2.
6. Plot a graph with the force of kinetic friction F_{fr} on the *y*-axis and force of gravity F_g on the *x*-axis. Determine the slope of the graph and write a specific equation for your graph. Include the units for the slope, if any.

Concluding Questions

1. When you doubled the force of gravity on the object sliding over your bench, what happened to the force of friction? What happened to the force of friction when the force of gravity was tripled? quadrupled?
2. What is the equation for your graph? (Remember to use the proper symbols and units.)
3. The slope of your graph is the coefficient of kinetic friction. What is the coefficient of kinetic friction between the block and the tabletop you used?
4. Name three situations where you need to have
   (a) a low coefficient of friction, and
   (b) a high coefficient of friction.

Challenge

1. Measure the coefficient of kinetic friction between your blocks and a different horizontal surface.

Part 2

Purpose

To determine how the force of kinetic friction varies with the area of contact between two smooth, flat surfaces, when all other factors are controlled

Procedure

1. Make a prediction: If you double the area of contact between two smooth, flat objects, will the force of friction (a) stay the same, (b) double, (c) be cut in half, or (d) change in some other way?
2. Pile four blocks on top of one another as in Figure 3.2.b(a). Loop a string around the blocks, attach a spring balance, and measure the force of friction as in Part 1.

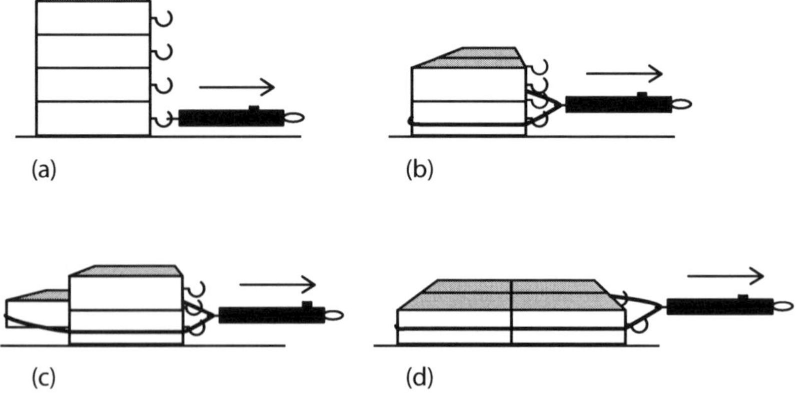

Figure 3.2.b *Friction — Part 2*

3. Prepare a table of data like Table 3.2.3. Record your results.

Table 3.2.3 *Data for Investigation, Part 2*

Number of Blocks	Area	Total Force of Gravity (N)	Force of Friction (N)
4	1 × A	constant	
4	2 × A	constant	
4	3 × A	constant	
4	4 × A	constant	

4. Double the surface area by arranging the blocks as in Figure 3.2.b(b). Notice that the force of gravity is still the same; only the area has changed. Measure and record the force of friction. Measure it several times until you are satisfied that you have an acceptable average.
5. Arrange the blocks so that the surface area is tripled, then quadrupled without changing the force of gravity. See Figure 3.2.b. Measure and record the force of friction each time.

Concluding Questions

1. After comparing your results for Part 2 with several other groups doing the same experiment, write a conclusion about the effect that varying the surface area has on the amount of friction between a smooth flat object of constant force of gravity and another smooth surface.
2. Discuss sources of error in this experiment.

3.2 Review Questions

1. (a) Where on a bicycle do you want to reduce friction? How is this done?

   (b) Where on a bicycle do you want friction?

2. (a) What is meant by the coefficient of kinetic friction?

   (b) Why are there no units attached to values of μ?

3. A force of 120 N is needed to push a box along a level road at a steady speed. If the force of gravity on the box is 250 N, what is the coefficient of kinetic friction between the box and the road?

4. The coefficient of kinetic friction between a steel block and an ice rink surface is 0.0100. If a force of 24.5 N keeps the steel block moving at a steady speed, what is the force of gravity on the block?

5. A copper block has dimensions 1 cm × 2 cm × 4 cm. A force of 0.10 N will pull the block along a table surface at a steady speed if the 1 cm × 4 cm side is face down on the table. What force will be needed to pull the same block along when its 2 cm × 4 cm side is face down?

6. A 48 N cart is pulled across a concrete path at a constant speed. A 42 N force is required to keep the cart moving. What is the coefficient of kinetic friction between the path and the cart?

3.3 Hooke's Law

Warm Up

Take three different known masses and a rubber band. Measure the length of the rubber band as it hangs from a hook. Add the smallest mass and measure the distance the rubber band stretches. Predict how far the rubber band will stretch with your other two masses. Test each one and record your predictions and results below.

____

____

____

Spring Constant

Figure 3.3.1 is a graph showing how the stretch of a certain spring varies with the force of gravity acting on it. This is not only a linear graph, but also a direct proportion. When the force of gravity on the spring is 1.0 N, the stretch is 0.75 cm. When the force is doubled to 2.0 N, the stretch doubles to 1.50 cm. If the force is tripled to 3.0 N, the stretch also triples to 2.25 cm.

If a force is exerted on an object, such as a spring or a block of metal, the object will be stretched or compressed. If the amount of stretching or compression, *x*, is small compared with the length of the object, then *x* is proportional to the force, *F*, exerted on the object. Figure 3.3.1 illustrates this proportionality. In Figure 3.3.1, stretch is given the symbol *x*, and the straight-line graph through (0,0) suggests that $F_g \propto x$ or that $F_g = kx$. The slope of the graph is the **spring constant**, *k*.

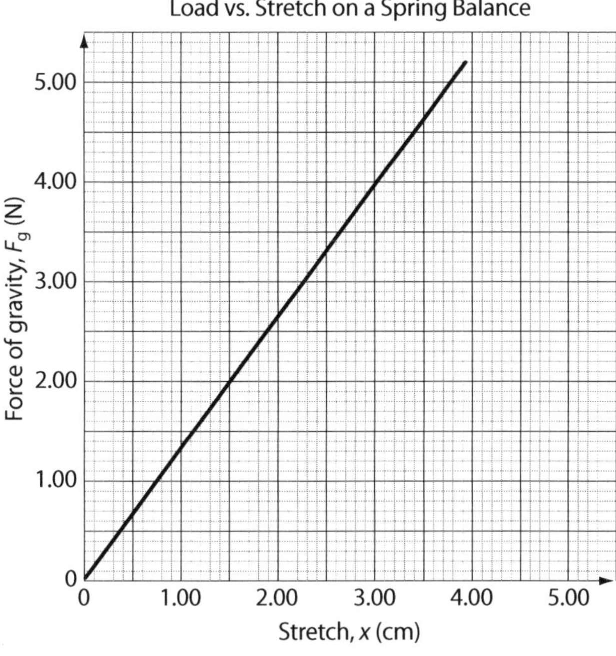

Figure 3.3.1 *The amount of stretch in a spring is proportional to the amount of force exerted on the spring.*

The English scientist Robert Hooke (1635–1703) first noticed the direct proportion between the force exerted on a solid object and the change in length of the object caused by the force. If too much force is applied, and an object is stretched or compressed excessively, the direct proportion breaks down. In that case, the object may be permanently stretched or compressed. **Hooke's law** is written with force as the subject of the equation:

$$\boldsymbol{F = k\Delta x}$$

where *F* is the applied force, *x* is the change in length, and *k* is the spring constant.

Quick Check

1. What is the applied force on a spring when it is stretched 0.20 cm and the spring constant is 3.2 N/m?

2. On Figure 3.3.1, the slope of the line is the spring constant (*k*). What is *k* for the spring used in that example?

3. A 2.5 kg mass stretches a spring 10 cm. How far will the spring stretch when it supports 5.0 kg?

Investigation 3.3.1 – Another Way to Weigh

Purpose

To make a "gravity measurer" out of a metre stick

Introduction

In an earlier course, you may have done an experiment where you added known masses to a spring and graphed the stretch of the spring against the force of gravity on the masses. In this Investigation, you will learn how you can measure the force of gravity using a metre stick.

Procedure

1. Set up the apparatus in Figure 3.3.a. Clamp a metre stick horizontally so that 80.0 cm overhangs the edge of your bench. (Use a piece of cardboard to protect the metre stick from damage by the clamp.) Tape a large paper clip to the end of the metre stick and bend the clip so that masses can be hung from it.

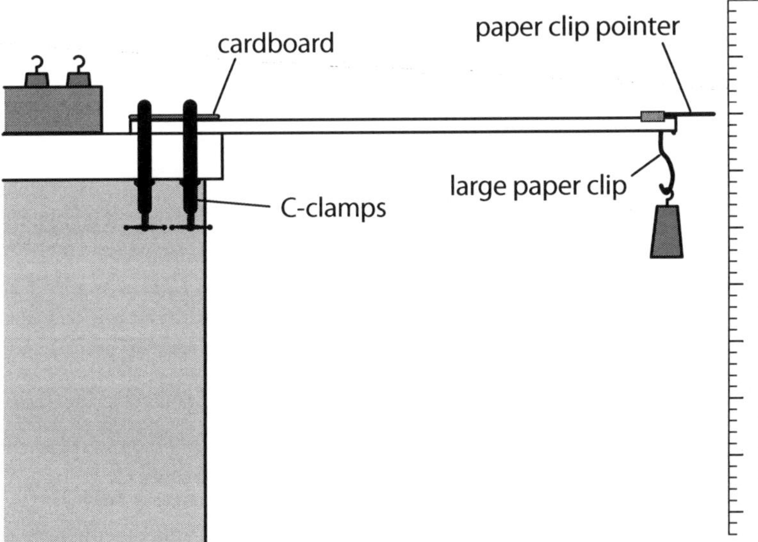

Figure 3.3.a *Step 1*

2. Mount another metre stick or ruler vertically so that the depression of the horizontal metre stick can be measured. Align the top edge of the horizontal metre stick with a convenient point on the vertical metre stick, such as 0.0 cm. Another paper clip could be used as a pointer.

3. Hang a 50.0 g mass on the paper clip and measure the depression or vertical drop of the end of the horizontal metre stick, estimating to the nearest one-tenth of a millimetre. The force of gravity on a 50.0 g mass is 0.490 N. Record the force of gravity and the depression in a table like Table 3.3.1.

4. Measure the depression caused by each of the forces of gravity listed in Table 3.3.1. When you finish reading the depression for 4.90 N, remove the masses and see whether the depression returns to 0.00 cm. If it does not, check that the metre stick is securely clamped. If it is not, tighten the clamps and repeat your measurements. Do not dismantle your set-up yet.

Table 3.3.1 *Data for Investigation*

Mass (g)	Depression (y) (cm)	Force of Gravity (F_g) (N)
0		0
50		0.49
100		0.98
150		1.47
200		1.96
250		2.45
300		2.94
350		3.43
400		3.92
450		4.41
500		4.90

5. Prepare a graph of force of gravity (y-axis) vs depression (x-axis). Find the slope, and write a specific equation for the line you obtain.
6. Hang an object with an unknown force of gravity (such as a small C-clamp) from the metre stick and measure the depression it causes. Find out what the force of gravity on it is (a) by direct reading of your graph and (b) by calculation using the equation for the line.
7. Measure the force of gravity on the object with the unknown force of gravity using a commercial laboratory spring balance.

Concluding Questions

1. (a) What is the equation for the graph you prepared of F vs. x? Remember to include the numerical value of your slope, with proper units.
   (b) Is the graph linear? Is the relationship between the two variables a direct proportion? Explain.
2. Calculate the percent difference between the unknown force of gravity as determined from the graph and as measured with a laboratory spring balance.

Challenge

1. Make a "letter weigher" using a strip of hacksaw blade instead of a metre stick. Calibrate it in grams instead of newtons. (The gram is a mass unit, but most postal rate scales are based on mass instead of force of gravity.)

3.3 Review Questions

1. Why are the units for the spring constant?

2. Using symbols "x" for stretch and "F" for force of gravity, write a specific equation for the line in Figure 3.3.1.

3. (a) Use your equation to solve for the stretch of the spring when a force of gravity of 4.0 N acts on it. Check your solution by looking at the graph in Figure 3.3.1.

   (b) Use your equation to solve for the force of gravity needed to stretch the spring 2.0 cm. Check your solution by looking at the graph in Figure 3.3.1.

4. In a direct proportion graph, the slope of the graph is called the spring constant. At any point on the line, the ratio of the stretch to the force of gravity will equal the constant of proportionality. By looking at the graph, find the spring constant when $F = 5.0$ N.

5. A wooden beam was clamped horizontally, so that masses could be hung from its free end. The depression x (in cm) caused by the force of gravity F_g (in N) on the masses was measured for loads up to 100 N. The graph below summarizes all the data.

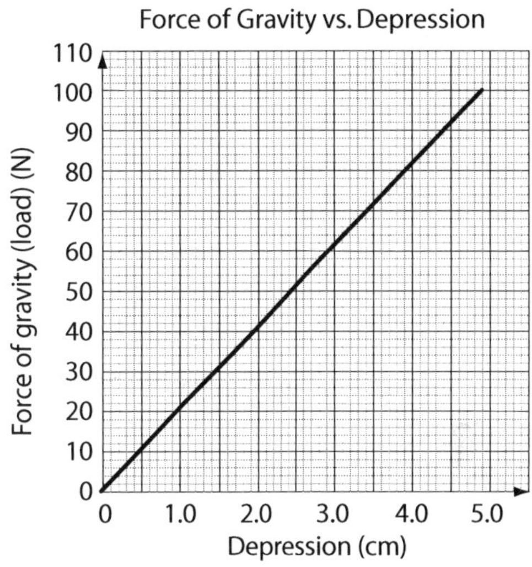

   a) What is the slope of the graph, expressed in appropriate units?

   (b) Write an equation specifically for this graph.

   (c) According to the above graph, how much will the beam be depressed by a load of 80.0 N?

   (d) According to the above graph, what load will cause the beam to be depressed by 3.0 cm?

Chapter 3 Conceptual Review Questions

1. Propose a force standard different from the example of a stretched spring discussed in the text. Your standard must be capable of producing the same force repeatedly.

2. The glue on a piece of tape can exert forces. Can these forces be a type of simple friction? Explain, considering especially that tape can stick to vertical walls and even to ceilings.

3. When you learn to drive, you discover that you need to let up slightly on the brake pedal as you come to a stop or the car will stop with a jerk. Explain this in terms of the relationship between static and kinetic friction.

Chapter 3 Review Questions

1. What is the force of gravity on a 70.0 kg man standing on Earth's surface, according to the law of universal gravitation? Check your answer using $F = mg$.

2. The force of gravity on a black bear is 2500 N on Earth's surface. The animal becomes so "unbearable" that it is transported four Earth radii from the *surface* of Earth. What is the force of gravity on it now?

3. Both G and g are constants. Why is G a *universal* constant and not g? Under what conditions is g a constant?

4. (a) Calculate the value of g at each of the locations shown in the table below. Express each answer as a multiple or a decimal fraction of Earth's g.

   (b) Would the force of gravity on you be greatest on the Moon, on Ganymede, or on Mercury?

5. What is the force of gravitational attraction between a 75 kg boy and a 60.0 kg girl
   (a) when they are 2.0 m apart?

   (b) when they are only 1.0 m apart?

6. Planet Mars has a mass of 6.4×10^{23} kg, and you have a mass of 5.0×10^{1} kg. What force of gravity is exerted between you and Mars, if you are standing on its surface? The radius of Mars is 3.4×10^{6}m.

	Mass	Radius	Value of g
On the Moon	7.34×10^{22} kg	1.74×10^{6} m	
On planet Mercury	3.28×10^{23} kg	2.57×10^{6} m	
On Ganymede*	1.54×10^{23} kg	2.64×10^{6} m	
On the Sun's surface	1.98×10^{30} kg	6.95×10^{8} m	

* One of Jupiter's moons

7. To slide a metal puck across a greased sheet of metal at constant speed requires a force of 0.525 N. If the force of gravity on the puck is 5.00 N, what is the coefficient of friction between the puck and the greased metal?

8. (a) The force of gravity on a wooden crate is 560 N. It can be pushed along a certain floor at steady speed if a horizontal force of 224 N is applied to it. How much horizontal force will be needed to move a stack of two crates at the same steady speed?

   (b) What force will be needed if the two crates are not stacked but tied to one another side by side?

9. The coefficient of kinetic friction between a rubber disc and the ice is 0.0050. If the force of friction is 0.25 N, what is the force of gravity on the rubber disc?

10. A student added masses to the end of a hanging spring, then measured the amount of extension, or stretch, caused by the force of gravity on each mass. The following readings were obtained:

Mass (kg)	0.200	0.400	0.600	0.800	1.000
Force of gravity (N)	1.96	3.92	5.88	7.84	9.80
Extension (cm)	0.47	0.93	1.41	1.89	2.35

   (a) Plot a graph with force of gravity (F_g) on the *y*-axis and extension (*x*) on the *x*-axis. Determine the slope of the graph in appropriate units. Write an equation describing how the force of gravity varies with the extension.

   (b) Use both your graph and your equation to figure out the force of gravity that would stretch the spring 1.50 cm.

   (c) Use both your graph and your equation to figure out how much stretch would occur in the spring when the force of gravity is 6.50 N.

4 Vectors

In this chapter the focus will be on the Big Ideas:

An object's motion can be predicted, analyzed and described.
Forces influence the motion of an object.

The content learning standard will include:

- vector and scalar quantities

By the end of this chapter, you should know the meaning of these **key terms**:

- scalar quantities
- vector quantities

By the end of this chapter, you should be able to use and know when to use the following formulae:

$a^2 + b^2 = c^2$

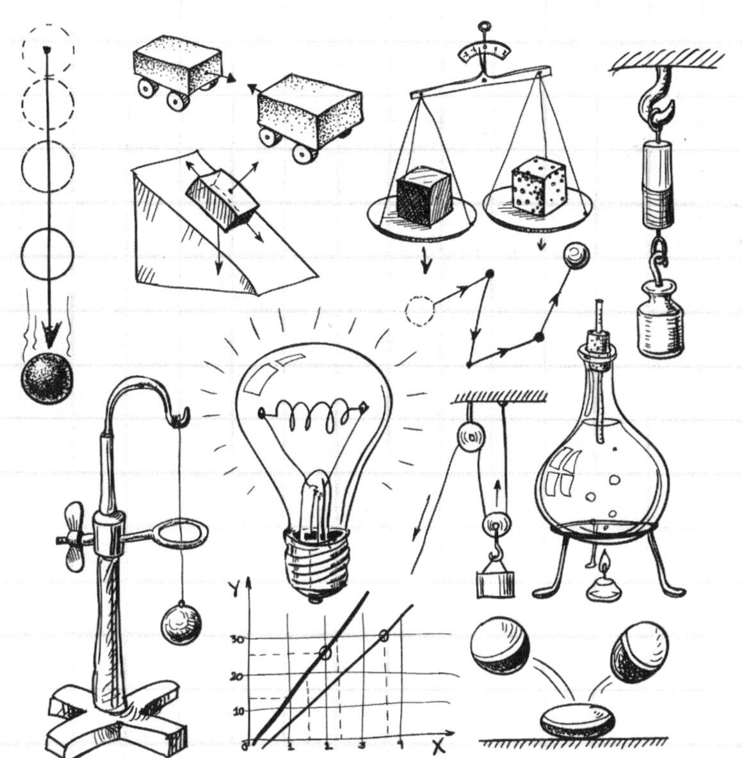

4.1 Scalars and Vectors

Warm Up

Your teacher will place an object in the classroom. Use only written directions to explain to someone who is blindfolded how to get from your chair to the object.

____

____

____

Scalar and Vector Quantities

If you add 5 L of water to another 5 L of water, you end up with 10 L of water. Similarly, if you add 5 kg of salt to 5 kg of salt, you will have 10 kg of salt. Volumes and masses are added by the rules of ordinary arithmetic. Volume and mass are **scalar quantities**. Scalar quantities have magnitude (size) only. Other scalar quantities with which you may be familiar are: length, energy, density, and temperature.

If you add a 5 N force to another 5 N force, the two forces together *may* add up to 10 N, but they may also add up to 0 N or to any value between 0 N and 10 N! This is because forces have *direction* as well as magnitude. Quantities that have both direction and magnitude are called **vector quantities.** Forces and other vector quantities must be added by the special rules of **vector addition,** which take into account direction as well as magnitude.

In addition to forces, other vector quantities you will encounter in this course include: velocity, displacement, acceleration, momentum, electrical field strength and magnetic field strength.

When you describe velocity, displacement, acceleration, force, momentum, or any other vector quantity, you must specify both magnitude and direction.

Watch Your Language

There are a few quantities where a different word is used for the scalar and the vector measurements. In day-to-day life, most people use one or both terms without wondering which term is correct. It is very important that you use them correctly from now on. This is important because some new concepts will seem much harder than they actually are if you use the terms incorrectly.

For now, there are two sets of scalar and vector quantities to focus on: distance and displacement, and speed and velocity. Distance and speed are scalar quantities. They only have an amount or magnitude. Think of a road sign that says 200 km to Vancouver or shows a speed limit of 30 km/h. Displacement and velocity are vector quantities and include both magnitude and direction. For example, to get to the arena, go 2 km [north].

Adding Vectors

In Figure 4.1.1, an object is hanging from a spring balance. Two forces pull on the object. Earth exerts a 10 N force of gravity downward on it, and the spring balance exerts a 10 N force up on it. Both Earth and the spring balance exert the same *size* of force on the object. The **net force** on the object is not 10 N or 20 N as one might expect. It is, in fact, 0 N!

To understand why the **net** or **resultant force** is zero in this situation, you must know (a) what a vector is and (b) how vectors are added.

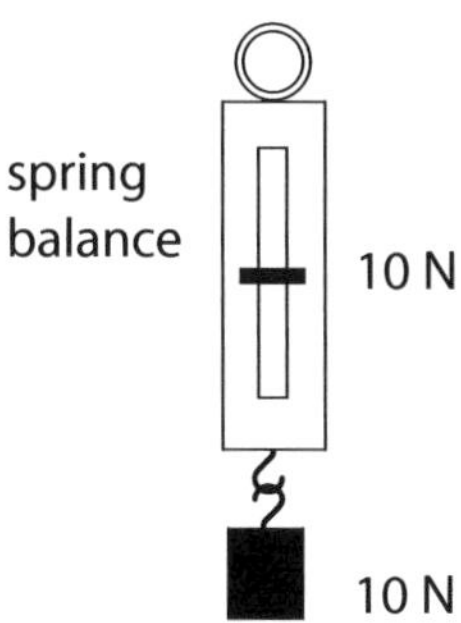

Figure 4.1.1 *The object hanging from this spring balance has forces acting on it in two directions, up and down.*

To show a vector, you must draw a line segment whose length is proportional to the magnitude of the quantity being represented. In Figure 4.1.2, this quantity is a force. You draw a segment in the direction the quantity is acting, and place an arrow tip at one end of the line segment to show its direction. The line segment, drawn to an appropriate scale complete with arrow tip, is a **vector.**

Figure 4.1.2 shows how the two forces in Figure 4.1.1 can be represented with vectors. Figure 4.1.2 (a) shows vectors representing the upward force $\vec{F}_1$ exerted by the spring balance and the downward gravitational force $\vec{F}_2$ individually. Figure 4.1.2(b) shows the two forces added together by **vector addition**.

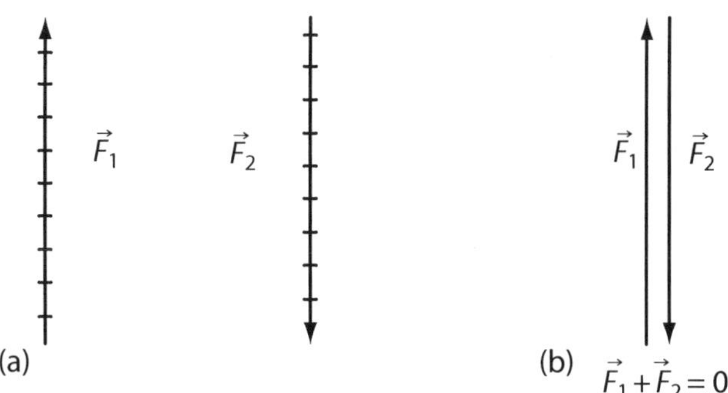

Figure 4.1.2 *Representing forces with vectors*

> Note: There are two ways to indicate that a quantity is a vector quantity. In diagrams or in handwritten notes, a small arrow may be drawn above the symbol for the quantity. For example, $\vec{F}$ indicates that a force vector is being discussed. In some textbooks, the symbol for a vector quantity may be typed in ***bold italics***, like this: ***F***. This symbol also indicates that a force vector is being discussed. If only the *magnitude* of a vector is of importance, the symbol *F* (*italics*, but not bold) is used.

To add vector $\vec{F}_1$ to vector, $\vec{F}_2$ draw vector $\vec{F}_1$ first, to scale and in the proper direction. Then draw vector $\vec{F}_2$ so that its tail begins at the tip of vector $\vec{F}_1$ and the line segment of $\vec{F}_2$ points in the proper direction. Be sure to draw the tip of an arrow to show which way $\vec{F}_2$ points. The net or resultant force is the vector going from the tail of $\vec{F}_1$ to the tip of $\vec{F}_2$.

In Figure 4.1.2, the resultant is clearly zero. When two or more forces acting on a body have a resultant of zero, the body is said to be in **equilibrium.** In this example, $\vec{F}_2$ is a force that balances one or more other forces and creates a condition where there is no net force. This type of force is called the **equilibrant.**

In Figure 4.1.3(a), strings connected to two different spring balances suspend a 10 N object. The strings form an angle of 120° where they are attached to the object. Notice that *both* scales read 10 N. Can the object possibly be in equilibrium if there are *two* 10 N forces pulling it up, and just *one* 10 N force pulling it down?

To find out what the **resultant** of the two upward forces is, use the rule for adding vectors again. In Figure 4.1.3(b), vectors $\vec{F}_1$, $\vec{F}_2$, and $\vec{F}_3$ have been drawn acting at a single point where the three strings meet. The vectors are all drawn to a suitable scale and are aimed in the proper directions relative to one another.

Vector $\vec{F}_1$ (dashed line) has been added to vector $\vec{F}_2$. The tail of vector $\vec{F}_1$ starts at the tip of vector $\vec{F}_2$ and vector $\vec{F}_1$ is aimed in the direction it acts, which is 60° left of the vertical.

The resultant of $\vec{F}_1$ and $\vec{F}_2$ starts at the tail of $\vec{F}_2$, and ends at the tip of $\vec{F}_1$. The resultant is drawn with a bold line and is labeled $\vec{F}_R$. Notice that $\vec{F}_R$ is equal in magnitude but *opposite in direction* to $\vec{F}_3$. (You could call $\vec{F}_R$ the *equilibrant* of $\vec{F}_3$.)

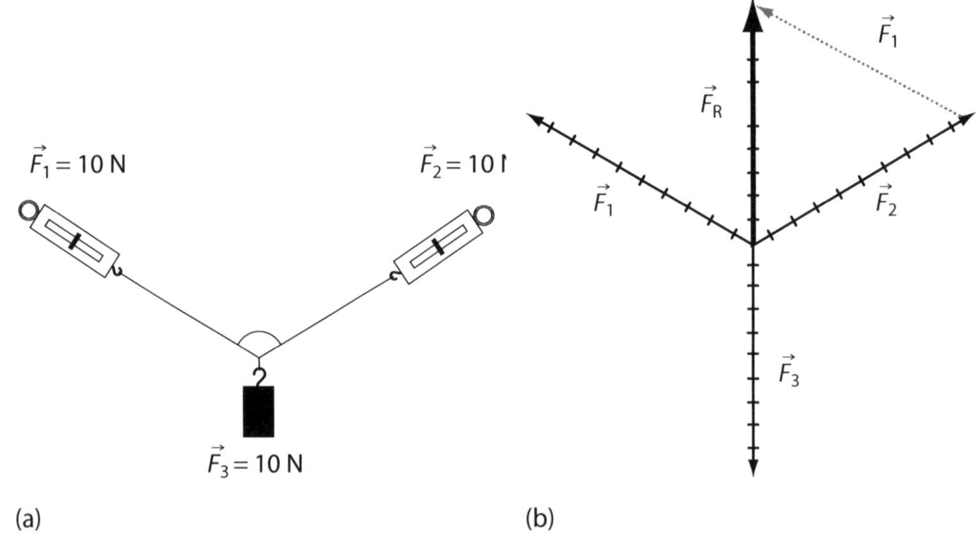

Figure 4.1.3 *Finding the resultant of two upward forces*

Quick Check

1. What would the resultant be in Figure 4.1.3(b) if you added $\vec{F}_2$ to $\vec{F}_1$ instead of $\vec{F}_1$ to $\vec{F}_2$?

2. What would the resultant be if you added $\vec{F}_R$ to $\vec{F}_3$?

3. (a) When you draw the three vectors in Figure 4.1.3(b) tip to tail, what kind of triangle do you get?

   (b) What if the three forces were 6 N [E], 8 N [S], and 10 N. What kind of triangle would they form when added together?

Adding Three Vectors

Figure 4.1.4 shows another way of looking at the vector situation you saw in Figure 4.1.3(a). This time, all three forces have been added together by vector addition. The vector sum of the three forces is zero. The fact that the resultant force is zero should not surprise you. The point at which the three forces act was stationary, and you will recall that a body that is stationary will remain so if the net force on it is zero. This in consistent with Newton's first law of motion.

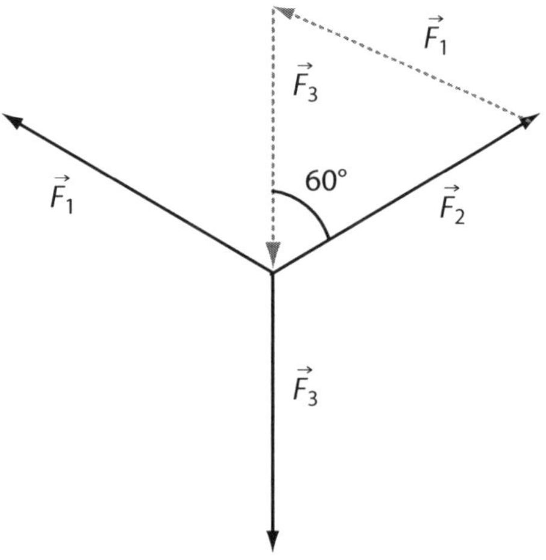

Figure 4.1.4 *In this example, the resultant force is zero.*

Two ways of writing the result of the vector analysis in Figure 4.1.4 are:

(1) $\vec{F}_1 + \vec{F}_2 + \vec{F}_3 = 0$

and (2) $\Sigma F = 0$

The symbol Σ means "the sum of." In this situation, it is the vector sum.

Quick Check

1. In how many ways could you add the vectors $\vec{F}_1$, $\vec{F}_2$, and $\vec{F}_3$?

2. Would it make any difference to the resultant you obtain if you added the three force vectors in a different order?

3. Displacement vectors are added in the same way as force vectors or any other vectors. If a golfer hits a drive 240 m toward the north, then hits a horrible second shot 100 m to the east, what is the resultant displacement of her golf ball? (Draw the two displacements to some suitable scale and then find their resultant.)

Quick Check continues

4. A dancer does the following Physics Jig move: 3 steps north, 2 steps west, 5 steps east, and 7 steps south. What is his
   (a) resultant displacement?

   (b) total distance travelled?

"Subtracting" Vectors

Method 1

Sometimes, you will have to find the difference between two vectors. For example, if the velocity of a body changes from $\vec{v}_1$ to $\vec{v}_2$, you may need to calculate the *change in velocity,* Δv. A vector *difference* is defined as the vector *sum* of the second vector and the *negative* of the first vector:

$$v = \vec{v}_2 + (-1)\vec{v}_1$$

or

$$v = \vec{v}_2 - \vec{v}_1$$

When "subtracting" vectors, simply remember that the negative of any vector is a vector of the same magnitude (size) but pointing in the opposite direction. The difference of two vectors is the sum of the first vector and the *negative* of the second vector. See Figure 4.1.5.

$$v \quad \vec{v}_2 - \vec{v}_1 \quad \vec{v}_2 \quad -\vec{v}_1$$

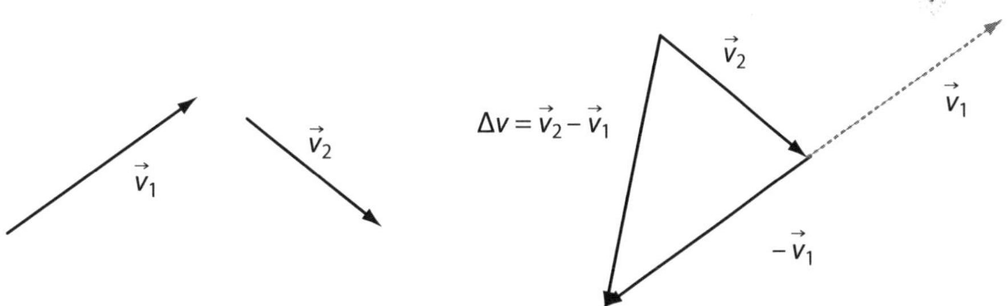

Figure 4.1.5 *Method 1 for "subtracting" vectors*

Method 2

The difference between two vectors can also be found by drawing the vectors "tail to tail," as shown in Figure 4.1.6. The resultant Δv is the vector drawn from tip to tip. From Figure 4.1.6,

$$\vec{v}_1 + \quad v = \vec{v}_2$$

$$v = \vec{v}_2 - \vec{v}_1$$

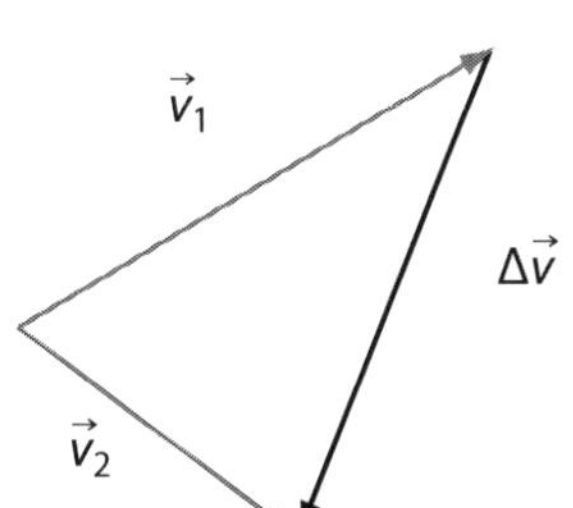

Figure 4.1.6 *Method 2 for "subtracting" vectors*

Vectors and Direction

To identify the direction of vectors, two common conventions are used: numerical and compass. Sometimes compass directions are also called cardinal directions.

Numerical directions use a positive and negative sign to indicate direction. If you think of a graph, the "up" direction on the y-axis and the "right" direction on the x-axis are positive. "Down" on the y-axis and "left" on the x-axis is negative. For example, a person walking 2 km right is walking +2 km and a person walking 2 km left is walking −2 km. The sign indicates direction.

Compass or cardinal directions are another way of indicating vector directions. As Figure 4.1.7 shows, there are four main directions on the compass: north, east, south, and west. North and west are usually positive, and east and south are negative. For example, if a person walking north encounters a person walking south, the two people are walking in opposite directions.

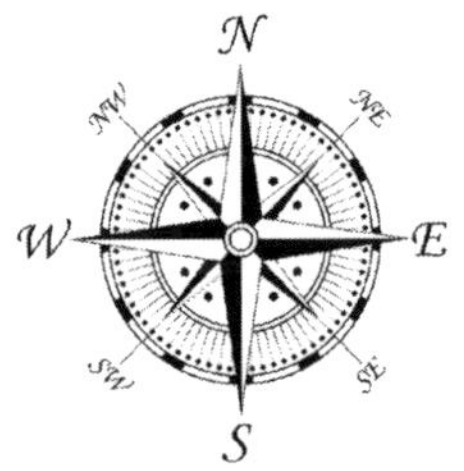

Figure 4.1.7 *The cardinal directions are north, east, south, and west, as shown on this compass.*

To determine the angle θ, you use trigonometric ratios. Three trigonometric ratios are particularly useful for solving vector problems. In the right-angled triangle ABC, consider the angle labelled θ. With reference to θ, AC is the opposite side (o), BC is the adjacent side (a), and AB is the hypotenuse (h). In any right-angled triangle, the hypotenuse is always the side opposite to the right angle.

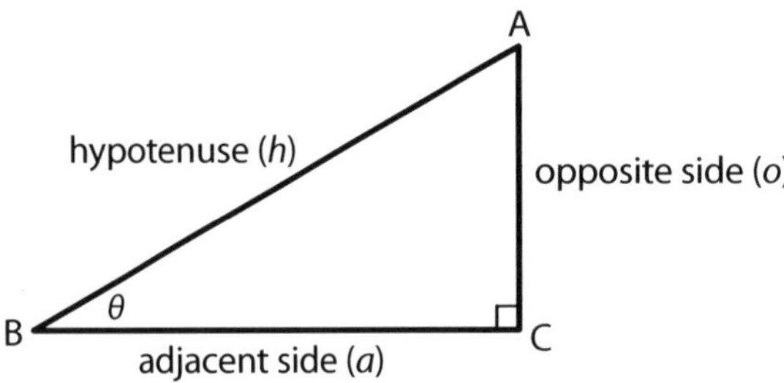

Figure 4.1.8 *The sides of a right-angled triangle are used to define trigonometric ratios.*

The three most commonly used trigonometric ratios are defined as follows:

$$\text{sine } \theta = \frac{\text{opposite side}}{\text{hypotenuse}} = \frac{o}{h}$$

$$\text{cosine } \theta = \frac{\text{adjacent side}}{\text{hypotenuse}} = \frac{a}{h}$$

$$\text{tangent } \theta = \frac{\text{opposite side}}{\text{adjacent side}} = \frac{o}{a}$$

Trigonometric ratios can help you solve vector problems quickly and accurately. Scientific calculators can provide you with the ratios for any angle.

Sample Problem — Vectors and Trigonometry

A rugby player is being pushed by one opponent with a force of 250.0 N and another opponent with a force of 600.0 N. Both forces are exerted horizontally and the player being tackled has her feet momentarily off the ground. If the two force vectors form an angle of 90°, what is the resultant force of the two forces exerted on the ball carrier?

What to Think About	How to Do It
1. Identify what you know and what you are solving.	$F_1 = 600.0$ N $F_2 = 250.0$ N $F_R = ?$
2. Represent the problem with a diagram.	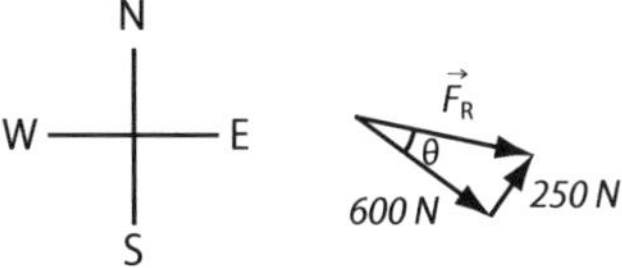 **Figure 4.1.9**
3. Solve using the Pythagorean theorem.	$c^2 = a^2 + b^2$ $F_R^2 = (250.0\ N)^2 + (600.0\ N)^2$ $F_R^2 = 422500\ N^2$ $F_R = \sqrt{422500\ N^2} = 650.0\ N$

Practice Problems — Vectors and Trigonometry

1. Two horses on opposite sides of a narrow canal are pulling a barge along the stream. Each horse pulls with a force of 720 N. The ropes from the horses meet a a common point on the front of the barge. What is the resultant force exerted by the two horses if the angle between the ropes is:

(a) 30°

(b) 45°

(c) 60°

4.1 Review Questions

1. Two boys are pulling a girl along on a toboggan. Each boy pulls on a rope attached to the same point on the front of the toboggan with a force of 360 N. Using a scale diagram, determine the resultant of the two forces exerted by the boys if their ropes form each of these angles with each other:

   (a) 0°

   (b) 60°

   (c) 120°

   (d) 180°

2. What is the *magnitude* of the resultant of the three forces acting at point X?

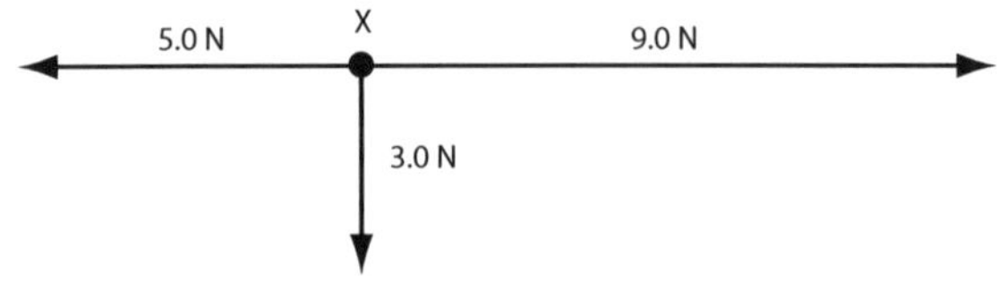

3. A football player is pushed by one opponent with a force of 50.0 N toward the east. At the same time, a second tackler pushes him with a force of 120.0 N toward the north. What is the magnitude and direction of the resultant force on the first player?

4. The following three forces act simultaneously on the same point: 100.0 N toward the north, 50.0 N toward the east, and 220.0 N toward the south. What will their resultant be?

4.2 Projectile Motion

Warm Up

Place the bottom of a bill in line with your friend's hand as shown in the drawing. Without warning, release the bill. Can your friend grab the bill? Human reaction time is about one seventh of a second. How long would the bill have to be to make it "catchable"?

____

____

____

____

Describing Projectile Motion

If you throw a baseball, your arm exerts a force on the ball until the ball leaves your hand. Once the ball is free of your hand, it continues moving because of its inertia, and it will follow a curved path unless you throw it straight up. A baseball thrown into the air is a good example of a **projectile**. If a marble rolls off the edge of a table, it follows a curved path to the floor. The marble, too, is a projectile.

Any object (a rock, a ball, or a bullet) that is projected by some method and then continues moving because of its inertia, is a projectile. Figure 4.2.1 shows the path taken by a baseball thrown by highly skilled fielder. The dashed line shows the path the baseball would take if there were no force of gravity. The solid line shows the actual path taken by the baseball.

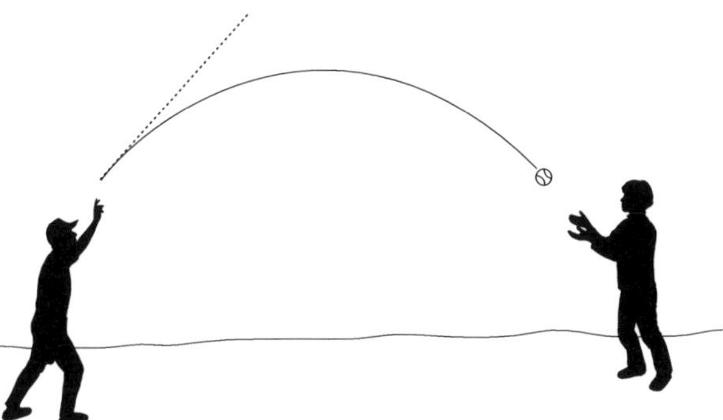

Figure 4.2.1 *The baseball follows a curved path rather than a straight one from the fielder's hand because of the force of gravity.*

At first glance, it may appear to be a complicated matter to describe the motion of a projectile. After you have done Investigation 4.2.1, you will understand that the motion of a projectile can be described very simply if you look at the vertical motion and the horizontal motion separately. This is called resolving the vector motion into components.

Vectors and Projectile Problems

You will use the four equations for uniform acceleration frequently when solving problems involving projectile motion. For your convenience, these laws are summarized here:

I	$\vec{v}_f = \vec{v}_0 + \vec{a}t$
II	$d = \frac{v_0 + v_f}{2} \cdot t$
III	$d = v_0 t + \frac{1}{2}at^2$
IV	$v_f^2 = v_0^2 + 2ad$

When solving projectile problems, you must remember that velocities, displacements, and accelerations are vector quantities. Upward motion is generally considered positive (+) and downward motion is negative (–). On or near Earth's surface, the magnitude of the acceleration due to gravity is $\vec{g} = 9.80\ \text{m/s}^2$, and since it is always acting downward, you should use

$$\vec{a} = -9.80\ \text{m/s}^2$$

When analyzing the motion of a projectile, the velocity is almost always resolved into its *horizontal* and *vertical* components. The laws of uniform acceleration may be applied to the vertical motion of the object. The horizontal motion is simple to deal with, since horizontal velocity is constant (ignoring air resistance).

The Parabolic Nature of Projectile Motion

When a projectile is fired, its path is *parabolic* if air resistance is negligible. This can be shown quite simply for a situation where an object is thrown horizontally (Figure 4.2.2).

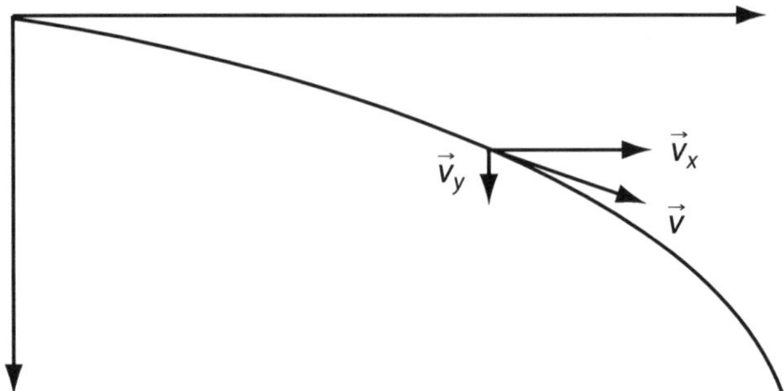

Figure 4.2.2 *Parabolic motion can be resolved into an x component and a y component for motion.*

Let the magnitude of the horizontal displacement of an object thrown horizontally be *x*. Horizontal velocity, which has magnitude v_x is constant.

$$v_x = \frac{x}{t} \text{ so } t - \frac{x}{v_x}$$

Let the magnitude of the vertical displacement be *y*. Assuming the object starts from rest so that $\vec{v}_0 = 0$, then

$$y = \tfrac{1}{2}at^2 \text{ or } y = \frac{1}{2}a\left[\frac{x}{v_x}\right]^2$$

Now, ½, a, and v_x are all constant, therefore we can say that $y = kx^2$.

This is the simplest possible equation for a *parabola.* A ball thrown out by a pitcher, or a stream of water issuing from a hose will follow a parabolic path. If air resistance is negligible, any object, given a horizontal motion in a gravitational field, will move along a parabolic path.

Sample Problem — Projectile Motion

A golf ball was struck from the first tee at Lunar Golf and Country Club, a private golf course for astronauts stranded on the Moon. It was given a velocity of 48 m/s at an angle of 40° to the horizontal. On the Moon, the magnitude of $g = 1.6\ m/s^2$.

(a) What is the vertical component of the golf ball's initial velocity?
(b) For what interval of time is the ball in flight?
(c) How far will the ball travel horizontally?

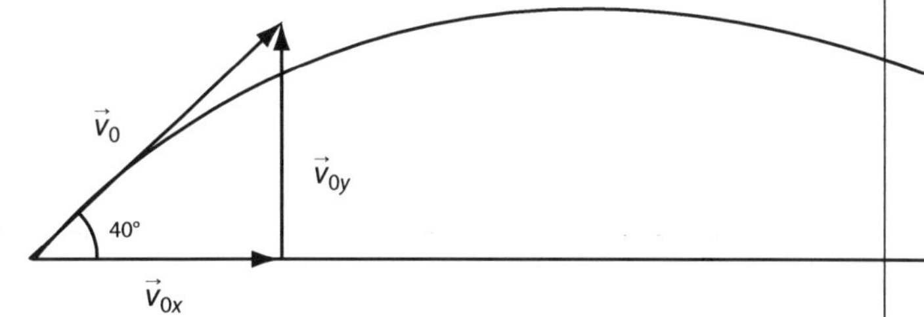

Figure 4.2.3

What to Think About	How to Do It
(a)	
1. Since the velocity of the ball is initially 48 m/s, find $\vec{v}_{0y}$. (*Keep one extra significant figure for now.)	$\vec{v}_{0y} = \vec{v}_0 \sin 40°$ $\vec{v}_{0y} = (48\ m/s)(0.6428)$ $\vec{v}_{0y} = 30.9\ m/s$ *
(b)	
1. The most direct way of solving for time is to use Equation III for uniform acceleration.	$d = v_0 t + \frac{1}{2}at^2$
2. Since the ball will eventually return to ground level, its displacement for the entire trip, in a vertical direction, is zero ($d = y = 0$). (*Keep one extra significant figure for now.)	Therefore, $0 = (30.9\ m/s)t + ½(-1.6\ m/s^2)t^2$ or $(0.80\ m/s^2)t^2 = (30.9\ m/s)t$ $t = \frac{30.9\ m/s}{0.80\ m/s^2} = 38.6\ s$ *
(c)	
1. Horizontal displacement: $x = v_{0x}t$ Horizontal velocity remains constant: $v_{0x} = v_0 \cos 40°$	$x = (v_0 \cos 40°)t$ $x = (48\ m/s)(0.7660)(38.6\ s)$ $x = 1.42 \times 10^3\ m$
Summary Round the final answers to two significant figures. The golf ball would travel 1.4 km on the Moon!	(a) 31 m/s (b) 39 s (c) 1.4×10^3 m or 1.4 km

Practice Problems — Projectile Motion

1. A girl throws a rock horizontally from the top of a cliff 98 m high, with a horizontal velocity of 27 m/s.
   (a) How many seconds will the rock be in the air?

   (b)How far out from the base of the cliff does the rock land?

2. A golfer gives a golf ball a velocity of 48 m/s at an angle of 45° with the horizontal.
   (a) What is the vertical component of the ball's initial velocity?

   (b) How long is the ball in the air?

   (c) What is the horizontal distance covered by the ball while in flight?

   (d) Compare your result with that for the same question on the Moon. (See Sample Problem 2.2.1.)

Investigation 4.2.1 Projectiles

Purpose

To study the two-dimensional motion of a projectile

Procedure

1. Set up the projectile apparatus in Figure 4.2.4. When the horizontal bar is released by a spring mechanism, ball A falls straight down and ball B is projected horizontally. Once "fired," both balls experience one force only (ignoring air resistance) — the force of gravity. Watch and listen as the two balls are projected simultaneously. Repeat the procedure several times.

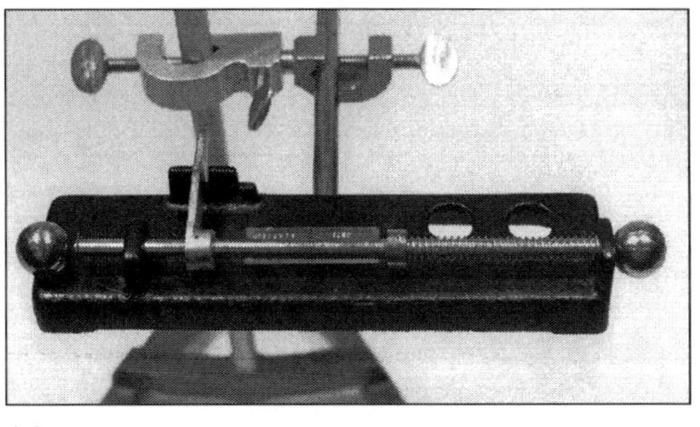

(a)

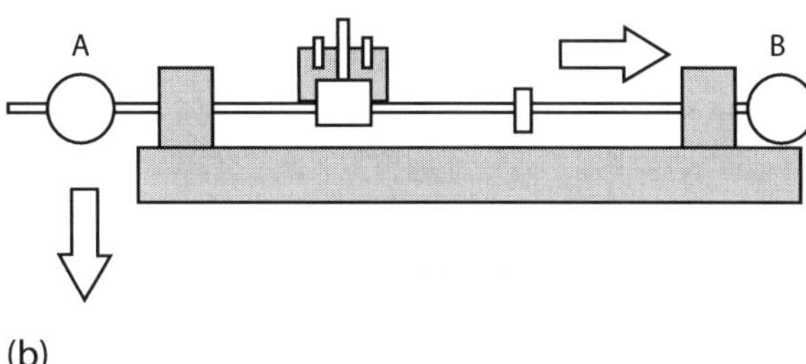

(b)

Figure 4.2.4

2. Figure 4.2.5(a) could be a tracing from a strobe photograph of two balls released simultaneously by a projectile apparatus similar to the one you just used. Make or obtain a copy of this tracing. Use a sharp, penciled dot to mark the position of the centre of each image of the balls. Figure 4.2.5(b) shows what to do.

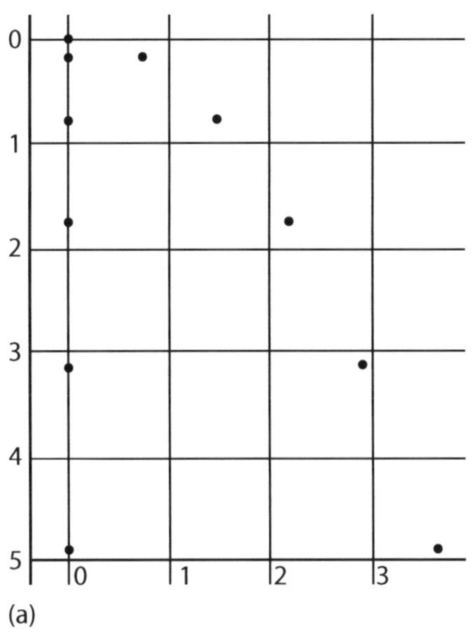

(a)

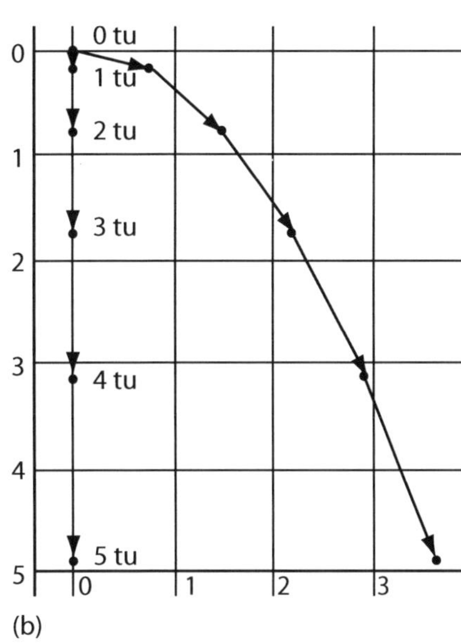

(b)

Figure 4.2.5 *A tracing of a stroboscopic photograph made of a projected ball, falling simultaneously with a ball falling straight down, might look like this.*

3. Consider ball A first. (It is the one falling straight down.) Find out if its acceleration is uniform as follows: Call the time interval between images one "time unit" (tu). Measure the displacement of the ball during each successive tu. Since average velocity equals displacement divided by time, the average velocity during each successive time interval simply equals displacement divided by 1 tu.

4. Make a graph of the average vertical velocity $\bar{v}_y$ vs. time, *t*. Find out if the acceleration of falling ball A is uniform. Remember that, since this is average velocity, you should plot velocities *midway* through each time interval.
5. Now, consider ball B, which was projected horizontally. On your tracing, draw in successive velocity vectors as shown in Figure 4.2.5(b) above. These vectors are cute to look at, but they do not help you understand what is happening to ball B! Therefore, construct both horizontal and vertical components of each of the velocity vectors. See Figure 4.2.6.

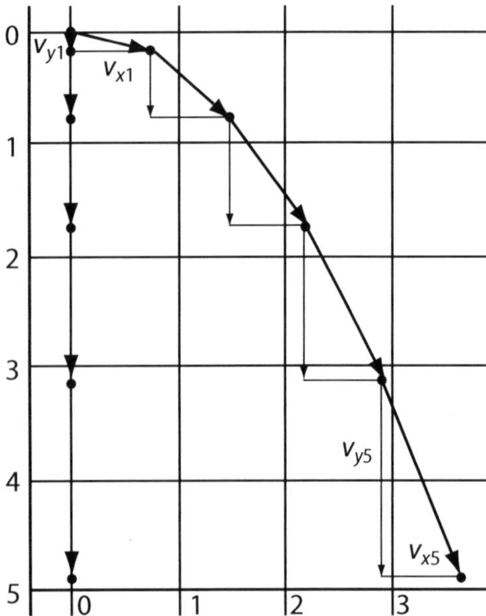

Figure 4.2.6

6. Compare successive vertical components of ball B's velocities with the corresponding vertical velocities of ball A. Plot a graph of $\bar{v}_y$ vs. *t* for ball B.
7. Compare successive horizontal components ($\bar{v}_x$) with each other. Plot $\bar{v}_x$ vs. *t*.

8. (a) Plot total vertical displacement from rest (d_y) vs. time (*t*) for the vertical motion of either ball.
   (b) Plot d_y vs. t^2.
9. Plot total horizontal displacement from rest (d_x) vs. time (*t*) for ball B.

Concluding Questions

1. A rifle fires a bullet horizontally on level ground. Just as the bullet leaves the rifle, the rifle falls to the ground. Which will hit the ground first, the bullet or the rifle? Explain your answer.
2. When a ball is projected horizontally, what conclusions do you arrive at regarding
   (a) its horizontal velocity components?
   (b) its vertical velocity components?
3. Write a simple mathematical relationship (such as $d_x = kt$, where k is the constant of proportionality) connecting the two variables in each of the following projectile situations:
   (a) v_y vs. *t*
   (b) v_x vs. *t*
   (c) d_y vs. *t*

Challenges

1. Build a "monkey gun" apparatus. See Figure 4.2.7. The projectile is a small marble, which is propelled by a "blow gun" made of a copper pipe, the diameter of which is just slightly larger than the marble. When the marble leaves the gun, it breaks a thin piece of aluminum foil, which opens an electric circuit. An electromagnet holding up a tin can target (the "monkey" in a tree?) is deactivated. Just as the marble leaves the gun, the "monkey" starts to fall to the ground. Will the marble hit the monkey or miss it? Explain your answer. Now test your prediction!

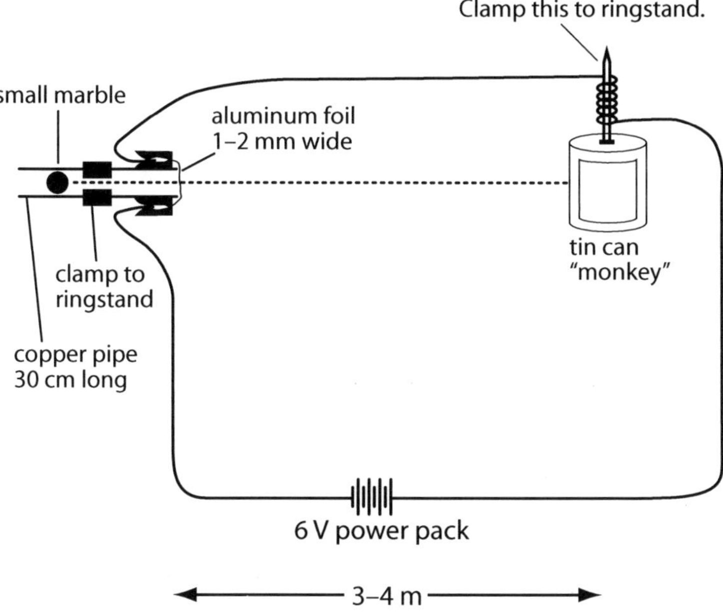

Figure 4.2.7

2. Imagine that the "blow gun" is aimed upward at some angle greater than zero relative to the horizontal. It is aimed at the "monkey" to begin with. Will it still hit the monkey if the monkey falls at the instant the marble leaves the gun? Explain your answer.

4.2 Review Questions

1. A rescue pilot has to drop a package of emergency supplies so that it lands as close as possible to a downed aircraft. If the rescue plane travels with a velocity of 81 m/s and is flying 125 m above the downed craft, how far away (horizontally) from the downed craft must the rescue pilot drop his package? (Assume negligible air resistance.)

2. An archer standing on the back of a pickup truck moving at 28 m/s fires an arrow straight up at a duck flying directly overhead. He misses the duck. The arrow was fired with an initial vertical velocity of 49 m/s relative to the truck.
   (a) For how many seconds will the arrow be in the air?

   (b) How far will the truck travel while the arrow is in the air?

   (c) Where, in relation to the archer, will the arrow come down? (Ignore air friction.) Will the archer have to "duck"? Explain.

3. A bullet is fired with a horizontal velocity of 330 m/s from a height of 1.6 m above the ground. Assuming the ground is level, how far from the gun, measured horizontally, will the bullet hit the ground?

4. A ball is thrown with a velocity of 24 m/s at an angle of 30° to the horizontal.
   Assume air friction is small enough to be ignored.
   (a) What is the horizontal component of the initial velocity?

   (b) What is the vertical component of the initial velocity?

   (c) How long will the ball be in the air?

(d) What horizontal distance (range) will the ball travel?

(e) To what maximum height will the ball rise?

5. Solve question 4 for angles of (i) 45° and (ii) 60°. Which of the three angles results in the greatest range? It can be shown that, for a given initial velocity, this angle is the best of all angles for obtaining the maximum range in the ideal, "no air resistance" situation.
   (i) 45°
      (a) What is the horizontal component of the initial velocity?

      (b) What is the vertical component of the initial velocity?

      (c) How long will the ball be in the air?

      (d) What horizontal distance (range) will the ball travel?

      (e) To what maximum height will the ball rise?

   (ii) 60°
      (a) What is the horizontal component of the initial velocity?

      (b) What is the vertical component of the initial velocity?

      (c) How long will the ball be in the air?

      (d) What horizontal distance (range) will the ball travel?

      (e) To what maximum height will the ball rise?

6. A student measured the horizontal and vertical components of the velocity of a projectile in a laboratory situation. The data is given below. Times and velocities are "true" (not scaled).

Time, t (s)	**Horizontal velocity, v_x (m/s)**	**Vertical velocity, v_y (m/s)**
0.10	2.12	3.58
0.20	2.12	4.56
0.30	2.13	5.54
0.40	2.11	6.52
0.50	2.12	7.50

(a) Plot vertical velocity vs. time.

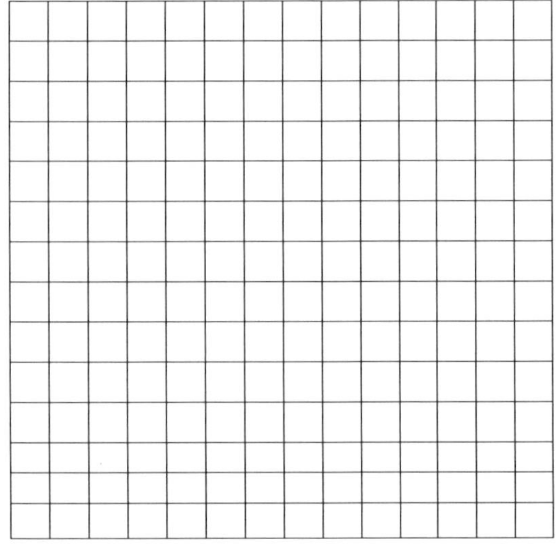

(b) Find the slope and y-intercept of your graph.

(c) Write an equation specifically describing your graph.

(d) On the same graph sheet, plot horizontal velocity vs. time.

(e) Write an equation specifically describing your second graph.

Chapter 4 Conceptual Review Questions

1. When walking, a person's speed can stay the same as he or she rounds a corner and changes direction. Using only this information, explain if speed is a scalar or a vector quantity?

2. If your friend (a fellow Physics fan) said 1 + 1 does not always equal 2, would you agree or disagree with them?

3. Is temperature a scalar or temperature measurement?

4. A bird has an airspeed of 15 km/hr. How fast would the bird be moving over the ground if it experienced a headwind of 15 km/hr?

5. Give an example in which velocity is zero yet acceleration is not.

Chapter 4 Review Questions

1. What is the difference between a scalar quantity and a vector quantity?

2. A man walks 1.00×10^2 m south, then 2.4×10^2 m east. What is his resultant displacement?

3. Two forces act on point Q. One is 5.0 N toward the south and the other is 3.0 N toward the east. Find the magnitude and direction of the third force that will be needed to produce static equilibrium.

4. What is the resultant force on a falling skydiver at an instant when the force of gravity on the skydiver is 720 N and the force of friction is 480 N?

5. Two dogs are pulling on the same bone. A poodle is pulling toward the south with a force of 7.0 N. A spaniel is pulling toward the east with a force of 24.0 N. With what force and in what direction must a colllie pull on the same bone, if the bone is to have a net force of zero on it? Express your answer in degrees relative to north.

6. A pebble is fired from a slingshot with a velocity of 30.0 m/s. If it is fired at an angle of 30° to the vertical, what height will it reach? If its fall is interrupted by a vertical wall 12 m away, where will it hit the wall in relation to the starting position of the pebble in the slingshot?

7. A firefighter is standing on top of a building 20.0 m high. She finds that if she holds the hose so that water issues from it horizontally at 12.0 m/s, the water will hit a burning wall of an adjacent building, at a height of 15.0 m above the ground. What is the horizontal distance from the firefighter to the burning wall?

8. The firefighter in question 7 wants the water from the same hose to reach the burning wall at the same level above the ground as she is standing. At what angle must she aim the hose relative to the horizontal?

9. An observer records time (t), displacement (d), and velocity (v) of a skier sliding from rest down a ski slope, with uniform acceleration. Sketch graphs using the following different variables.

(a) d vs. t

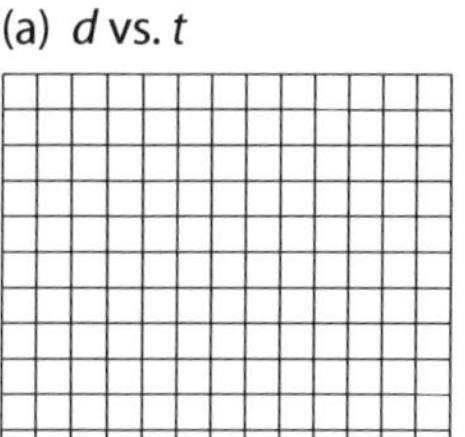

(b) d vs. t^2

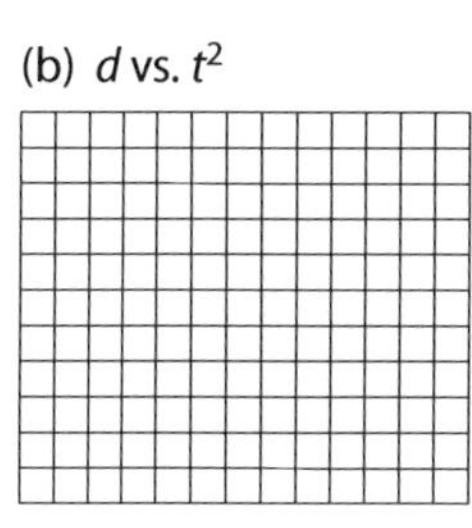

(c) v vs. t

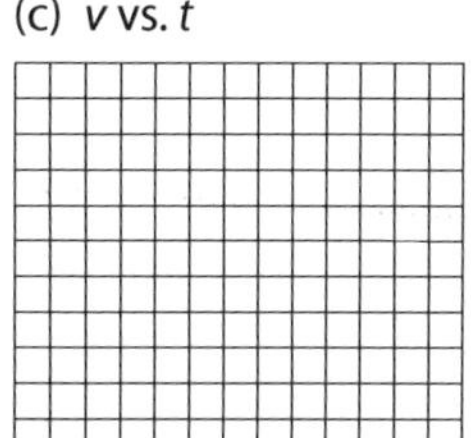

(d) v^2 vs. d

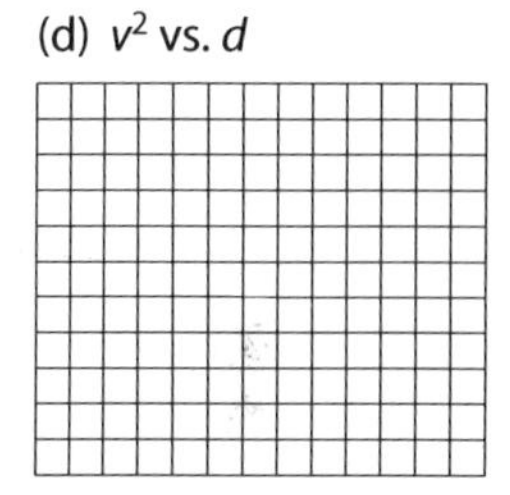

(e) In which case will the observer not obtain a straight line?

10. You drop a penny down a very deep well and hear the sound of the penny hitting the water 2.5 s later. If sound travels 330 m/s, how deep is the well?

11. A youngster hits a baseball, giving it a velocity of 22 m/s at an angle of 62° with the horizontal. Ignoring air friction, how far will the ball travel before a fielder catches it? Would this hit be a likely home run? Explain.

12. A stone is thrown straight up with a speed of 15.0 m/s.
    (a) How fast will it be moving when its altitude is 8.0 m above the point from which it was thrown? How much time elapses while the stone is reaching that height?

    (b) Is there one answer or are there two answers? Why?

5 Newton's Laws of Motion

In this chapter the focus will be on the Big Ideas:

An object's motion can be predicted, analyzed and described.
Forces influence the motion of an object.

The content learning standards will include:

- Newton's laws of motion and free-body diagrams
- Balanced and unbalanced forces in systems

By the end of this chapter, you should know the meaning to these **key terms**:

- action force
- gravitational mass
- impulse
- inertia
- inertial mass
- law of action and reaction
- law of conservation of momentum
- law of inertia
- momentum
- newton
- Newton's first law of motion
- Newton's second law of motion
- Newton's third law of motion
- reaction force

By the end of this chapter, you should be able to use and know when to use the following formulae:

$F = ma$ $p = mv$ $\Delta p = F\Delta t$

This device is called Newton's cradle, named after Sir Isaac Newton, the British scientist. When a ball at one end is lifted and released, it hits the ball next to it but that ball doesn't move. Only the ball at the end of the row is pushed upward as shown here. In this chapter you'll learn about Newton's laws of motion and momentum, which help to explain how this device works.

5.1 Inertia and Newton's First Law

Warm Up

You are attending a magic show and the magician stands beside a table set with fancy plates, cups, and silverware. Grabbing the edge of the tablecloth she quickly pulls the cloth out, and the plates, cups, and silverware stay in place. Is this magic or just physics in action? Explain your answer.

____

____

____

Inertia

Imagine you are a passenger in a car, and the driver makes a sudden left turn. What sensation do you feel during the left turn? From your own experience, you might recall that you feel as if you are being pushed to the right. Contrary to what you feel, you are not being pushed to the right at all.

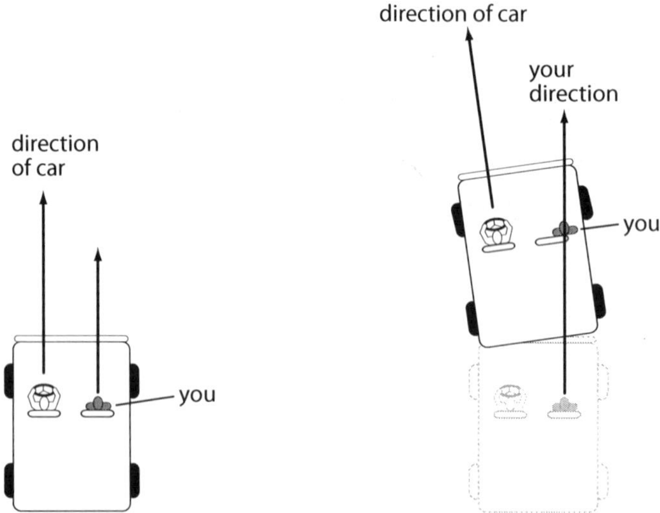

Figure 5.1.1 *As the car turns, your body wants to keep moving straight ahead.*

Figure 5.1.1 illustrates what happens and explains why you feel the force acting on your body. The car starts out by going straight and then the driver steers the car to the left. The car is moving to the left but your body wants to carry on in a straight line. What's stopping you? The door of the car is moving left with the rest of the car so it is pushing you in the direction the car is going. You feel as if you are pushing against the door, but this feeling is not what is happening. What is happening is that your body is trying to continue along its original straight path while the car is turning left. The result is that you are being pulled along with the car rather than continuing in a straight line.

As a general rule, any object tends to continue moving with whatever speed and direction it already has. This can include zero speed. When a driver accelerates a car, a body in the car tends to keep doing what it was already doing. So if the car is stopped, you are stopped. As the car starts to move and speeds up, you feel as if you are being pushed back into your seat.

The tendency that all objects have to resist change in their states of motion is called **inertia**. Every object in the universe that has mass has this property of inertia. Galileo Galilei (1564–1642) was the first person to describe this property of nature, which is called the **law of inertia**.

Some objects have more inertia than others because they have more mass. A logging truck has much more inertia than a mountain bike. Because it has so much more inertia, the logging truck is

(a) more difficult to get moving,
(b) more difficult to stop,
(c) more difficult to turn at a corner.

Measuring Inertia

Is there a way to measure inertia? You have measured it many times in science class. The way to measure inertia is to measure the object's mass. When you measure the mass of an object using a balance, that mass is equal to the object's **inertial mass**.

Strictly speaking, what the balance measures is called **gravitational mass**. This is because the unknown object is placed on one pan, and a standard mass is placed on the other pan. The masses are assumed to be equal when the force of gravity on the unknown mass balances the force of gravity on the standard mass. Gravitational mass is numerically equal to inertial mass, so a balance can be used to measure inertial mass as well.

Quick Check

1. Why does it hurt more to kick a rock shaped like a soccer ball than a soccer ball?

____

____

2. When astronauts are living in the International Space Station (ISS) they are in orbit around Earth at a minimum altitude of 278 km. They live in an environment of apparent weightlessness. Compare the inertial mass of the astronauts when they live on the ISS to their inertial mass when they are on Earth.

____

____

Newton's First Law

Isaac Newton (1642–1727) is considered one of the greatest scientists of all time. In any physics class you ever take, you will come across his name at some time. This is impressive, given that all his work was done more than 350 years ago. Newton is probably best known for his laws of motion. Newton's three laws describe motion as we experience it on Earth. They are also the foundation for helping to send humans to the Moon and deep-space vehicles out beyond our solar system.

Newton's first law of motion incorporated Galileo's law of inertia. The first law of motion, or law of inertia, can be stated this way:

> A body will continue to move at the same speed and in the same direction for as long as there are no unbalanced forces acting on it.

Ideal Conditions

Put another way, an object wants to keep doing what it is already doing. This means if a basketball is placed on the floor, it will not move until another force acts on it. Someone picking up the ball is an example of a force acting on the ball.

Sometimes it appears that Newton's first law does not apply. For example, when coasting on your bicycle along a flat part of the road, you have probably noticed that you slow down even though it appears no forces are acting on the bicycle. In fact, the force of friction between the road and tires is responsible for slowing the bicycle. If there were no friction, the bicycle would continue at the same speed until another force acted on it. That is why in many physics problems about motion, you will see the assumption that there is no friction. A situation that is assumed to have no friction is called *ideal conditions*. Using ideal conditions, we can focus on the motion being observed. By specifying ideal conditions, we also show we know that friction would have to be considered under normal conditions.

Quick Check

1. A car you are driving in encounters a patch of ice just as the car enters a corner turn. Using your knowledge of Newton's first law of motion, explain what will happen to the car.

2. You are a judge listening to an injury claim from a bus passenger. The passenger claims to have been hurt when the bus driver slammed on the brakes and a suitcase came flying from the front of the bus to hit the passenger. Do you believe the passenger's description of what happened? Explain your answer.

3. When you receive a drink for a take out order, usually there is a lid on the cup. Use Newton's first law to explain why the lid is necessary to prevent spills.

Investigation 5.1.1 Investigating Inertia

Purpose
To answer problems that will help you develop an understanding of inertia and Newton's first law of motion

Problem 1: How does a seatbelt work?

Figure 5.1.2 *Problem 1*

Procedure
1. Place a small toy human figure on a toy car or truck as shown in Figure 5.1.2. Do not fasten the figure to the vehicle. Let the vehicle move toward an obstruction like another toy vehicle or a brick and collide with it. Observe what happens to the unattached passenger.
2. Repeat step 1, but this time give the toy human figure a "seatbelt" by taping it to the vehicle.

Questions
1. How does this procedure illustrate inertia?
2. How does a seatbelt work?
3. Why are you more likely to survive a collision with a seatbelt than without one?

Problem 2: Does air have inertia?

Procedure
1. Fill a large garbage bag with air, and hold it as shown in Figure 5.1.3.
2. Quickly jerk the bag to one side. What happens to the air in the bag
   (a) when you start moving the bag?
   (b) when you stop moving the bag?

Question
1. What evidence have you observed from this procedure that supports the claim that air has inertia?

Figure 5.1.3 *Problem 2*

Problem 3: Inertia on an air track

Procedure

1. Place a glider on an air track as shown in Figure 5.1.4. Turn on the compressed air supply and check that the track is absolutely level. When the track is level the glider should have no tendency to move in one direction or the other. It should sit still.
2. Place the glider at one end of the track. Give it a slight nudge, and let it go.
3. Observe the motion of the glider.

Questions

1. Are there any unbalanced forces on the glider?
2. Describe its motion.
3. How does this demonstration illustrate Newton's first law?

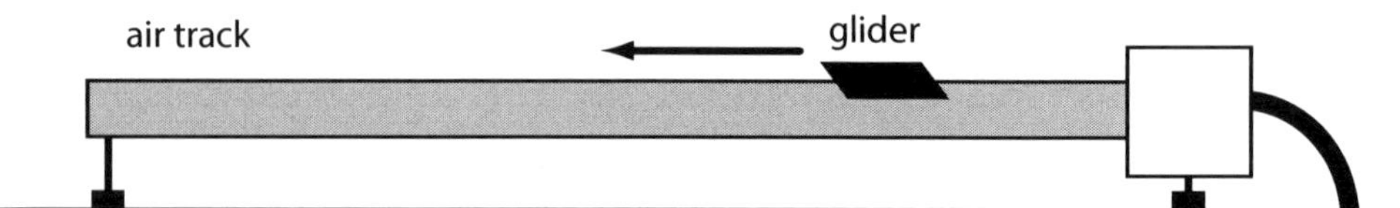

Figure 5.1.4 *Problem 3*

Problem 4: Get on the right track.

Procedure

1. Place a battery-powered toy train on a circular track, and let it run a few full circles.
2. Predict which way the train will go if one of the sections of curved track is removed. Which one of the following will the train do? Explain your answer.
   (a) continue to move in a circle
   (b) move off along a radius of the circle
   (c) move off in a straight line tangent to the circle
   (d) follow some other path
3. Now test your prediction by setting up a section of track as shown in Figure 5.1.5.

Question

1. What happens to the toy train when it leaves the track? Explain this in terms of inertia.

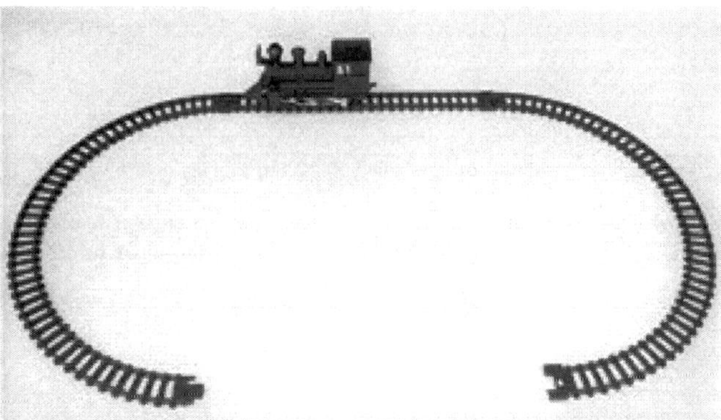

Figure 5.1.5 *Problem 4*

Problem 5: Where will the string break? Getting the "hang" of inertia

Procedure

1. Attach two equal masses, either 500 g or 1 kg, to a supporting rod, as shown in Figure 5.1.6. Use string that is strong enough to support the hanging masses, but not so strong that you cannot break it with a moderate pull with your hand. Add a 50 cm length of the same kind of string to the bottom of each mass.
2. Predict where each string will break, above or below the mass, if you pull on the end of the string first gently and then abruptly. Test your predictions by experiment.

Pull string here.

Figure 5.1.6 *Problem 5*

Questions

1. Explain what happened, in terms of inertia.
2. Which action illustrates the weight of the ball and which illustrates the mass of the ball?

Problem 6: The pop-up coaster

(a)

(b)

Figure 5.1.7 *Problem 6*

Procedure

1. The cart in Figure 5.1.7 contains a spring that can fire a steel ball straight up in the air. The cart is given a steady horizontal speed when pulled with a string. This also activates the trigger for the spring-loaded cannon. When the cart is moving with a steady speed, giving the string a sudden pull will release the spring and fire the ball up in the air.
2. Predict whether the ball will land ahead of the cannon, behind the cannon, or in the cannon. Explain your prediction.
3. Test your prediction.

Questions

1. What forces are acting on the ball when it is in the air?
2. How does this procedure illustrate Newton's first law of motion?
3. Why does the ball sometimes miss the cart after it is released? Does this mean Newton's first law sometimes does not apply?

Concluding Question

Use your understanding of inertia to explain the following situation: You are carrying a carton of milk with one hand and need to get a section of paper towel off the roll in your kitchen. You can only use one hand to tear off the paper towel. Why does a quick, jerking motion work better than a slow pulling motion when removing the paper towel section from the roll?

5.1 Review Questions

1. In the Warm Up of this section, you were asked to explain why the magician was able to pull the tablecloth out from the under the plates, cups and silverware. Using the concepts of inertia and Newton's first law, explain why this "magic act" succeeds.

2. Does 2 kg of apples have twice the inertia or half the inertia of 1 kg of apples? Explain your answer.

3. If the pen on your desk is at rest, can you say that no forces are acting on it? Explain your answer.

4. If the forces acting on the pen are balanced, is it correct to say that the pen is at rest? Explain your answer.

5. If you place a ball in the centre of a wagon and then quickly push the wagon forward, in what direction does the ball appear to go? Why?

6. Why do headrests in cars help protect a person from head and neck injury in a car accident?

7. A hockey puck moving a constant velocity across the ice eventually comes to a stop. Does this prove the Newton's first law does not apply to all situations?

8. You are travelling in a school bus on a field trip. The driver has to apply the brakes quickly to prevent an accident. Describe how your body would move in response to this rapid braking action.

9. While travelling in Africa you are chased by a very large elephant. Would it make more sense to run in a straight line to get away or in a zigzag motion? Explain your answer.

5.2 Newton's Second Law of Motion

Warm Up

Take an empty spool of thread and wrap a string or thread around it three or four times, leaving the end loose so you can pull on it. Place the spool on the floor and pull on the thread horizontally to make the spool move to the right.

1. Based on your observations, what can you say about the direction of the force applied to the spool and the acceleration of the spool?

___

___

2. Would the direction of the force or the acceleration of the spool be affected if the thread were wrapped around the spool in the opposite direction? Explain your answer.

___

___

Defining Newton's Second Law of Motion

In his second law of motion, Newton dealt with the problem of what happens when an unbalanced force acts on a body. **Newton's second law of motion** states: If an unbalanced force acts on a body, the body will accelerate. The rate at which it accelerates depends directly on the unbalanced force and inversely on the mass of the body.

$$\boldsymbol{a} = \frac{F}{m}$$

The direction in which the body accelerates will be the same direction as the unbalanced force. The measuring unit for force is the **newton (N)**. The measuring unit for mass is the kilogram (kg) and for acceleration is m/s^2. Therefore, using $F = ma$, one newton can be defined as the force needed to accelerate one kilogram at a rate of one metre per second per second.

Whenever Newton's second law is used, it is understood that the force F in the equation $F = ma$ is the unbalanced force acting on the body. This unbalanced force is also called the net force. To calculate the unbalanced force acting on a 1.0 kg mass falling due to gravity, you use Newton's second law:

$$F = ma = 1.00 \text{ kg} \times 9.81 \text{ m/s}^2 = 9.81 \text{ kg•m/s}^2 = 9.81 \text{ N}$$

To calculate the rate at which the mass accelerates, you rearrange Newton's second law to give:

$$a = \frac{F}{m} = \frac{9.81 \text{ N}}{1.00 \text{ kg}} = \frac{9.81 \text{ kg•m/s}^2}{1.00 \text{ kg}} = 9.81 \text{ m/s}^2$$

The acceleration of the mass is g or 9.81 m/s^2.

Quick Check

1. A single engine plane has a mass of 1500 kg and acceleration of 0.400 m/s^2. What is the thrust, or unbalanced force, from the engine?

2. What is the mass of a rocket that accelerates at 2.0 m/s^2 and has a thrust of 25 000 N?

3. Find the acceleration of a passenger jet that has a mass of 250 000 kg and an engine thrust that provides an unbalanced force of 50 000 N.

Multiple Forces

The example and problems in the Quick Check above involve only one unbalanced force. In other situations, like Sample Problem on the next page, there are more forces to consider.

Remember that, in these problems, it is important to identify the forces that create the unbalanced force. Figure 5.2.1 shows four different forces acting on a block. The two vertical forces are the force of gravity and the normal force (the force exerted by the floor on the block). The two horizontal forces are the applied force and the force of friction.

The two vertical forces balance each other because the force of gravity and the normal force equal each other in size and act in opposite directions. The unbalanced force is the difference between the applied force and the friction force opposing the applied force.

Sample Problem — Multiple Forces Acting on a Body

A 45.0 N block is being pushed along a floor, where the coefficient of kinetic friction is 0.333. If a force of 25.0 N is applied, at what rate will the block accelerate? The mass of the block is 4.60 kg.

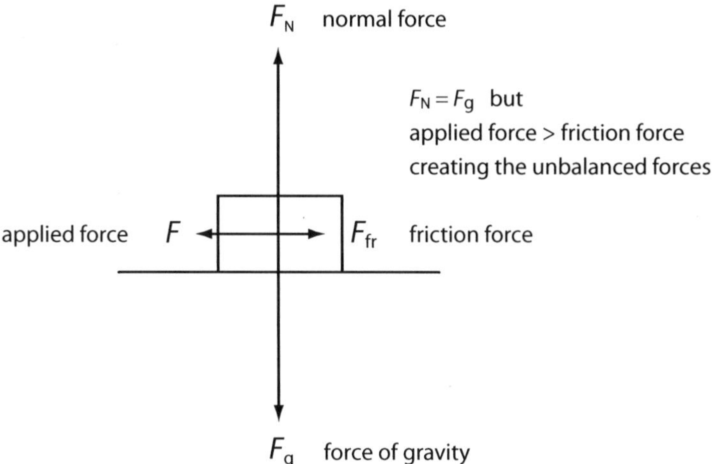

Figure 5.2.1 *Forces acting on block*

What to Think About	How to Do It
1. Find the force of friction.	$F_{fr} = \mu F_N = \mu F_g = (0.333) \times (45.0\ \text{N}) = 15.0\ \text{N}$
2. Find the unbalanced force.	unbalanced force = applied force – friction force $F = 25.0\ \text{N} - 15.0\ \text{N} = 10.0\ \text{N}$
3. Find the acceleration.	$a = \frac{F}{m} = \frac{10.0\ \text{N}}{4.60\ \text{kg}} = 2.17\ \text{m/s}^2$

Practice Problems — Multiple Forces Acting on a Body

1. A falling object of 20 N experiences air resistance of 6.0 N. If acceleration due to gravity is 9.8 m/s^2, what is the mass of the object?

2. A 900 N person stands on two scales so that one foot is on each scale. What will each scale register in Newtons?

3. What is the mass of a paratrooper who experiences an air resistance of 400 N and an acceleration of 4.5 m/s^2 during a parachute jump.

4. A force of 50 N accelerates a 5.0 kg block at 6.0 m/s^2 along a horizontal surface.
   (a) What is the frictional force acting on the block?

   (b) What is the coefficient of friction?

Investigation 5.2.1 Newton's Second Law of Motion

Purpose

To investigate how the change in speed of a cart is affected by
(a) the amount of unbalanced force, and (b) the amount of mass in the cart

Procedure

Part 1: Setting up and moving the cart

1. Set up the apparatus as shown in Figure 5.2.2(a). Start with three 200 g masses in the cart. Suspend a mass of 200 g from the end of a string, which passes over a pulley at the end of the bench. The force of gravity on this mass is 1.96 N or approximately 2.0 N.
2. Lift one end of your laboratory table so that the cart rolls toward the pulley at a steady speed. This can be checked with a ticker tape and your recording timer. If your bench cannot be lifted, do the experiment on a length of board, which can be raised at one end. What this lifting does is balance friction with a little help from gravity.
3. The class will now share the task of preparing and analyzing ticker-tape records of speed vs. time for each of the situations in Figure 5.2.2. Each lab group of two students will choose one of the eight set-ups and prepare two tapes or one for each partner. Note that the whole system of cart-plus-string-plus-hanging-mass moves as one unit. The mass of the whole system must be kept constant. This means that once you build your system you must not add any additional masses.

Varying the Unbalanced Force

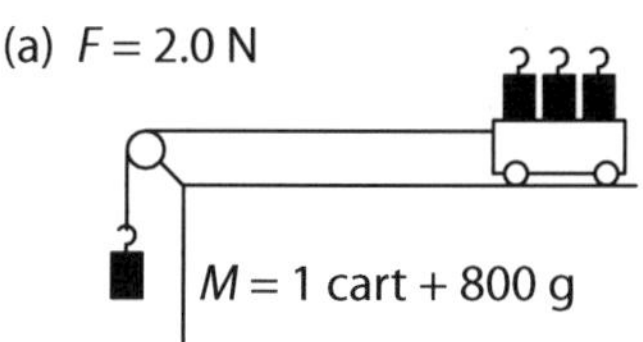

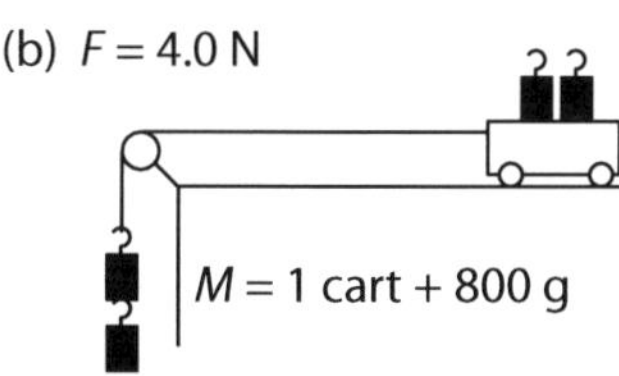

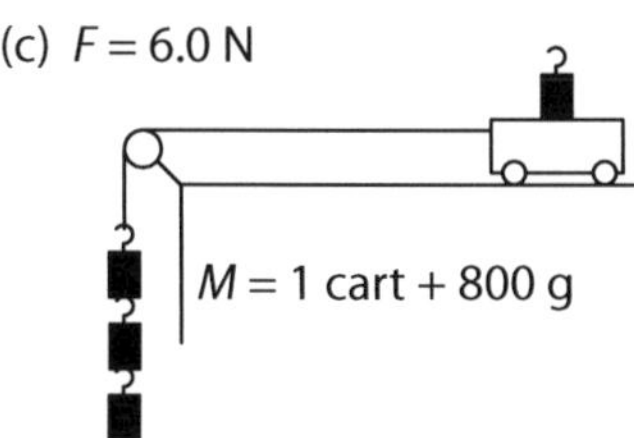

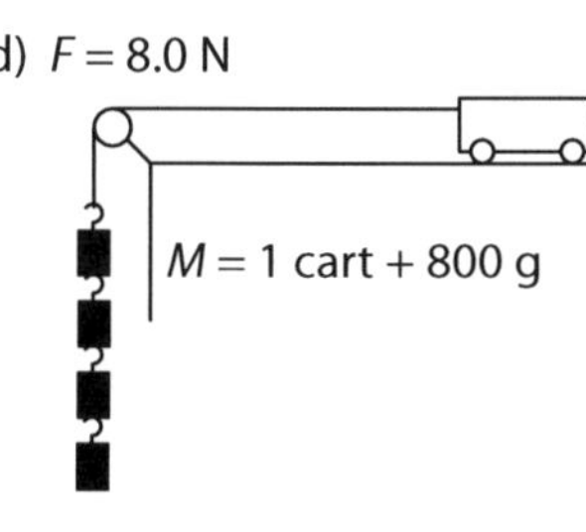

Varying the Mass

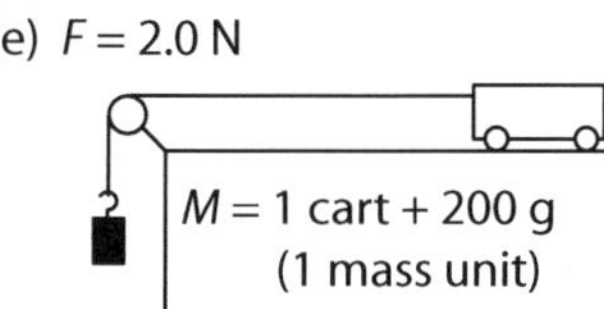

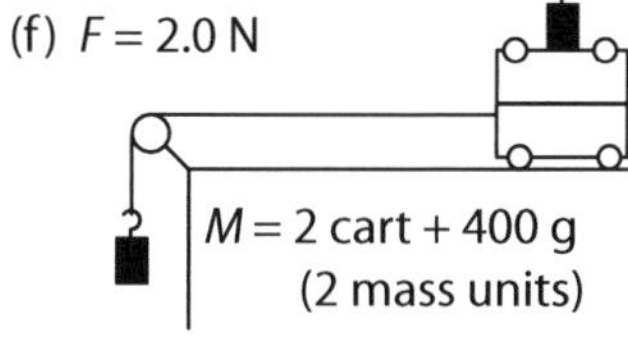

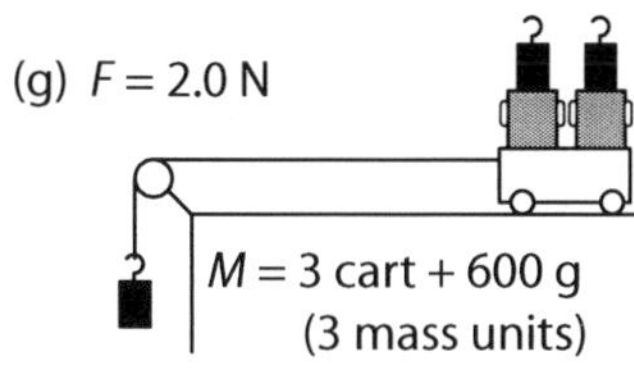

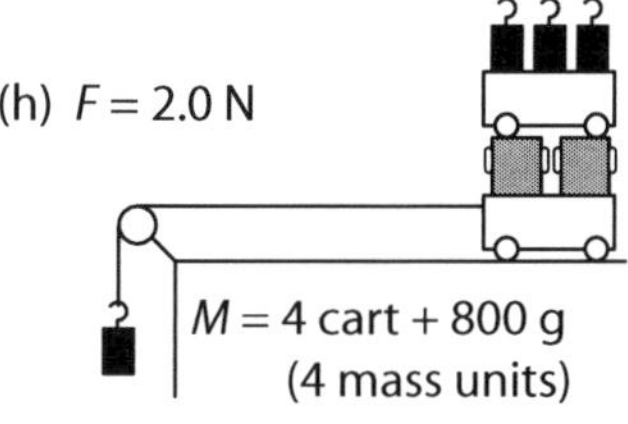

Figure 5.2.2 *Cart and mass set-ups*

Part 2: Preparing Your Own Tape

1. The class as a team will prepare and analyze tapes for each of the situations in Figure 5.2.2. If your class is large enough, compare duplicated data for any potential sources of error.
2. Use the technique you used to measure acceleration in an earlier chapter. Remember that a group of six dots represents 0.10 s and that the average speeds for each interval are plotted mid-way through each time interval and not at the end of the interval.
3. Prepare your graph. Label it carefully with the unbalanced force used (2.0 N, 4.0 N, 6.0 N, or 8.0 N) and the mass of the cart system.
4. The most important measurement you need is the acceleration of the cart. You get this from the slope of the graph. Express the acceleration in cm/s^2. You will share this information with the rest of the class.

Part 3: Analyzing Class Data

1. Prepare the following tables of data, summarizing class results.

Table 5.2.1 *Acceleration vs. Unbalanced Force (mass constant)*

Unbalanced Force F (N)	**Acceleration** a (cm/s^2)
0	0
2.0	
4.0	
6.0	
8.0	

Table 5.2.2 *Acceleration vs Mass (unbalanced force constant)*

Mass, m (mass units)	**Acceleration,** a (cm/s^2)	$\frac{1}{\text{mass}}, \frac{1}{m}$ (mass units^{-1})
1.0		1.0
2.0		0.50
3.0		0.33
4.0		0.25

2. Plot a graph of acceleration (y-axis) against unbalanced force (x-axis).
3. Plot a graph of acceleration against mass.
4. Plot a graph of acceleration against the reciprocal of mass ($1/m$).

Concluding Questions

1. Describe how the speed of a cart changes when a constant unbalanced force pulls it.
2. According to your first graph (a vs. F), how does acceleration depend on unbalanced force? Does your graph suggest that acceleration is directly proportional to unbalanced force? Support your answer with your data.
3 According to your second and third graphs, how does the acceleration of the cart vary when the mass is doubled, tripled, and quadrupled?
4 Write an equation for the third graph, complete with the numerical value and units for the slope.
5 What were some of the experimental difficulties you encountered in this investigation, which would make it difficult to obtain ideal results?

5.2 Review Questions

1. What unbalanced force is needed to accelerate a 5.0 kg cart at 5.0 m/s^2?

2. A net force of 7.5×10^4 N acts on a spacecraft of mass 3.0×10^4 kg.
   (a) At what rate will the spacecraft accelerate?

   (b) Assuming constant acceleration is maintained, how fast will the spacecraft be moving after 25 s, if its initial speed was 5.0×10^3 m/s?

3. A model rocket has a mass of 0.12 kg. It accelerates vertically to 60.0 m/s in 1.2 s.
   (a) What is its average acceleration?

   (b) What is the unbalanced force on the rocket?

   (c) If the force of gravity on the rocket is 1.2 N, what is the total thrust of its engine?

4. What is the mass of a rock if a force of 2.4×10^3 N makes it accelerate at a rate of 4.0×10^1 m/s^2?

5. A fully loaded military rocket has a mass of 3.0×10^6 kg, and the force of gravity on it at ground level is 2.9×10^7 N.
   (a) At what rate will the rocket accelerate during lift-off, if the engines provide a thrust of 3.3×10^7 N?

   (b) Why will this acceleration not remain constant?

6. A boy and his skateboard have a combined mass of 60.0 kg. After an initial shove, the boy starts coasting at 5.5 m/s along a level driveway. Friction brings him to rest in 5.0 s. The combined force of gravity on the boy and skateboard is 5.9×10^2 N. What is the average coefficient of rolling friction between the driveway and the skateboard wheels?

5.3 Newton's Third Law of Motion

Warm Up

1. Consider the following situations. Draw a sketch of each situation and, on each diagram, indicate the forces being described. Share your results with the class.
   (a) If you wish to climb stairs, in which direction do *you* push? Which way to you move?
   (c) If you are rowing a boat, which way must your oars push if the boat is to move forward? Which way to do you move?
   (b) If you wish to swim forward, in which direction must your arms push? Which way do you move?
   (d) When a car is moving forward, in which direction do the *wheels* push on the road? Which way to do you move?

Action and Reaction Forces

Isaac Newton observed that whenever forces exist between two bodies, the forces are mutual. If one body pushes on another, the other body exerts an equal force on the first body, but in the opposite direction. To do push-ups, for example, you push down on the floor. The floor exerts an equal force up on you. The floor lifts you up! Earth exerts a force of gravity on the Moon. What evidence is there that the Moon exerts an equal force on Earth?

Newton studied situations involving forces between pairs of bodies and he stated his conclusions about mutual forces between pairs of bodies as his third law. **Newton's third law of motion** is also called the **law of action and reaction**.

> If two bodies interact, the force the first body exerts on the second body will equal the force the second body exerts on the first body. The two forces will be opposite in direction and will act simultaneously over the same interval of time.

The first force is called the **action force**, and the second force is called the **reaction force**. If we call the first body A and the second body B, then the law of action and reaction can be expressed mathematically like this:

$$F_{\text{A on B}} = -F_{\text{B on A}}$$

where the minus sign indicates opposite direction.

It is important to remember that for both forces, each force is exerted on the other body. The forces do not cancel. This is a really important point. For example, imagine a horse pulling a cart. If we just consider the force the horse exerts on the cart, then Newton's third law tells us that the cart exerts an equal and opposite force on the horse. The two forces are illustrated in Figure 5.3.1.

You might look at the picture and say that the horse and cart do not move because the two forces seem to cancel each other out. They are equal and opposite. But remember that the horse is exerting an action force on the cart and the cart is exerting a reaction force on the horse. That is why the horse feels the heavy cart on its harness when it starts pulling.

When applying Newton's third law, always ask yourself what object or thing applies the force and what body or object receives the force. There must be two different bodies or objects.

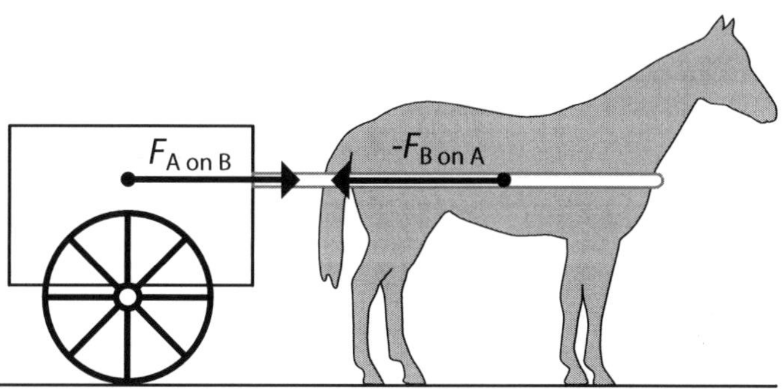

Figure 5.3.1 *Movement occurs when the horse's feet exert a force on Earth's surface and Earth exerts an equal and opposite force back on the horse.*

Quick Check

1. Review your diagrams from the Warm Up activity. In each diagram, label the action force and reaction force.
2. When you are walking, you are producing an action force toward the ground. Why do you move in the opposite direction?

   ____

   ____

3. You see a large dog running along a floating log. If the dog is running to your right, what, if anything, is happening to the log?

   ____

   ____

Investigation 5.3.1 Newton's Third Law

Purpose
To observe demonstrations of Newton's third law and identify the action and reaction forces

Procedure

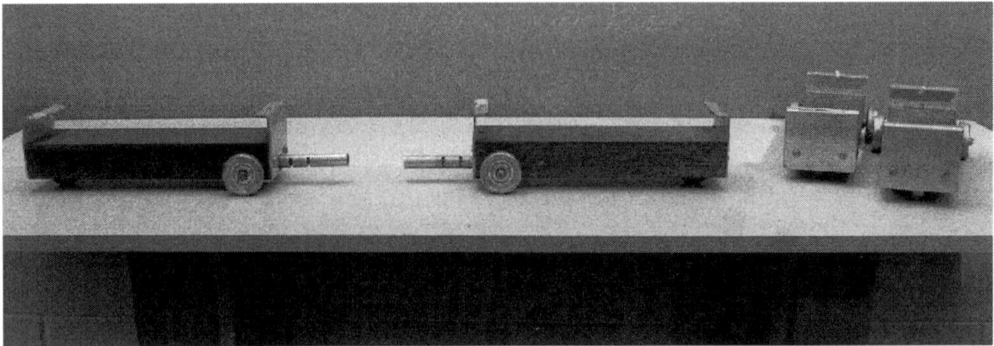

Part 1: Exploding Carts

Figure 5.3.2 *Laboratory carts*

1. Push two identical laboratory carts together so that their spring bumpers are compressed. Release the carts on a flat table or floor. Observe as they accelerate away from each other.
   (a) What force makes the carts accelerate?
   (b) Why do the two carts, of identical mass, accelerate at the same rate?
   (c) How does this demonstration illustrate Newton's third law?
2. Predict what will happen if you double the mass of one of the carts by placing an extra cart on top of it. Test your prediction.
   (a) Has the force repelling the carts changed?
   (b) What has changed?
3. Try making the mass of one of the carts much greater than the mass of the other.
   (a) Is the force changed?
   (b) What has changed?

Part 2: Motion from Rest

Figure 5.3.3 Set-up for part 2

1. Place a piece of light plastic insulating Styrofoam board (50 cm × 25 cm × 2.5 cm) at one end of an air table as shown in Figure 5.3.3. Place a wind-up toy car or a radio-controlled car at one end of the board. Turn on the air table and start the car moving. Observe and describe what happens:
   (a) to the car
   (b) to the "road" under the car
2. How does this demonstration illustrate Newton's Third Law?

Part 3: Tug of War

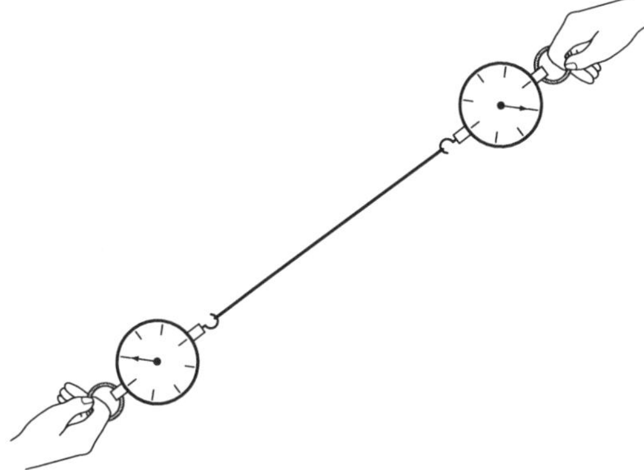

Figure 5.3.4 *Students stretching the string*

1. Tie a string between two 20 N spring balances. Have two students stretch the string between them as shown in Figure 5.3.4. What do the two spring balances read?
2. Try pulling with different forces. Compare the forces on each spring balance each time you pull on the string with a different force. Does it matter who does the pulling?
3. Try adding a third spring balance in the middle of the string. How does this demonstration illustrate Newton's third law?

Concluding Questions

1. When a car moves forward, in which direction do the wheels of the car push on the road? What force actually makes the car move forward?
2. List and discuss three examples of situations from your own everyday experience, that involve Newton's third law.

5.3 Review Questions

1. You are playing softball and your friend throws a ball to you. You catch the ball. The action force is the impact of the ball against your glove. What is the reaction force?

2. During a golf swing, is the club impacting on the ball the action force or the reaction force? Use a diagram to illustrate your answer.

3. If a soccer player kicks a ball with a force of 100 N, what is the magnitude of the reaction force?

4. Spiderman is having a tug of war with a grade 2 student. Both are pulling very hard from opposite ends. Who exerts a greater force on the rope? Explain your answer.

5. In a demolition derby a Hummer SUV collides head-on with a SMART car. Which car experiences a greater impact force? Explain your answer.

6. During a martial arts demonstration, a black belt uses a karate chop to break a large board with her hand by exerting a force of 2000 N. What force did the board exert on her hand?

7. A few years from now after much hard work, you are an astronaut and are completing a repair of some solar panels. To do this you have to take a space walk outside the International Space Station. By accident, you find yourself disconnected from the support rope and need to get back to the station. All you have is your tools with you. How can you propel yourself back to safety?

5.4 Momentum

Warm Up

Consider the following objects and motion in the two columns below:

feather	fast (10 m/s)
marble	average (5 m/s)
softball	slow (2 m/s)

1. Connect an object in the first column with a motion in the second column for the following situations.
   (a) The combination that will cause the most pain if the object hits your leg

   ______________________ + ______________________

   (b) The combination that will cause the least pain if the object hits your leg

   ______________________ + ______________________

2. Explain your reasoning for each answer.

   (a) ____

   ____

   (b) ____

   ____

Mass × Velocity = Momentum

One of the most important concepts in physics is that of momentum**.** Isaac Newton first used the idea when he wrote his second law of motion. In his original version, the second law looks like this:

$$F = \frac{m\Delta v}{t}$$

Newton called the product of mass and velocity (*mv*) a quantity of motion. Thus, his second law stated that the unbalanced force on an object is equal to the rate of change of a quantity of motion with respect to time. We now call the product of mass × velocity **momentum** and we give it the symbol *p*. The unit of measurement for momentum is kg•m/s.

$$p = m\Delta v$$

Newton's second law can be written this way:

$$F = ma = \frac{m\Delta v}{t} = \frac{\Delta p}{t}$$

Thus, the unbalanced force equals the rate of change of momentum with respect to time.

Quick Check

1. What is the momentum of a 100 kg motorbike travelling at 10 m/s?

2. What is the mass of plane that is travelling at 200 km/h and has a momentum of 1.1×10^6 kg•m/s?

3. How fast does a 0.01 kg bug have to fly to have a momentum of 0.25 kg•m/s? Is this possible?

Impulse

According to Newton's second law, in its original form $F = \frac{mv}{t}$. This can be rearranged to:

$$\boldsymbol{\Delta p = F\Delta t = m\Delta v = \text{impulse}}$$

The product of the force and the time interval during which it acts is called the **impulse**. The last equation shows that the impulse is equal to the change in momentum it produces.

This is an important relationship when considering an object that is undergoing a change in momentum. An object's momentum changes because an impulse has been placed on the object. For example, if you are driving down a road at a constant velocity, you and your vehicle have a momentum. When you press on the gas pedal, the velocity of the vehicle increases. The momentum has also increased. This increased momentum was caused by a force being exerted on the vehicle over a period of time. Or put another way, the vehicle experienced an impulse. The amount of impulse equals the change in momentum in the vehicle.

Units for Momentum and Impulse

Momentum is measured in kg•m/s because these units have the dimensions of mass and velocity. Impulse is measured in N•s because these units have the dimensions of force and time. Since impulse is equal to change in momentum, these units must be equivalent. It can easily be shown that this is true:

$$(\text{N}\bullet\text{s}) = (\text{kg}\bullet\text{m/s}^2)\bullet(\text{s}) = (\text{kg}\bullet\text{m/s})$$

Momentum and impulse may be expressed in either unit.

Quick Check

1. (a) What is the momentum of a 112 kg football player running with a velocity of 3.6 m/s?

   (b) What impulse must a tackler impart to the football player to bring him to a stop?

   (c) If the tackle was completed in 0.80 s, what average force did the tackler exert on the other player?

   (d) Why is the force negative in question 1(c)?

   ____

   ____

Law of Conservation of Momentum

Any moving body has momentum equal to the product of the body's mass and its velocity. What makes momentum such an important quantity in nature is the fact that in a closed system, momentum is conserved. A closed system is one where no outside forces act on the system. This is the **law of conservation of momentum**. In other words, the total change in momentum within the closed, two-body system is zero. This means that the total momentum is constant, or that momentum is conserved.

Scientists have done many, many experiments with momentum and are convinced that momentum truly is a conserved quantity in nature. At the subatomic level in experiments done with high-energy particle accelerators, physicists rely heavily on the law of conservation of momentum in interpreting the results of collisions of particles.

Conservation of Momentum and Newton's Third Law

Newton's third law is a special case of the law of conservation of momentum. This can be shown by using a proof. A proof is a mathematical solution that logically demonstrates something to be true. The following is a proof showing that Newton's third law is a special case of the law of conservation of momentum.

Consider two bodies interacting such that body A exerts a force on body B, and body B exerts an equal force on body A, but in the opposite direction.

$$F_{\text{A on B}} = -F_{\text{B on A}}$$

$$\text{action force} = -\text{reaction force}$$

The minus sign indicates that the direction of the reaction force is opposite to that of the action force. Using Newton's second law, written in terms of momentum:

$$\frac{m_B v_B}{t} = -\frac{m_A v_A}{t}$$

The time intervals on both sides of the equation are the same because both forces act over the same interval of time. So the equation can be simplified to:

$$m_B v_B = -m_A v_A$$

Therefore, $$m_A v_A + m_B v_B = 0$$

or $$p_A + p_B = 0$$

Other Examples of the Law of Conservation of Momentum

If you have ever played pool or billiards you will be familiar with the law of conservation of momentum. When the cue ball, or white ball, hits another ball, momentum is conserved. For example, if all the momentum is transferred from the cue ball to the billiard ball, the cue ball will stop and the billiard ball will move.

Sample Problem — Conservation of Momentum

A railway car of mass 6.0×10^3 kg is coasting along a track with a velocity of 5.5 m/s when suddenly a 3.0×10^3 kg load of sulphur is dumped into the car. What is its new velocity?

What to Think About	How to Do It
1. What do I know about the problem?	The momentum of the railway car will not change because of the law of conservation of momentum. Let initial mass be m_1 and initial velocity be v_1. The final mass of the railway car will be m_2 and the final velocity v_2.
2. What am I trying to solve?	Solve for the final velocity v_2.
3. What formula applies to this situation?	$m_1 v_1 = m_2 v_2$
4. Find the final velocity v_2.	$(6.0 \times 10^3 \text{ kg})(5.5 \text{ m/s}) = (6.0 \times 10^3 \text{ kg} + 3.0 \times 10^3 \text{ kg})(v_2)$ $33 \times 10^3 \text{ kg•m/s} = (9.0 \times 10^3 \text{ kg})(v_2)$ $v_2 = \frac{33\ 10^3 \text{ kg•m/s}}{9.0\ 10^3 \text{ kg}}$ $= 3.7 \text{ m/s}$ The rail car's new velocity is 3.7 m/s

Practice Problems — Conservation of Momentum

1. Two identical air track gliders each have a mass of 100 g and are sitting on an air track. One glider is at rest and the other glider is moving toward it at a velocity. When they collide they stick together and move off at 2.0 m/s. What was the initial velocity of the moving glider?

2. A 1.0 kg ball of putty is rolling towards a resting 4.5 kg bowling ball at 1.5 m/s. When they collide and stick together, what is the resulting momentum of the two objects stuck together?

3. A ball rolls at a velocity of 3.5 m/s toward a 5.0 kg ball at rest. They collide and move off at a velocity of 2.5 m/s. What was the mass of the moving ball?

5.4 Review Questions

1. What is the momentum of a 75 g mouse running across the floor with a velocity of 2.6 m/s?

2. What is the impulse of a 55 N force exerted over a time interval of 1.0 ms?

3. A 0.060 kg rifle bullet leaves the muzzle with a velocity of 6.0×10^2 m/s. If the 3.0 kg rifle is held very loosely, with what velocity will it recoil?

4. A 53 kg skateboarder on a 2.0 kg skateboard is coasting along at 1.6 m/s. He collides with a stationary skateboarder of mass 43 kg, also on a 2.0 kg skateboard, and the two skateboarders coast off in the same direction that the first skateboarder was travelling.What velocity will the combined skateboarders now have?

5. What impulse is needed to change the velocity of a 10.0 kg object from 12.6 m/s to 25.5 m/s in a time of 5.00 s? How much force is needed?

6. A 1.5×10^3 kg car travelling at 44 m/s collides head-on with a 1.0×10^3 kg car travelling at 22 m/s in the opposite direction. If the cars stick together on impact, what is the velocity of the wreckage immediately after impact? (Hint: Let the velocity of the second car be –22 m/s, since it is moving in a direction opposite to the first car.)

7. (a) What impulse must be imparted by a baseball bat to a 145 g ball to change its velocity from 40.0 m/s to –50.0 m/s?

   (b) If the collision between the baseball and the bat lasts 1.00 ms, what force was exerted on the ball? (1 ms = 10^{-3} s)

Chapter 5 Conceptual Review Questions

1. Which statement is correct – (a) or (b)? Explain and support your answer with an example.

   (a) Net force causes change in motion.

   (b) Net force causes motion.

2. You throw a small ball straight up. What is the net external force acting on the rock when it's at the top of it's trajectory?

3. When a car accelerates rapidly, there is a sensation of being pushed back into your seat. Explain why you move backward in the seat. Is there really a force being exerted backwards on you?

4. Explain in terms of momentum and Newton's laws how a car's air resistance is due in part to the fact that it pushes air in its direction of motion.

5. How can a small force impart the same momentum to an object as a large force?

Chapter 5 Review Questions

1. A person who does not wear a seatbelt may crash through the windshield if a car makes a sudden stop. Explain what happens to this person in terms of Newton's first law of motion. Explain why it is wise to wear a seatbelt.

2. In a frame of reference where there are no external, unbalanced forces, show that Newton's second law *includes* the law of inertia.

3. What unbalanced force is needed to accelerate a 2.0×10^3 kg vehicle at 1.5 m/s^2?

4. What is the acceleration of a 5.8×10^3 kg vehicle if an unbalanced force of 1.16×10^2 N acts on it?

5. What is the mass of a space satellite if a thrust of 2.0×10^2 N accelerates it at a rate of 0.40 m/s^2 during a small steering adjustment?

6. At what rate will a 5.0 kg object accelerate if a 12.8 N force is applied to it, and the friction force opposing its motion is 2.8 N?

7. A rope is strong enough to withstand a 750 N force without breaking. If two people pull on opposite ends of the rope, each with a force of 500 N, will it break? Explain.

8. State Newton's third law of motion. Describe an example of a situation involving the law of action and reaction that you have not already used.

9. Two tug-of-war teams are at opposite ends of a rope. Newton's third law says that the force exerted by team A will equal the force that team B exerts on team A. How can either team win the tug-of-war?

10. (a) Define momentum.

(b) Why is momentum considered a very important quantity in physics?

11. (a) Define impulse.

(b) What is the impulse due to a force that causes the velocity of a 46 g golf ball to change from 0 m/s to 60.0 m/s in 0.50 ms?

(c) What force was applied to the ball?

12. A hunter who fails to hold the rifle firmly against a shoulder may be injured when shooting. Explain in terms of Newton's third law.

13. A 4.2 kg rifle shoots a 0.050 kg bullet at a velocity of 3.00×10^2 m/s. At what velocity does the rifle recoil?

14. A 0.250 kg ball of Plasticine moving at 5.0 m/s overtakes and collides with a 0.300 kg ball of Plasticine, travelling in the same direction at 2.0 m/s. The two balls of Plasticine stick together on collision. What is their velocity after the collision?

15. A railroad car of mass 12 000 kg is travelling at a velocity of 6.0 m/s when it collides with an identical car at rest. The two cars lock together. What is their common velocity after the collision?

6 Energy

In this chapter the focus will be on the Big Idea:

Energy is found in different forms, is conserved and has the ability to do work

The content learning standards will include:

- Conservation of energy, principle of work and energy
- Power and efficiency
- Simple machines and mechanical advantage

By the end of this chapter, you should know the meaning to these **key terms**:

- conduction
- convection
- efficiency
- energy
- gravitational potential energy
- heat
- kinetic energy
- law of conservation of energy
- mechanical advantage
- power
- radiation
- specific heat capacity
- temperature
- thermal energy
- watt
- work

By the end of the chapter, you should be able to use and know when to use the following formulae:

$W = Fd$

$E_p = mgh$

$P = \frac{W}{\Delta t} = \frac{\Delta E}{\Delta t}$

$W = \Delta E$

$E_k = \frac{1}{2}mv^2$

$efficiency = \frac{W_{out}}{W_{in}} = \frac{P_{out}}{P_{in}}$

An explosion is an example of chemical, sound, light, and thermal energy being released all at the same time.

6.1 Do You Know the Meaning of Work?

Warm Up

Bounce a rubber or tennis ball up and down several times. List all the different forms of energy you observe.

____

____

____

What is Energy?

Energy appears in a variety of forms. Some forms you are familiar with include light, sound, thermal energy, electrical energy, elastic potential energy, gravitational potential energy, chemical potential energy, nuclear energy, and mechanical energy. What is energy? Your experience tells you it is associated with movement or with the potential for motion. Energy is what makes things move. The usual definition of energy says that energy is the capacity to do work.

In physics, **work** has a specific meaning. If work is to be done on an object, two things must happen: (1) a force must act on the object and (2) the object must move through a distance in the direction of the force. The amount of work done is equal to the product of the force exerted and the distance the force causes the object to move, measured in the direction of the force.

$$\textbf{work} = \textbf{force} \times \textbf{distance}$$

$$W = Fd$$

Since force is measured in newtons (N) and distance in metres (m), work can be measured in newton-metres. One newton-metre (N·m) is called a **joule (J)** after James Joule (1818–1889), an English physicist.

$$1\text{ J} = 1\text{ N·m}$$

Sample Problem — Calculating Work

How much work does a golfer do lifting a 46 g golf ball out of the hole and up to his pocket (0.95 m above the ground)?

What to Think About	How to Do It
1. Find the correct formula.	$W = Fd$
2. Find the force in newtons.	$F = mg = (0.046\text{kg})(9.81\text{ m/s}^2)$ $F = 0.45\text{ N}$
3. Find work done.	$W = Fd = (0.45\text{ N})(0.95\text{ m})$ $= 0.43\text{ J}$ The golfer does 0.43 J of work lifting the golf ball from the hole to his pocket.

Practice Problems — Calculating Work

1. How much work will you do if you push a block of concrete 4.3 m along a floor, with a steady force of 25 N?

2. If your mass is 70.0 kg, how much work will you do climbing a flight of stairs 25.0 m high, moving at a steady pace? (g = 9.81 N/kg)

3. Your car is stuck in the mud. You push on it with a force of 300.0 N for 10.0 s, but it will not move. How much work have you done in the 10.0 s?

Power

A machine is powerful if it can do a lot of work in a short time. **Power** is the measure of the amount of work a machine can do in one second.

$$\text{power} = \frac{\text{work}}{\text{time}}$$

$$P = \frac{W}{\Delta t}$$

Power could be measured in joules per second (J/s), but one joule per second is called one **watt (W)**, after James Watt (1736–1819), a Scottish engineer.

1 W = 1 J/s

Power can be measured in kilowatts (kW) or megawatts (MW).

1 kW = 1000 W (10^3 W)
1 MW = 1 000 000 W (10^6 W)

Sample Problem — Calculating Power

The power of a small motor in a toy can be calculated by the amount of work it does in a period of time. What is the power rating of a toy motor that does 4200 J of work in 70.0 s?

What to Think About	How to Do It
1. Find the correct formula.	$P = \frac{\Delta W}{\Delta t}$
2. Calculate the power.	$P = \frac{4200\text{ J}}{70.0\text{ s}} = 60\text{ W}$ The power rating of the toy motor is 60 W.

Practice Problems — Calculating Power

1. An airport baggage handler lifts 42 pieces of luggage, averaging 24 kg each, through a height of 1.6 m onto a baggage cart, in a time of 3.6 min. In this situation, what is the power of the baggage handler?

2. How much work or energy (in J) does a 150 W light bulb convert to heat and light in 1.0 h?

3. A mechanical lifting system is approximately 25% efficient. This means that only 25% of the energy used to lift a mass is converted into useable energy. The rest is mostly lost as heat. If 1.5×10^8 W is used for 2.0 h, how much energy (in J) of useable work is produced? How much heat is produced?

What's Watt?

Power is commonly measured in **horsepower**. Eventually, horsepower may be replaced by the **kilowatt**, which is a metric unit, but the horsepower (non-metric) will persist for some time because it is firmly entrenched in our vocabulary.

The Scottish engineer James Watt is famous for his improved design of a steam engine, invented earlier by Thomas Newcomen. Watt's new engine was used at first for pumping water out of coal mines, work that previously had been done by horses. Customers wanted to know how many horses Watt's new engines would replace. So that he could answer their questions, Watt did the following:

1. He measured the force, in pounds, exerted by the average horse over a distance, measured in feet.
2. He calculated the amount of work the horse did, in a unit he called foot-pounds.
3. He measured the time it took the horse to do the work.
4. He calculated how much work the horse would do in one second, which is the average power of the horse. He found this to be 550 foot-pounds per second. This was taken to be the average power of one horse equal to one horsepower.

$$1 \text{ horsepower} = 550 \frac{\text{foot-pounds}}{\text{second}}$$

The modern unit for power is the watt (W). One horsepower is equivalent to 746 W, which is almost 3/4 kW. The following example finds the power in an electric motor and them shows how to convert watts to horsepower.

Sample Problem — Calculating Horsepower An electric motor is used, with a pulley and a rope, to lift a 650 N load from the road up to a height of 12 m. This job is done in a time of 11 s. What is the power output of the motor?	
What to Think About	**How to Do It**
1. Find the correct formula.	$P = \frac{work}{time} = \frac{W}{\Delta t}$
2. Calculate the power in watts.	$P = \frac{Fd}{\Delta t} = \frac{(650\ N)(12\ m)}{11\ s}$ $= 7.1\ 10^2\ W$
3. Calculate the horsepower.	The often-used unit of power, 1 horsepower, is equivalent to 7.5×10^2 W. The motor in this question would have a horsepower of $\frac{7.1 \times 10^2\ W}{7.5 \times 10^2\ W/HP} = 0.95\ HP$

Investigation 6.1.1 Getting Work Done with Pulleys

Machines such as pulleys are used to get work done, but you must do some work to operate these simple machines.

Purpose

To compare the amount of work that you do using a pulley system with the amount of work the pulley does for you

Procedure

1. Set up the pulley system in Figure 6.1.1. The pulley system will be used to lift a 200 g mass up to a height of 10.0 cm (0.100 m). The force of gravity on the mass is approximately 2.0 N. The work that the pulley system will do is therefore:

   $W = Fd = (2.0\ \text{N})(0.10\ \text{m}) = 0.20\ \text{J}$

2. Your task is to see how much work you have to do when you operate the pulley system to do the 0.20 J of work.
   (a) Pull gently on the spring balance until the string is tight and the load is just about to lift. Mark the position of the bottom of the spring balance hook. Pull up on the spring balance until the load has been raised 10.0 cm. Write down the force you had to exert (**effort force**) and the distance through which you had to exert it (**effort distance**).
   (b) Calculate how much work you did by multiplying your effort force by your effort distance. Express your answer in joules (J).

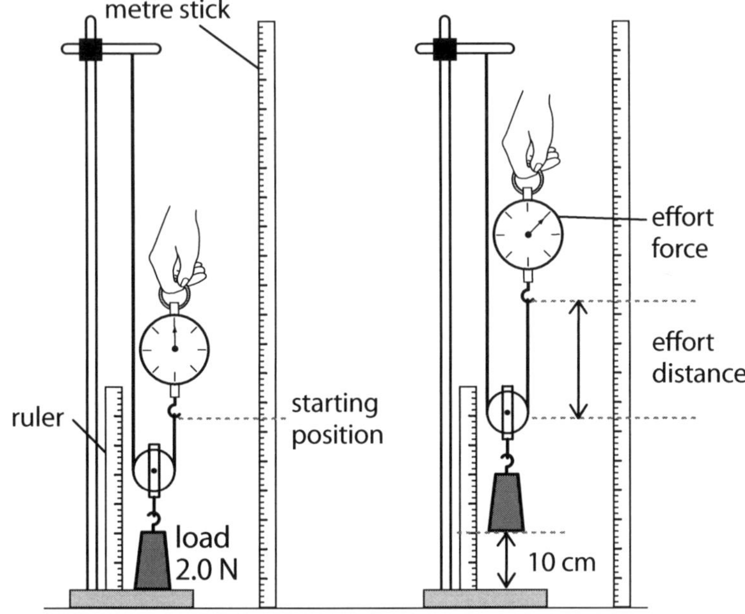

Figure 6.1.1 *Pulleys Step 1*

3. Repeat Procedure 2 using each of the pulley arrangements in Figure 6.1.2. In each trial, use the pulley system to lift a 2.0 N load a distance of 10.0 cm (0.100 m), so that the work done by each pulley system is 0.20 J. Measure your effort force and your effort distance with each system. Record all your data in a copy of Table 6.1.1.

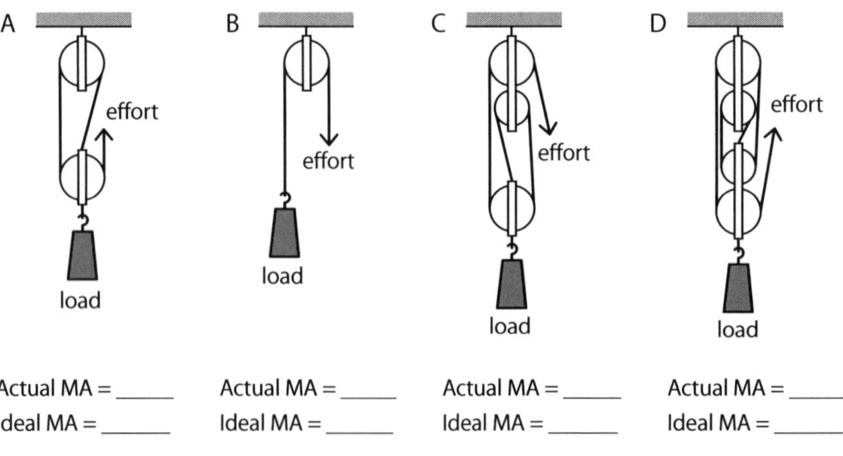

Actual MA = ____ Ideal MA = ____ (A)

Actual MA = ____ Ideal MA = ____ (B)

Actual MA = ____ Ideal MA = ____ (C)

Actual MA = ____ Ideal MA = ____ (D)

Figure 6.1.2 *Pulleys Step 3*

Table 6.1.1 *Data for Investigation 6.1.1*

System Used	Load Lifted (N)	Load Lifted This Distance (m)	Work Done By Pulley System (J)	*Your* Effort Force (N)	*Your* Effort Distance (m)	Work Done by *You* (J)
Fig. 6.1.1	2.0	0.10	0.20			
Fig. 6.1.2A	2.0	0.10	0.20			
Fig. 6.1.2B	2.0	0.10	0.20			
Fig. 6.1.2C	2.0	0.10	0.20			
Fig. 6.1.2D	2.0	0.10	0.20			

Concluding Questions

1. According to your results and those of your classmates, is the work that *you* do operating the pulley systems greater than, equal to, or less than the work done by the pulley systems?
2. Does a pulley system "save" you work? Explain. Why are pulley systems used to lift heavy loads?
3. If a pulley system allows you to lift a load that is twice your effort force, we say that it has a **mechanical advantage (MA)** of 2. Mechanical advantage is equal to the load divided by the effort force:

$$\textbf{MA} = \frac{\textbf{load}}{\textbf{effort force}}$$

   Calculate the mechanical advantage of each of the five pulley systems you used.

4. Examine the diagrams in Figures 6.1.1 and 6.1.2. Note the number of sections of rope that are exerting an upward force on the load. Considering that these sections of rope share the load equally, can you figure out a quick and easy way to predict the **ideal mechanical advantage** of each system? Test your prediction against the actual mechanical advantage you calculated for each pulley system.
5. How might the effort distance and the load distance be used to calculate the ideal MA of a pulley system? Write a formula for calculating MA from effort distance and load distance.

Challenges

1. Predict what the mechanical advantage of the pulley system in Figure 6.1.3 will be. Test your prediction by experimenting.
   Hint: Is it really just *one* pulley system?
2. Draw a pulley system that has a mechanical advantage of less than one. For what purpose might it be used?

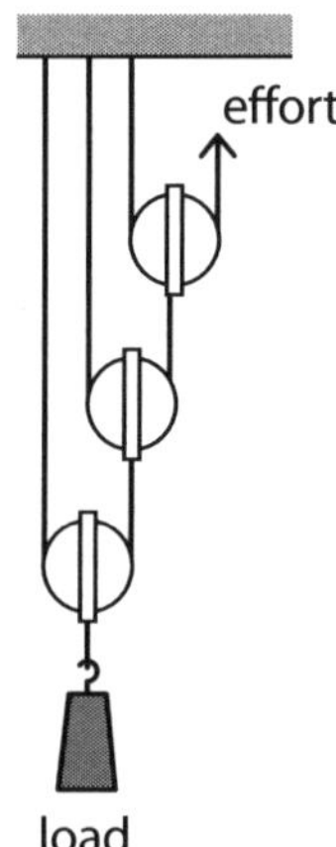

Figure 6.1.3 *Pulleys Challenge 1*

Investigation 6.1.2 Measuring the Power of a Small Motor

Purpose

To measure the rate at which a small electric motor does work and thus determine its power output

Procedure

1. Use a small electric motor equipped with a special shaft on which a 2.0 m length of string can be wound. Clamp the motor to a ring stand (Figure 6.1.4).

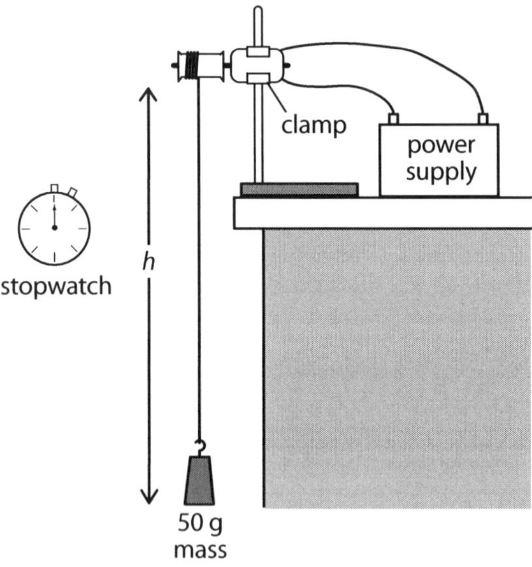

Figure 6.1.4 *Power Step 1*

2. Try different source voltages with the motor to see what you need so that the motor will lift a mass of 50.0 g up from the floor in a time of approximately 2.0–3.0 s.
3. To measure the useful power of the motor, you will need to know the force of gravity on the mass, the height through which the mass will be raised, and the time it takes to lift the mass through that height. (Remember that 1 kg of mass has a force of gravity on it of 9.8 N.)
4. Calculate the power of the motor for at least three different sets of conditions, using

   $\text{power} = \frac{\text{work}}{\text{time}}$. Try different loads and/or different source voltages to vary the conditions.

Concluding Questions

1. What is the maximum power output you measured for your motor?
2. What was the maximum power a member of your class achieved with the motor?

6.1 Review Questions

1. How much work is done on a 10.0 kg mass by Earth's gravitational field when the mass drops a distance of 5.0 m?

2. A girl uses a 3.0 m long ramp to push her 110 kg motorbike up to a trailer. The floor of the trailer is 1.2 m above the ground. How much work is done on the motorbike?

3. The force of gravity on a box of apples is 98.0 N. How much work will you do
   (a) if you lift the box from the floor to a height of 1.2 m?

   (b if you carry the box horizontally a distance of 2.0 m?

4. A hiker carries a 25 kg load up a hill at a steady speed through a vertical height of 350 m. How much work does she do on the load?

5. The force of gravity on a box is 100.0 N. The coefficient of friction between the floor and the box is 0.250. How much work is done when the box is pushed along the floor, at a steady speed, for a distance of 15.0 m?

6. Which of the variables below would improve in your favour if you used a pulley system of MA = 8 to lift a load, compared with a pulley system of MA = 2? Explain your answer.
   (a) effort distance
   (b) effort force
   (c) work done by you
   (d) your power
   (e) work done by the machine

7. Draw a pulley system that has a mechanical advantage of 1/2. For what purpose might you use such a system?

8. How powerful is a motor that can lift a 500.0 kg load through a height of 12.0 m in a time of 12 s?

9. A motor does 25 MJ (megajoules) of work in one hour.
   (a) What is the power rating of the motor?

   (b) How many horsepower is this motor, if 1 HP = 750 W?

10. How much energy is consumed by a 100.0 W light bulb, if it is left on for 12.0 h?

11. An appliance that consumes electrical energy at the rate of 1500 J/s, accomplishes 1200 J/s of useful work. How efficient is the appliance?

6.2 Mechanical Energy

Warm Up

Fill a coffee can with three or four handfuls of dry sand. Measure the temperature of the sand. Now shake the can vigorously for three minutes. Take the temperature of the sand. Describe what happened to the temperature and explain why you think it occurred.

____

____

____

Kinetic Energy

A moving object can do work. A falling axe does work to split a log. A moving baseball bat does work to stop a baseball, momentarily compress the ball out of its normal shape, then reverse its direction, and send it off at high speed.

Since a moving object has the ability to do work, it must have energy. We call the energy of a moving object its **kinetic energy.** A body that is at rest can gain kinetic energy if work is done on it by an external force. To get such a body moving at speed v, a net force must be exerted on it to accelerate it from rest up to speed v. The amount of work, W, which must be done can be calculated as follows:

$$W = Fd = (ma)d = m(ad)$$

Remember that for an object accelerating from rest at a uniform rate, $v_f^2 = 2ad$.

Therefore,
$$(ad) = \frac{v_f^2}{2}$$
and
$$W = m(ad) = m\left(\frac{v_f^2}{2}\right) = \frac{1}{2}\,mv^2$$

The work done on the object to accelerate it up to a speed v results in an amount of energy being transferred to the object, which is equal in magnitude to $\frac{1}{2}\,mv^2$. This is the object's kinetic energy, E_k.

$$E_k = \frac{1}{2}\,mv^2$$

Once an object has kinetic energy, it can do work on other objects.

Quick Check

1. A golfer wishes to improve his driving distance. Which would have more effect? Explain your answer.
   (a) doubling the mass of his golf club
   OR
   (b) doubling the speed with which the clubhead strikes the ball

2. How much work must be done to accelerate a 110 kg motorbike and its 60.0 kg rider from 0 to 80 km/h?

3. How much work is needed to slow down a 1200 kg vehicle from 80 km/h to 50 km/h? What does this work?

4. How much work is needed to accelerate a 1.0 g insect from rest up to 12 m/s?

Gravitational Potential Energy

Figure 6.2.1 shows an extremely simple mechanical system. A basketball player lifts a basketball straight up to a height h. The ball has mass m, so the force of gravity on the ball is mg. In lifting the ball, the basketball player has done work equal to mgh on the ball. He has transferred energy to the ball. Chemical energy in his cell molecules has been changed into gravitational potential energy because of the work he did.

Work is always a measure of energy transferred to a body. When the basketball is held up at height *h*, it has gravitational potential energy (E_p) equal to *mgh*.

$$E_p = mgh$$

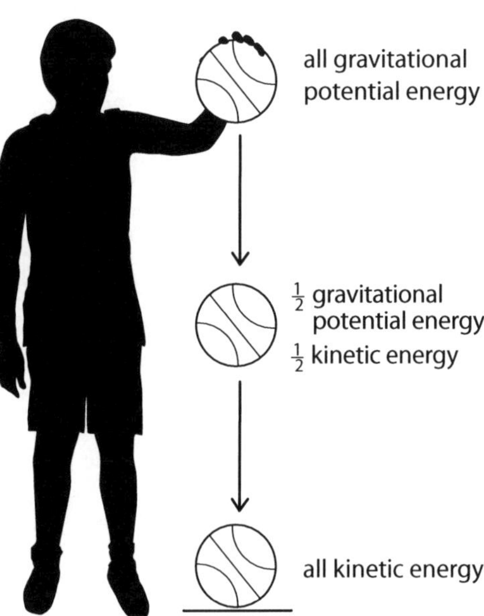

Figure 6.2.1 *At its highest point, the ball has only gravitational potential energy. Once it starts dropping, it has kinetic energy as well.*

Reference Point

When calculating gravitational potential energy, the height an object moves is always measured from the starting point of the movement. This is called the **reference point**. This is important because it means, the amount of potential energy in an object is relative to where the measurement occurs. For example, a table 1.0 m high has a 1.0 kg book on it. If the book is lifted 0.5 m above the table, how much gravitational potential energy does the book have? If h is measured from the table, it has 4.5 J of potential energy because $h = 0.5$ m or $E_p = (91.0 \text{ kg})(9.8 \text{ m/s}^2)(0.5 \text{ m})$. If h is measured from the ground, the book has 14.7 J of potential energy because $h = 1.5$ m or $E_p = (91.0 \text{ kg})(9.8 \text{ m/s}^2)(1.5 \text{ m})$.

Both answers are correct. What is important that the reference point is identified and only the vertical height is measured when determining the amount of gravitational potential energy in an object.

Quick Check

1. A box of bananas is lifted 5 m and gains a certain amount of potential energy. If the box is lifted another 5 m, describe how the potential energy changes.
2. What is the mass of a television if it takes 620 J to lift it 2.5 m.
3. If it takes 240 J to lift a 4 kg object, how high is the object lifted?

Work Energy Theorem

If a force is applied to an object over a distance, the amount of kinetic energy in the object changes. For example, a car speeds up because the force of the engine turns the wheels faster over a distance. The increased speed of the car represents the increase in the car's kinetic energy. You may have noticed that when the formula for kinetic energy was derived, work equaled the amount of kinetic energy:

$$W = \frac{1}{2}mv^2$$

The work-energy theorem states that the work done on a system the energy changes or:

$$\boldsymbol{W = \Delta E}$$

Law of Conservation of Energy

Now consider what happens when the basketball you saw in Figure 6.2.1 is allowed to fall under the influence of the force of gravity. The unbalanced force, ignoring air friction, is equal to the force of gravity on the ball. For any situation where an object of mass *m* is pulled by an unbalanced force *F*, there will be an acceleration, *a*. Newton's second law of motion tells us that $F = ma$.

In our example, the basketball is a free-falling body, and $a = g$. As the ball falls through height *h*, its speed increases from 0 to v_f. For uniform acceleration,

$$v_f^2 = 2ad$$

For this situation, $v_f^2 = 2gh$. Since the unbalanced force pulling the ball down is *mg*, the work done on the ball by Earth's gravitational field is *mgh*.

$$\text{If } v_f^2 = 2gh, \text{ then } gh = \frac{v_f^2}{2}$$

$$\text{Therefore, } mgh = m\left(\frac{v_f^2}{2}\right) = \frac{1}{2}mv_f^2$$

When the ball is at the top of its path, all its energy is gravitational potential energy. The ball is not moving. It has energy only because of its position above the floor from which it was lifted. As the ball falls, it loses its potential energy and gains energy of motion, kinetic energy. Just before it collides with the floor, all the energy of the ball is kinetic energy, and the potential energy is zero. The amount of kinetic energy (E_k) at the bottom of its fall is given by:

$$E_k = \frac{1}{2}mv_f^2$$

On the way down, the kinetic energy of the ball at any time depends on the speed the ball has reached. For any speed *v*, kinetic energy $E_k = mv_f^2$. As the ball gains kinetic energy, it loses gravitational potential energy. At all times the sum of the gravitational potential energy and the kinetic energy is constant.

$$E_p + E_k = \text{constant}$$

This is an example of the **law of conservation of energy**, which states:

> The total energy of a mechanical system is constant. Energy can be transformed from one form into another, but the total amount of energy is unchanged.

As the ball falls through positions 1, 2, 3, etc., the sum of the potential energy and the kinetic energy remains constant:

$$mgh_1 + \frac{1}{2}mv_1^2 = mgh_2 + \frac{1}{2}mv_2^2 = mgh_3 + \frac{1}{2}mv_3^2 = \dots$$

Notice that mechanical energy can be either potential or kinetic. For a mechanical system, the total mechanical energy is constant.

Sample Problem — The Law of Conservation of Energy

The pendulum bob in Figure 6.2.2 is pulled back far enough that it is raised 0.36 m above its original level. When it is released, how fast will it be moving at the bottom of its swing?

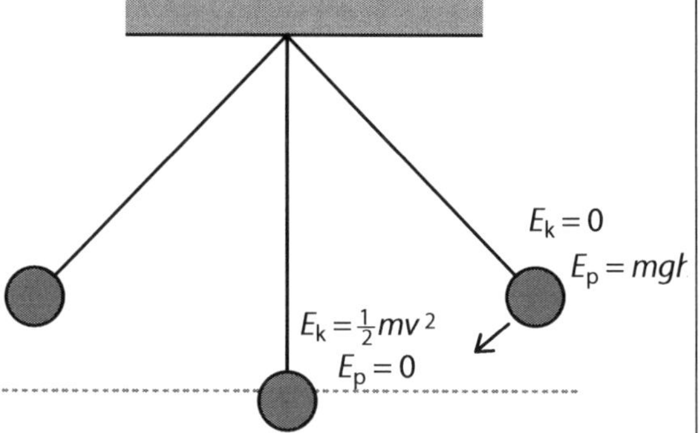

Figure 6.2.2 *Moving pendulum*

What to Think About	How to Do It
1. When the pendulum is pulled back, it is also lifted through a height *h*, and work *mgh* is done in lifting the bob against the force of gravity. The bob gains gravitational potential energy equal to the work done on it, so $E_p = mgh$. When the bob is released, its gravitational potential energy is transformed into kinetic energy. At the bottom of the swing, $E_p = 0$, and, $E_k = \frac{1}{2} mv^2$ but the kinetic energy at the bottom of the swing must equal the gravitational potential energy at the top according to the law of conservation of energy.	$E_p = mgh = \frac{1}{2} mv^2$
2. Rearrange to find speed.	Therefore, $v^2 = 2gh$ and $v \sqrt{2gh}$
3. Solve to find the speed of the bob at the bottom of the swing.	$v = \sqrt{2gh}$ $= \sqrt{2(9.8 \text{ m/s}^2)(0.36 \text{ m})}$ $= 2.7 \text{ m/s}$ The pendulum bob will be moving 2.7 m/s at the bottom of its swing.

Practice Problems — The Law of Conservation of Energy

1. Spiderman shoots a web line 9 m long and swings on the end of it, like a pendulum. His starting point is 3.0 m above the lowest point in his swing. How fast is Spiderman moving as he passes through the bottom of the swing?

2. A vehicle moving with a speed of 90 km/h (25 m/s) loses its brakes but sees a runaway hill near the highway. If the driver steers his vehicle into the runaway hill, how far up the hill (vertically) will the vehicle travel before it comes to a stop? (Ignore friction.)

3. A 500 kg roller coaster car is going 10 m/s at the bottom of its run. How high can you build the next hill on the track so that it can get over without any additional work being done on the car? (Ignore friction.) Is your answer reasonable?

6.2 Review Questions

1. How much kinetic energy does the 80.0 kg skier sliding down the frictionless slope shown below have when he is two-thirds of the way down the ramp? The vertical height of the ramp is 60.0 m.

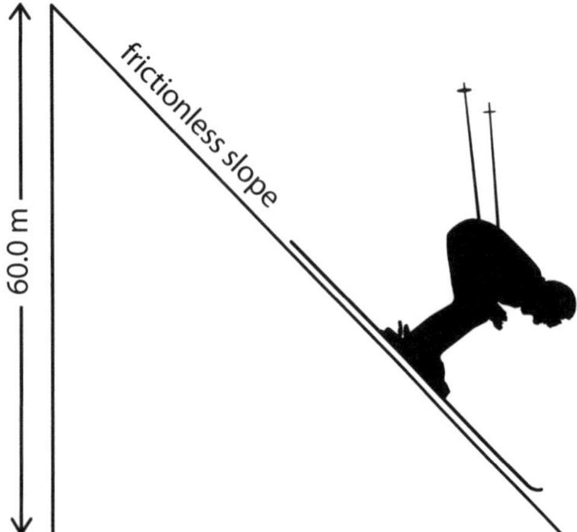

2. (a) How much potential energy is gained when a 75 kg person takes a ski lift up a mountain for 600 m?

   (b) At another ski hill, a 50 kg person gains 3.68×10^5 J when she travels up a ski lift for 1500 m at a 30° angle. What is the vertical height gained by the skier?

3. In a computer simulation, a Moon exploration robot lifted 0.245 kg of Moon rock 60 cm. This action required 0.24 J. What is the acceleration due to gravity on the Moon?

4. A physics student lifts his 2.0 kg pet rock 2.8 m straight up. He then lets it drop to the ground. Use the law of conservation of energy to calculate how fast the rock will be moving (a) half way down and (b) just before it hits the ground.

5. A 65 kg girl is running with a speed of 2.5 m/s.
   (a) How much kinetic energy does she have?

   (b) She grabs onto a rope that is hanging from the ceiling and swings from the end of the rope. How high off the ground will she swing?

6. A rubber ball falls from a height of 2.0 m, bounces off the floor and goes back up to a height of 1.6 m.
   (a) What percentage of its initial gravitational potential energy has been lost?
   (b) Where does this energy go? Does this contradict the law of conservation of energy? Why or why not?

7. How much work must be done to increase the speed of a 12 kg bicycle ridden by a 68 kg rider from 8.2 m/s to 12.7 m/s?

8. A 2.6 kg laboratory cart is given a push and moves with a speed of 2.0 m/s toward a solid barrier, where it is momentarily brought to rest by its spring bumper.

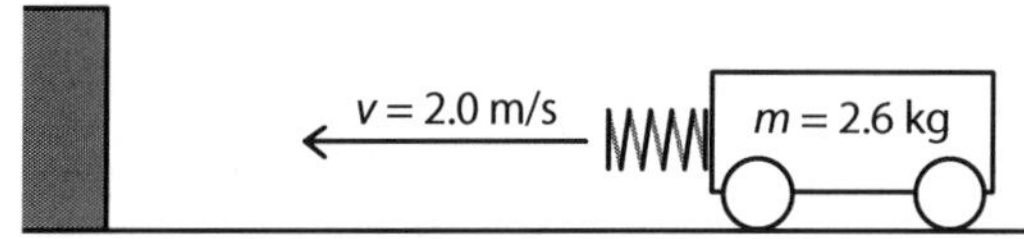

   (a) How much elastic potential energy will be stored in the spring at the moment when the spring is fully compressed?
   (b) What is the average force exerted by the spring if it is compressed 0.12 m? Why is it necessary to specify average force in this situation?

6.3 Temperature, Heat, and Thermal Energy

Warm Up

On a hot summer day, you may have noticed that if you walk on concrete with your bare feet, it will be hotter than the grass. If you go inside, a tile floor will feel cooler on your feet than the rest of the house. Why do you experience these differences if the temperature is not changing dramatically?

____

____

____

Kinetic Molecular Theory

According to the **kinetic molecular theory**, all matter is made up of tiny particles that are constantly moving. The particles — molecules or atoms — attract each other to some extent. The particles can move in a number of ways (Figure 6.3.1):

- They can move in straight lines (translational motion between collisions).
- They can rotate.
- They can vibrate.

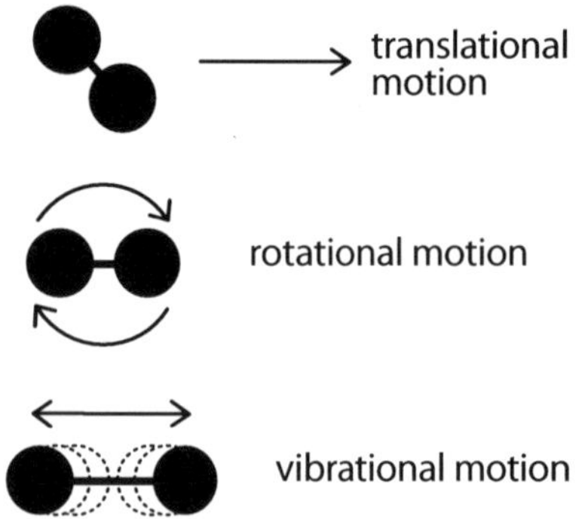

Figure 6.3.1 *Particles in matter can move in three different ways.*

Molecules may have **translational kinetic energy**, which is energy due to motion in straight lines, **rotational kinetic energy** and **vibrational kinetic energy**. They may also have **potential energy**, which arises from attractions between molecules or repulsions at very close range.

The **total energy** of all the molecules in an amount of material is called the **thermal energy** of the material. When thermal energy is transferred from one material to another material, the amount of energy transferred is called **heat**. For a transfer of energy to occur, there must be a difference in temperature between the body from which the thermal energy is being transferred and the body to which the thermal energy is being transferred. Heat is transferred from a hotter body to a cooler body.

The way we describe how hot or cold a body is to use a number we call the body's **temperature** on a standard temperature scale. The **Celsius** scale is named after Anders Celsius (1704–1744), a Swedish astronomer who first suggested its use. In the Celsius scale, 0°C is assigned to the temperature at which ice melts or water freezes, and 100°C is assigned to the temperature at which water boils at standard sea level air pressure. On a typical mercury or alcohol thermometer, the space between 0°C and 100°C is divided into 100 equal divisions called **degrees**.

What does temperature really measure? Temperature depends on the average translational kinetic energy of all the molecules in a material. Imagine a drop of boiling hot water spilled from a large bucket of boiling water. The bucket of boiling water has far more thermal energy in it, and its **total kinetic energy** is far greater than the total kinetic energy in the drop of boiling water. The molecules in the bucket of water and those in the drop of water, however, have the same **average translational kinetic energy**, so both have the same **temperature.**

Absolute Zero

What would happen if a substance were cooled so much that the average translational kinetic energy of its molecules was zero? The substance would have almost no energy to transfer to any other body. If its average translational kinetic energy were zero, its temperature would be the lowest it could possibly be. On the Celsius scale, this temperature would be about –273°C. This temperature is called **absolute zero**.

On another temperature scale called the **Kelvin** scale, after British physicist Lord Kelvin (1824–1907), absolute zero is assigned a value of 0 K. On this scale, the unit for temperature is not called a degree, but instead a kelvin (K). Therefore, 0 K = –273°C. A kelvin is the same size as a Celsius degree. This means that a temperature of 0°C would be equal to 273 K. Water boils at 100°C, or 373 K. To scientists, the Kelvin scale is useful because on this scale, the temperature of an "ideal" gas in kelvins is directly proportional to the average translational kinetic energy of the molecules in the gas. Helium is a gas that behaves like an ideal gas. It is monatomic, which means that its smallest particles consist of just one atom.

Quick Check

1. (a) Explain the difference between temperature, thermal energy, and heat.

   (b) Why is it incorrect to say that a body contains heat?

2. A sample of helium gas has a temperature of 20°C.
   (a) What is its temperature in kelvins (K)?

   (b) In another helium sample, the atoms have twice the average translational kinetic energy. What is the temperature of this sample in
   (i) kelvins?

   (ii) °C?

3. A large pot of near-boiling water has a small, red-hot nail dropped into it.

   (a) Which has more thermal energy to begin with — the pot of water or the nail?

   (b) Which has the higher average kinetic energy to begin with?

   (c) Which will lose heat, and which will gain heat when the nail is dropped into the pot of boiling water?

   (d) After five minutes, which will have
   (i) more thermal energy?

   (ii) higher average kinetic energy?

Heat Transfer by Conduction

Imagine that you hold one end of a glass rod in your hand and heat the other end with the flame of a Bunsen burner (Figure 6.3.2). Molecules near the heated end have thermal energy transferred to them from the flame. These glass molecules gain kinetic energy, collide with their neighbours, and pass the increased kinetic energy on. Eventually, the whole rod will be warmed up and the end you are holding may in time become too hot to hold.

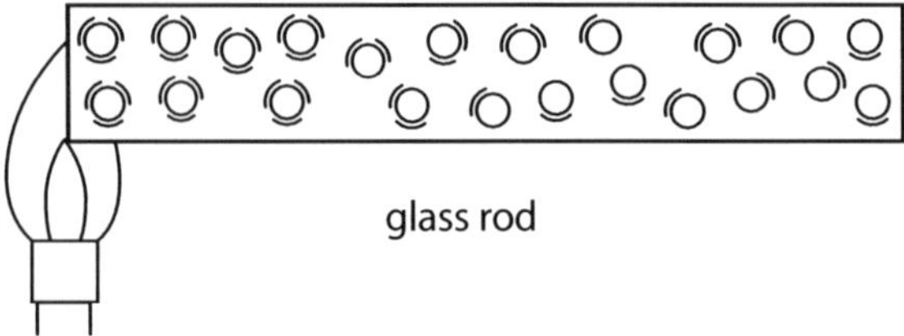

Figure 6.3.2 *The heat from the Bunsen burner transfers through the kinetic energy of the glass molecules.*

Heat is transferred through the glass rod slowly by **conduction.** Conduction is the transfer of heat from molecule to molecule or atom to atoms through a material. Glass is not a particularly good conductor. The best **conductors** are metals. Metals conduct heat and electricity well, because atoms of metals have loosely attached electrons, called free electrons. These free electrons can move easily throughout the length of the metal. When these free electrons gain kinetic energy, they can transfer their energy easily to other electrons and atoms with which they collide.

Heat Transfer by Convection

Thermal energy is not easily transferred by conduction through gases and liquids. In conduction, the energy is transferred through collisions of atoms or molecules or electrons with neighbouring particles.

In fluids (gases or liquids), thermal energy can be transferred very efficiently by **convection.** In convection, the thermal energy "flows" with the molecules from one place to another. In convection, the substance being warmed moves, carrying the thermal energy with it. The movement of the substance is called a **convection current**. Investigation 6.3.2 demonstrates the nature of convection.

Convection in Everyday Life

Different parts of Earth's surface absorb the Sun's heat better than others, so the air near these parts of Earth will be warmed accordingly. Convection currents result from the uneven heating. Small-scale local winds and the larger continental wind patterns are convection currents resulting from uneven heating of air near Earth's surface.

Heat Transfer by Radiation

Our primary source of thermal energy is the Sun. Since the space between the Sun and our planet is for all practical purposes "empty," there is no way heat transfer by conduction or convection can occur. Heat transmission through a vacuum is possible, however, by the process of **radiation.** Any form of energy transmitted by radiation will be in the form of electromagnetic waves and will travel at the speed of light. The various forms of **radiant energy** that originate in the Sun include: radio waves, microwaves, infrared radiation (heat), visible light, ultraviolet light, X-radiation, and gamma radiation. You cannot see infrared radiation, of course, but you can often feel it on your skin. When you sit in front of a fireplace, the warming effect you sense is due to infrared radiation. Infrared radiation can also be detected by photography or by electronic means.

Radiation in Everyday Life

Radiant energy falling on materials may be absorbed or reflected. The absorbed radiation increases the average translational kinetic energy of the molecules in the object, and therefore its temperature. A perfectly black object would absorb all the radiant energy falling on its surface. Light-coloured objects reflect more radiant energy. On a hot, sunny summer day, a good choice of outer-wear would be white, since it will reflect much of the infrared and visible radiation falling on your clothes.

In some parts of the world, radiant energy from the Sun is reflected by well-placed mirrors to receivers in which water is heated and changed into steam. The steam is used to operate a turbine, which runs a generator to produce electricity.

Another way of collecting radiant energy from the Sun is to use a convex lens to focus the radiation to a small area. This type of lens, called a Fresnel lens, can be used to make a solar furnace. On a sunny day, one of these Fresnel lenses can produce a temperature of over 1000°C at its focus. You can find a small-scale example of a Fresnel lens in an overhead projector.

Quick Check

1. Water is a poor conductor, yet water is brought to a boil quickly in a pot or kettle. Explain.

2. The diagram below shows a seashore scene. Water temperature stays quite constant day and night, but the land warms up during the day, so it has a higher temperature than the sea. At night, the land cools rapidly and is cooler than the sea.

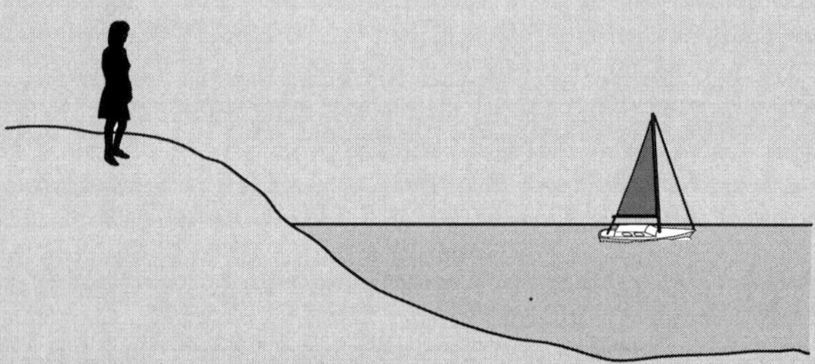

   (a) Sketch the direction of the convection current near the seashore in the daytime.
   (b) Using another colour or dotted arrows, sketch the direction of the convection current near the seashore at night.
   (c) When would you rather launch a sailboat to go out to sea—in the very early morning or in the evening? Why?

4. Carefully dismantle a thermos bottle and examine its construction. Assume it is filled with hot soup. How does the construction of the thermos bottle work to prevent heat loss by conduction, convection, and radiation?

5. Which will melt faster on a bright, sunny day—fresh snow or dirty snow? Why?

Investigation 6.3.1 Heat Transfer by Conduction

Purpose

To demonstrate conduction and conductors

Procedure

Your teacher may decide to do these activities as a demonstration.

Part 1

1. (a) Obtain a conduction apparatus like the one in Figure 6.3.3 and clamp it above an alcohol burner. Predict which of the metals will conduct heat fastest. Which will be the poorest conductor?
   (b) Test your prediction by heating the rods at the junction. Drops of candle wax have been used to attach small nails or paper clips to the ends of each of the metal rods. Record the order in which the rods drop their nails. Was your prediction correct?

Figure 6.3.3 *Conduction Part 1 — Step 1*

2. Touch the surface of your wooden workbench with the flat of your hand. Now touch the base of a metal ring stand or a sheet of aluminum foil. Which feels warmer to the touch? Is either surface at a different temperature than the other? Why does one surface feel cooler than the other?

Part 2

1. Place some crushed ice in a large test tube and use a few marbles to keep the ice at the bottom of the test tube. Add water to the level shown in Figure 6.3.4.
2. Use a Bunsen burner to carefully heat the test tube near the top. Can you make the water at the top of the test tube boil while the ice remains frozen at the bottom? Do your observations suggest that water is a good conductor or a poor conductor?

Figure 6.3.4 *Conduction Part 2*

Part 3

1. Set up the apparatus shown in Figure 6.3.5. Attach two rings to the same ring stand. Ring A is approximately 15 cm above the top of the Bunsen burner. Cover each ring with a sheet of copper gauze.
2. (a) Turn on the gas and use a match to light the gas at A. Observe what happens. Does the gas initially burn at B and/ or C? Turn off the gas.
   (b) Turn on the gas, and light the gas at B. Observe what happens. Turn off the gas.
   (c) Turn on the gas, and light the gas at C. Observe what happens. Turn off the gas.
   (d) Turn on the gas, and light the gas at A and C. Observe, then turn off the gas.

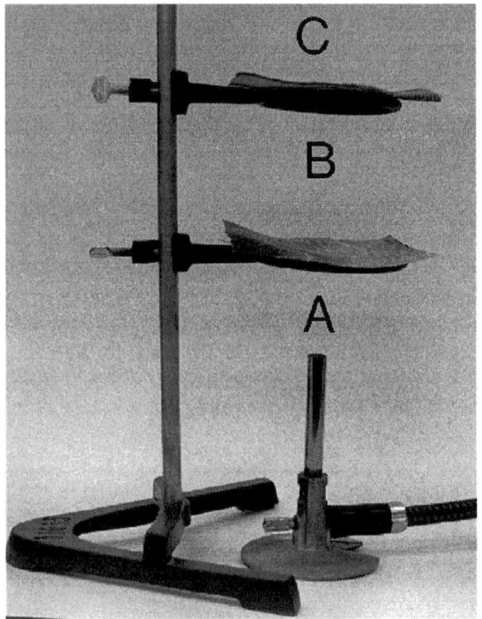

Figure 6.3.5 *Conduction Part 3*

Concluding Questions

1. Of the metals you tested for conductivity in Part 1, list the order in which they conduct heat, from best to worst.
2. List three metals that are used in cooking utensils because they conduct well.
3. Explain the results you observed in Part 3.

Challenge

1. Have a contest to see who can design a container that will keep an ice cube solid for the longest time.

Investigation 6.3.2 Convection (Demonstrations)

Purpose
To observe convection currents in fluids

Procedure

Part 1: Convection in a Liquid (Water)

1. Your teacher has filled the ring-shaped glass tube shown in Figure 6.3.6 with water. An alcohol burner or candle is arranged so that its flame will warm a bottom corner of the tube.
2. Predict which way the water in the tube will circulate when the flame is lit and the water is warmed.
3. Your teacher will light the flame. After allowing the water to warm up slightly, your teacher will add one drop of food colouring to the opening at the top of the tube. Sketch the tube and show the direction in which the water flows. The flow you observe is a convection current.

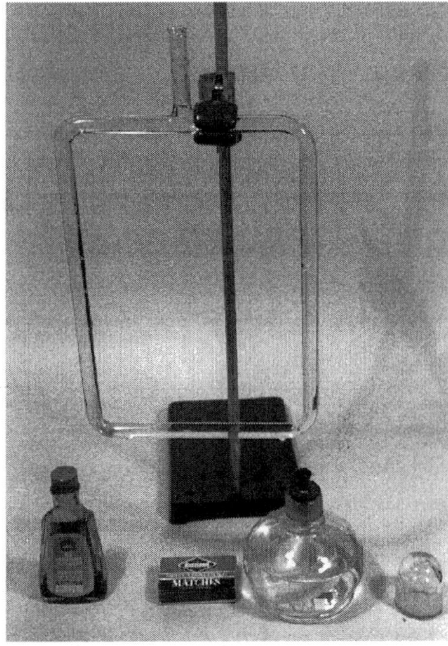

Figure 6.3.6 *Convection Part 1*

Part 2: Convection in a Gas (Air)

1. Figure 6.3.7 shows a convection box, which has a sliding front window and two glass chimneys. Light the candle and close the front window. Allow the candle to burn for a minute, then light a piece of touch paper (or other source of smoke) and hold the smoking source above each of the two chimneys in turn. Observe the pattern of motion of the air, as shown by the visible smoke carried by the air.

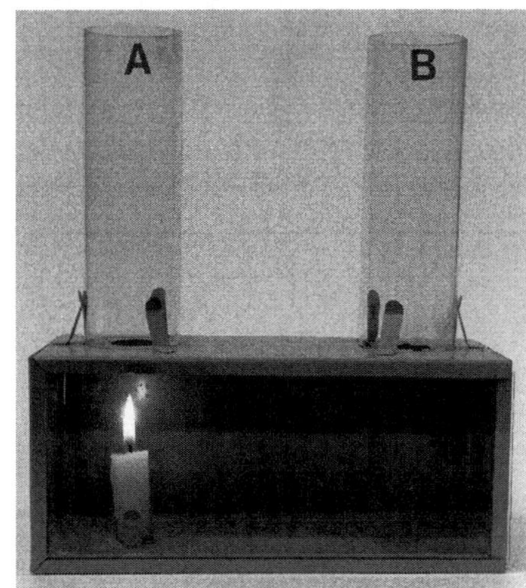

Figure 6.3.7 *Convection Part 2*

Concluding Questions

1. Explain, in terms of molecular motion and density (density = mass/volume), why a convection current in water or air moves in the direction that it does.
2. In Investigation 6.3.1, you were able to boil water at the top of a test tube while ice at the bottom of the tube remained frozen. What would happen if you heated the bottom of a test tube that has ice at the top? How would the heat be transferred to the ice?

Investigation 6.3.3 Absorbing Infrared Radiation

Purpose

To find out if a black surface or a shiny surface absorbs more infrared radiation in a given time

Procedure

1. Obtain two used, black plastic film containers. Leave one black, but cover the other container with aluminum foil, as shown in Figure 6.3.8.
2. Fill each container with water, and measure the temperature of the water in each one. Prepare a chart like Table 6.3.1. Enter the starting temperature in the column under 0 min.
3. Set the containers on insulating Styrofoam cups, the same distance (50 cm) from a source of infrared light, such as a 100-W lamp. After 1 min, measure the temperatures of the water in each container. Two students might read the temperatures simultaneously. Record these temperatures in your table.
4. Repeat the measurements after 2, 3, 4, and 5 min. If necessary, continue taking readings until a definite pattern is established.

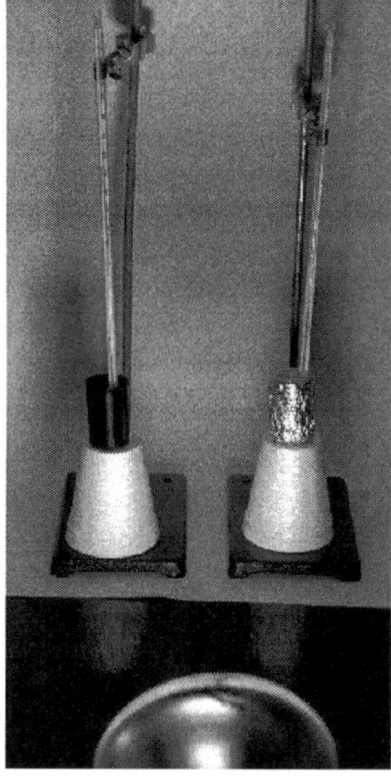

Figure 6.3.8 *Radiation*

Table 6.3.1 *Temperatures of Containers of Water Warmed by a Lamp*

Time (minutes)	0	1	2	3	4	5
Temperature (°C) BLACK						
Temperature (°C) SHINY						

Concluding Questions

1. Which container, if either, warmed up more?
2. Try to explain what you observed.

Challenge

1. A Crooke's radiometer, named after Sir William Crookes (1832–1919), is shown in Figure 6.3.9. Four vanes are connected to a pivot in a glass bulb, which is partially, but not completely, evacuated. There are some air molecules inside the container. One side of each vane is black. The other side may be white or silvered.

   Design an experiment using an infrared light source, a mirror, and a radiometer to test whether infrared radiation reflects from a shiny surface the way visible light does.

Figure 6.3.9 *Crooke's radiometer*

6.3 Review Questions

1. What are the three potential forms of kinetic energy that a molecule could have?

2. If the temperature of an object is 30°C, what is its temperature in kelvins?

3. By what method can heat be transferred without the presence of matter?

4. What is the direction of airflow at night in the situation shown below, assuming there are no major weather disturbances?

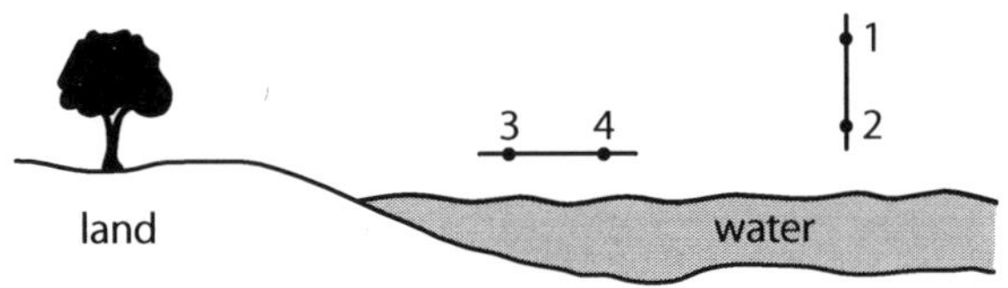

5. A cold weather emergency survival suit is made of a reflecting plastic material with a thin coating of regular plastic. Why is the shiny, reflecting plastic on the *inside* of the suit facing your body? Why is it *not* wise to place this suit on someone who is already suffering from hypothermia?

6. If you are sitting in front of an open fireplace, what is the main method by which heat is transferred to you?

7. When a pot of soup heats up, what is the main method by which heat is transferred within the soup?

8. In winter, why do the blades of your skates feel cooler to the touch than your boots do?

6.4 Measuring Thermal Energy

Warm Up

In the fall when the temperature drops below 0°C many lakes will not freeze over, but smaller puddles will freeze. Why does this happen?

____

____

____

Specific Heat Capacity

The amount of thermal energy in an object depends on several factors. First, it depends on the mass, m, of the object. Second, it depends on the temperature, T, of the object. Third, it depends on the nature of the material in the object. Different materials have different capacities for holding thermal energy. One material that has an exceptionally high capacity for holding thermal energy is water.

It can be shown that to raise the temperature of 1 kg of water by 1°C requires an input of 4200 J. For comparison, it only requires an input of 450 J to raise the temperature of 1 kg of iron by 1°C. The amount of heat required to raise the temperature of 1 kg of a substance by 1°C is called the **specific heat capacity** (c) of the substance. For example, the specific heat capacity of water is written as $c = 4200$ J/kg/°C. For iron, the specific heat capacity is $c = 450$ J/kg/°C.

The joule (J) is an appropriate unit for measuring heat, since the English scientist James Joule did the first experiments to compare the specific heat capacities of different materials. Table 6.4.1 lists some specific heat capacities.

Table 6.4.1 *Specific Heat Capacities*

Substance	J/kg/°C	Substance	J/kg/°C
water	4200	aluminum	920
methyl alcohol	2400	glass	840
ethylene glycol*	2200	iron	450
ice	2100	copper	430
kerosene	2100	lead	130
steam	2100		

*antifreeze

Since the specific heat capacity, c, is the amount of energy that must be transferred to raise the temperature of 1 kg of water by 1°C, then $c = \frac{\Delta E}{m\Delta T}$, where ΔE is the energy transferred, m is the mass of material, and ΔT is the change in temperature. This is commonly written as:

$$\Delta E = mc\Delta T$$

Sample Problem — Working with Specific Heat Capacity

If 25 kJ of heat is transferred to 50.0 kg of water initially at 20.0°C, what will the final temperature of the water be?

What to Think About	How to Do It
1. Find the formula	$\Delta E = mc\Delta T$
2. Identify what you know.	$\Delta E = 25$ kJ $m = 50.0$ kg $c = 4.2 \times 10^3$ J/kg/°C $T_1 = 20.0$°C $T_2 = ?$
3. To find the final temperature, determine how much the temperature will increase with 25 kJ of heat added.	$T_2 - 20.0°C = \frac{2.5 \times 10^4 \text{ J}}{(5.0 \times 10^1 \text{ kg})(4.2 \times 10^3 \text{ J/kg/°C})}$ $= 0.12°C$
4. Solve for T_2.	$T_2 = 20.0°C + 0.12°C$ $= 20.1°C$ The final temperature will be 20.1°C.

Practice Problems — Working with Specific Heat Capacity

1. How much heat is needed to raise the temperature of 90.0 kg of water from 18°C to 80°C?

2. If 1.0 MJ (megajoule) of heat is transferred to 10.0 kg of water initially at 15°C, what will the water's final temperature be?

3. If 12 kg of water cools from 100°C down to room temperature (20°C), how much heat will it release to the environment?

4. Why is water such a desirable material to use as a coolant in a car engine?

5. If it takes 1200 J to raise the temperature of 0.500 kg of brass from 20.0°C to 26.2°C, what is the specific heat capacity of brass?

Power of a Heat Source

Power is the rate at which energy is produced or consumed (or the rate at which work is done). For our present needs, power is the rate at which heat is transferred.

$$P = \frac{\Delta E}{\Delta t}$$

where P is power, ΔE is the energy transferred, and Δt is the time interval during which the energy is transferred.

Efficiency

For any energy-converting device, a convenient ratio to know is the ratio of the useful energy output of the device to the energy put into the device. This ratio is the **efficiency** of the device.

$$\text{efficiency} = \frac{\text{useful energy out of device}}{\text{energy put into device}}$$

$$\textbf{efficiency} = \frac{W_{out}}{W_{in}} = \frac{P_{out}}{P_{in}}$$

The efficiency rating gives us an idea of how much energy a device wastes as heat. One of the least efficient devices is an ordinary incandescent light bulb. Since it converts only 5% of its electrical energy into light and 95% into heat, a light bulb is only 5% efficient. An automobile might be only 10% efficient. Where does all its wasted energy go?

Electric motors may have efficiencies in the range between 60% and 90%, while transformers and generators may be 99% efficient.

Sample Problem — Calculating Efficiency

To lift a 1200 N motorcycle a vertical height of 1.3 m onto a pickup truck, a motocross rider pushes the bike up a ramp 2.4 m, requiring an effort force up the ramp of 820 N. What is the efficiency of the ramp?

What to Think About	How to Do It
1. Find the useful work done by the ramp.	$W_{out} = (1200\text{ N})(1.3\text{ m}) = 1560\text{ J}$
2. Find the work put into using the ramp.	$W_{in} = (820\text{ N})(2.4\text{ m}) = 1968\text{ J}$
3. Find the efficiency of the ramp.	$\text{efficiency} = \frac{1560\text{ J}}{1968\text{ J}} \times 100\% = 79\%$. The ramp is 79% efficient.

CONNECTIONS

Traditional Knowledge and Western Science

Practice Problems — Calculating Efficiency

1. You must do 500 J of work to operate a pulley system that lifts a 150 N load to a height of 3.0 m. How efficient is the pulley system?

2. A kettle that is 80% efficient is rated 1200 W. At what rate does the water in the kettle absorb energy (in watts)?

3. If a light bulb has an efficiency of 5.0%, at what rate does a 60 W bulb produce light energy?

4. For every megajoule of chemical potential energy in the fuel used to run a certain truck, only 120 kJ of useful work is done by the truck in making itself move. How efficient is the truck? Where are some of the places that the energy from the fuel is wasted?

Investigation 6.4.1 Measuring the Power of a Hot Plate

Purpose

To measure the power of a hot plate indirectly, by measuring the heat transferred to a known mass of water in a given time

Procedure

1. Measure out 300 mL of water into a 400 mL beaker using a graduated cylinder. Since water has a density of 1 g/mL, this will give you 300 g or 0.300 kg of water.
2. Arrange the thermometer as in Figure 6.4.1, so that it is not touching the bottom of the beaker.
3. Let the hot plate warm up for a minute or two, and then start your stopwatch and record the temperature of the water as precisely as you can. Record the temperature of the water every half-minute for 10 min. Stop the experiment if the water comes to a boil and use only your data for temperatures less than boiling temperature. Record your data in a table like Table 6.4.2.
4. Plot a graph with temperature on the *y*-axis and time on the *x*-axis.
5. Find the slope of your graph, which is $\Delta T/\Delta t$. Units will be °C/s.

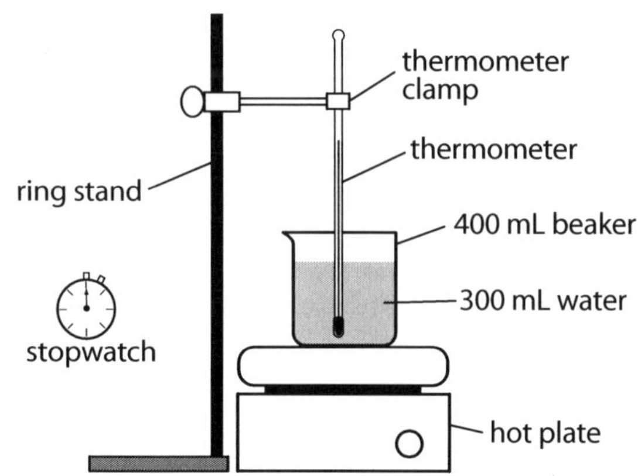

Figure 6.4.1 *Step 2*

Table 6.4.2 *Data for Investigation 6.4.1*

Time (s)	0	30	60	90	120	150	180	210	240	→
Temperature (°C)										

6. Since the energy transferred to the water from the hot plate is $E = mc\Delta T$, then the power of the hot plate would be:

$$P = \frac{\Delta E}{\Delta t} = \frac{mc\Delta T}{\Delta t} = mc \times (\text{slope})$$

Calculate the power of your hot plate using $m = 0.300$ kg, $c = 4200$ J/kg/°C, and the slope of your graph.

7. Find a cooled hot plate and read the label on it to see what the manufacturer's power rating is for it.

Concluding Questions

1. What was your calculated power for the hot plate?
2. Calculate the percent difference between your calculated power and the manufacturer's rating, as follows:

$$\%\text{ difference} = \frac{\text{manufacturer's rating} - \text{calculated power rating}}{\text{manufacturer's power rating}} \times 100\%$$

3. Assuming your calculations were correct, and the manufacturer's rating was also correct, what is the ratio of the power you calculated (heat absorbed by the water per second) to the hot plate's rated power (heat given off by the hot plate per second). This ratio is the efficiency of the hot plate. You can convert your decimal fraction to a percent by multiplying by 100.

$$\text{efficiency} = \frac{\text{calculated power rating}}{\text{manufacturer's power rating}} \times 100\%$$

4. Why is the efficiency less than 100%?

6.4 Review Questions

1. How much heat would be needed to warm 1.6 kg of ice from –15°C up to its melting point of 0°C?

2. A 5.0 kg block of lead at 250°C cools down to 20°C. How much heat does it give off in doing so?

3. How much heat must be transferred into 5.0 kg of water to raise its temperature from 20°C up to 97°C?

4. If water has a specific heat capacity of 4200 J/kg/°C, how much heat is needed to warm 50.0 kg of water from 15°C up to 85°C?

5. If 24 kJ of energy will warm 0.600 kg of a metal from 20° up to 220°C, what is the specific heat capacity of the metal?

6. A light bulb is immersed in 0.500 kg of water, which has a specific heat capacity of 4200 J/kg/°C. The apparatus is well insulated, so that essentially all of the radiated heat is used to warm the water. Every 100 s, the temperature of the water is recorded. The graph below summarizes the data.

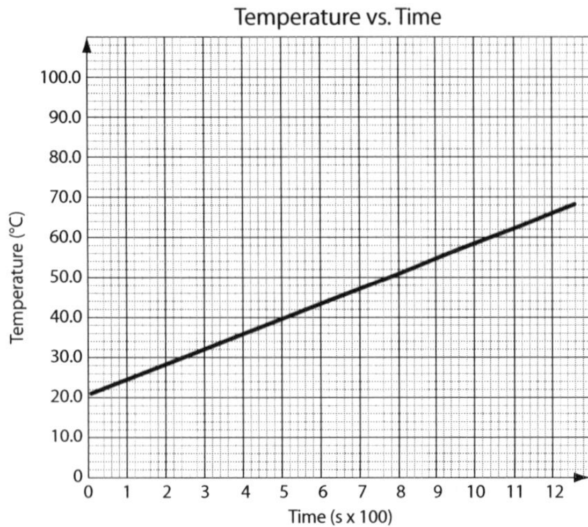

(a) What is the slope of the above graph, expressed in proper units and in correct significant figures?

(b) Use the slope to calculate the useful heating power of the light bulb.

(c) What is the approximate power rating of the bulb used in this experiment?

7. Why are coastal climates more moderate than inland climates?

8. A 60 W incandescent light bulb is 5% efficient. A 60 W fluorescent bulb is 15% efficient. How much more light will the fluorescent light bulb give off than the incandescent bulb, in the same period of time?

9. A 1500 W kettle warms 1.00 kg of water from 18°C to 88°C in a time of 3.6 min. How efficient is the kettle?

Chapter 6 Conceptual Review Questions

1. Give an example of a situation where there is a force and a displacement, but the force does no work. Explain why it does no work.

2. Describe a situation in which a force is exerted for along time, but does no work. Explain

3. Most electrical appliances are rated in Watts. Does this rating depend on how long the appliance is on? (When off, it is a zero-watt device). Explain in terms of the definition of power.

4. Work done on a system puts energy into it. Work done by a system removes energy from it. Give an example for each statement

5. Do devices with efficiencies of less than one violate the law of conservation of energy? Explain.

Chapter 6 Review Questions

1. (a) How much work will you do if you lift a 0.67 kg book from a table top up a distance of 1.5 m to a shelf?

   (b) How much work will be done on the book if you lift it and move it 1.5 m sideways to a spot on the same shelf?

2. If you push a 75 N block along a floor a distance of 4.2 m at a steady speed, and the coefficient of kinetic friction is 0.40, how much work will you do on the block?

3. Discuss the scientific accuracy of this statement: *I used a ramp to get my motorbike up on my truck, and the ramp saved me a lot of work!*

4. (a) What is the ideal mechanical advantage of the pulley system shown below??

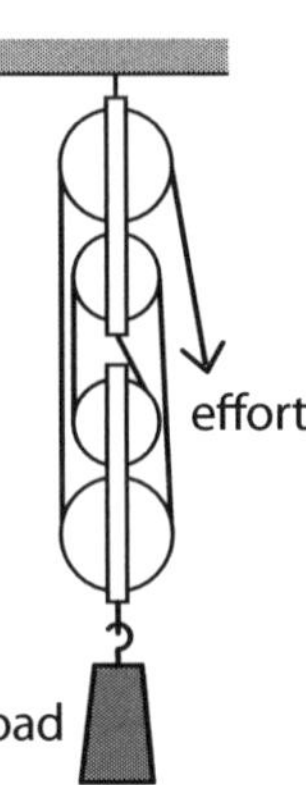

   (b) If the load is 240 N, what will the effort force be, ignoring friction?

   (c) If the load is lifted 2.8 m, how far will you have to pull down on the rope?

   (d) If the load is lifted 2.8 m in 1.6 s, what is the power rating of the pulley system?

5. With a pulley system, a mechanic can lift an 840 N engine using an effort force of only 70.0 N.
   (a) What is the mechanical advantage of the pulley system?

   (b) To lift the engine up 20.0 cm, how far down on the rope will the mechanic pull?

   (c) How much work is done on the 840 N engine when it is lifted a height of 20.0 cm?

   (d) What is the minimum amount of work the mechanic will have to do to lift the engine 20.0 cm?

6. One watt is equivalent to 1 J/s, so a joule is the same as a watt·second. How many joules are there in 1 kW·h?

7. A skier has 60 kJ of gravitational potential energy when at the top of the hill. Assuming no friction, how much kinetic energy does she have when she is one-third of the way down the hill?

8. The head of a golf club transfers a certain amount of kinetic energy to the ball upon impact. Let this be E_k. If the golfer lightens the mass of the club head by 1/3, and increases the club head speed so that it is 3 times it previous speed, how much kinetic energy will be transferred to the ball now?

9. A pendulum bob is moving 1.8 m/s at the bottom of its swing. To what height above the bottom of the swing will the bob travel?

10. The pendulum bob shown here must circle the rod, and the string must remain taut at the top of the swing. How far up must the bob be raised before releasing it to accomplish these goals?

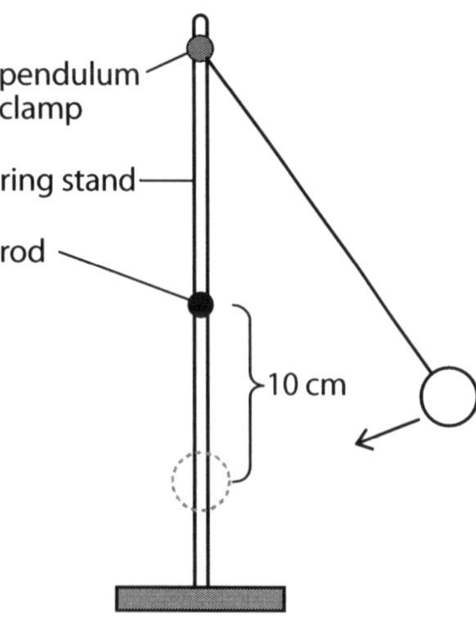

11. Tarzan grabs a vine 12 m long and swings on the end of it, like a pendulum. His starting point is 5.0 m above the lowest point in his swing. How fast is Tarzan moving as he passes through the bottom of the swing?

12. Change 250°C to kelvins.

13. A steel rod is at a temperature of 25°C. To what Celsius temperature must you raise it, in order to double its Kelvin temperature?

14. Why are metals such good conductors?

15. In your home, what method(s) of heat transfer are involved in the following situations?
    (a) Heat is distributed to your rooms from your furnace.
    (b) Heat escapes through the walls of your house.
    (c) Heat escapes from your roof to the atmosphere.

16. Why is the water at the top of a hot water tank warmer than the water at the bottom of the tank?

17. A certain metal has a specific heat capacity of 420 J/kg/°C, while water has a specific heat capacity of 4200 J/kg/°C. A kilogram of the metal and a kilogram of water are both at a temperature of 98°C. If both are allowed to cool to 18°C, which will give off more heat to the atmosphere, and how much more will it release?

18. If 10.0 kg of water at 25°C is heated by a 100% efficient 1500 W heater for 5.00 min, what will its final temperature be?

19. How much heat is supplied by a 100% efficient 1200 W kettle in 10.0 min?

20. What is the efficiency of a 1500 W kettle if it supplies heat at the rate of 1400 W to the water in it?

7 Electric Circuits

In this chapter the focus will be on the Big Idea:

Energy is found in different forms, is conserved and has the ability to do work

The content learning standard will include:

- electric circuits (DC), Ohm's law and Kirchhoff's laws

By the end of this chapter, you should know the meaning to these **key terms**:

- ammeter
- ampere
- conventional electric current
- electric current
- electric power
- electromotive force (emf)
- equivalent resistance
- internal resistance
- parallel circuit
- resistance
- series circuit
- terminal voltage
- voltmeter

By the end of the chapter, you should be able to use and know when to use the following formulae:

$I = \dfrac{Q}{t}$ $\qquad V = IR$

$P = IV$ $\qquad V_{terminal} = \quad \pm Ir$

These high voltage transmission lines have an important role in transporting electrical energy to your home and school where the energy is used to power a range of electrical devices including hybrid vehicles.

7.1 Static Electric Charges

Warm Up

Place a metre stick on a watch glass. Rub an inflated balloon on your hair and bring it close to the metre stick. Observe the result. Describe and provide a reason for what you observe.

___

___

___

Attraction and Repulsion Forces

If your hair is dry and you comb it briskly, your comb will attract not only your hair but also bits of dust, paper, or thread. The comb is probably made of plastic, but many kinds of material will produce the same effect. As long ago as 600 B.C., the Greeks observed the "attracting power" of amber when it was rubbed with cloth. Amber is a fossilized resin from trees that the Greeks used for decoration and trade. Of course, magnets also have an "attracting power," but they only attract certain metallic elements such as iron, nickel, and cobalt, and some of their alloys. Amber, if rubbed with cloth, will attract small bits of just about anything.

In the late 1500s, the Englishman Dr. William Gilbert was curious about this interesting property of amber, and he did many experiments with it and other materials. Gilbert discovered that many materials, if rubbed with certain fabrics, could be electrified. Words like *electrified, electricity, electron,* and *electronics* come from the Greek word for *amber,* which was *elektron*.

In the early 1700s, Charles du Fay, a French scientist, was probably the first person to figure out that there were two kinds of electricity. He observed that if two glass rods were rubbed with silk and brought near each other, they would **repel** one another. "Repel" means to push away. Two amber rods rubbed with fur would also repel one another. If, however, an "electrified" amber rod was brought close to an "electrified" glass rod, the two rods would **attract** each other. Du Fay correctly deduced that there must be two kinds of electricity. Later in the 1700s, Benjamin Franklin called these "positive electricity" and "negative electricity."

By convention, a glass rod rubbed with silk is said to have a **positive charge**. An amber rod rubbed with wool or fur has a **negative charge.**

In classroom experiments, a good way to get a positive charge is to rub an acetate plastic strip with cotton. A negative charge is easily obtained by rubbing a vinyl plastic strip with wool or fur (Figure 7.1.1).

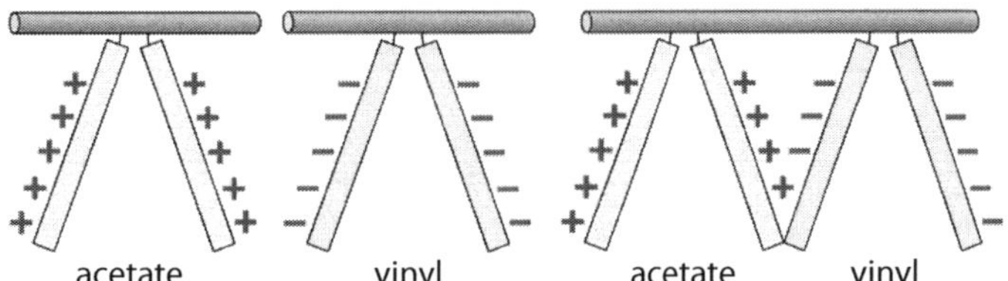

Figure 7.1.1 *Two charged acetate plastic strips (+), hanging freely from a supporting rod, repel each other. Two charged vinyl strips (–) also repel each other. However, a charged acetate strip will attract a charged vinyl strip.*

Since the electric charges on "electrified" objects are not moving, they are referred to as **static charges** or **static electricity**. "Static" means stationary or unmoving.

A charged object will attract any **neutral** body. A neutral body is one without any charge. It will also attract an oppositely charged body, but it will repel another body carrying the same charge.

> Bodies with the same charge repel each other.
> Bodies with opposite charges attract one another.
> A neutral body is attracted to either a positively charged body or a negatively charged body.

Elementary Atomic Structure

John Dalton's famous atomic theory assumed that all matter was made up of indivisible particles. A very important experiment by Ernest Rutherford showed that the atom actually had some internal structure to it. He was able to show that the atom had a **nucleus**, in which positive charge was concentrated. Since the atom as a whole is neutral, there must be negatively charged matter somehow distributed around the nucleus. Negatively charged particles were first identified by English physicist J. J. Thomson. These were later called **electrons**.

A simplified view of the atom as pictured in Rutherford's "planetary" model shows the nucleus of the atom with its positive charge, surrounded by negatively charged electrons. The positively charged particles in the nucleus are **protons**. Figure 7.1.2 also shows **neutrons**, but these were not discovered until 1932. An English physicist named James Chadwick, a contemporary of Rutherford, added this particle to the list of subatomic particles. Neutrons carry no electric charge, and their mass is just slightly greater than that of protons. Electrons are far less massive than protons or neutrons. The mass of a proton is 1.67×10^{-27} kg, which is 1836 times the mass of an electron.

The smallest atom is that of hydrogen. It has the simplest possible nucleus — one proton. The radius of the nucleus is approximately 10^{-15} m, compared with the radius of the hydrogen atom as a whole, which is approximately 10^{-10} m. Rutherford thought that the hydrogen nucleus might be the fundamental unit of positive charge. He was first to use the label proton for the hydrogen nucleus.

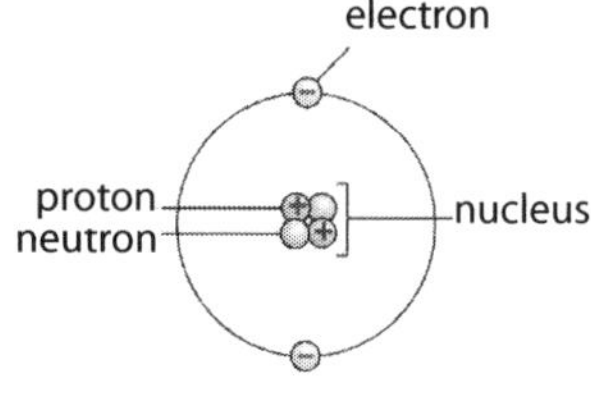

Figure 7.1.2 *The simple "planetary" model of the atom*

The normal state of an atom is neutral. However, atoms can gain or lose electrons, in which case they become electrically charged atoms called **ions.** Since protons are safely locked away in the nucleus of an atom, only electrons are transferred from one body to another during the "electrification" of normal objects.

Electrification of Objects

Figure 7.1.3 shows what happens when a vinyl plastic strip is rubbed on wool. Vinyl has a stronger affinity for electrons than wool. When vinyl contacts wool, some electrons leave the wool and go to the surface of the vinyl. This leaves the vinyl with an excess of electrons, so it has a negative charge. The wool, having lost electrons, has a positive charge.

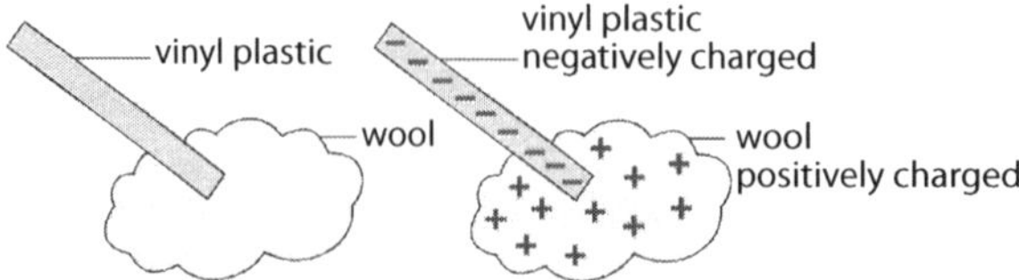

Figure 7.1.3 *Charging a vinyl rod with wool: the vinyl becomes negatively charged and the wool becomes positively charged.*

Similarly, if acetate plastic is rubbed with cotton, the cotton gains electrons from the acetate. The acetate becomes positively charged while the cotton becomes negatively charged.

All experiments show that there is no "creation" or "destruction" of electric charge during electrification. All that happens is a transfer of electrons from one body to another.

> According to the **law of conservation of charge**, electric charge is never created and never destroyed. Electric charge, like momentum and total energy, is a conserved quantity.

The Electrostatic or Triboelectric Series

Whether an object loses or gains electrons when rubbed with another object depends on how tightly the object holds onto its electrons. The electrostatic or triboelectric series lists various objects according to how tightly they hold onto their electrons (Figure 7.1.4). The higher up on the list the object is, the stronger its hold is on its electrons. The lower down on the list the object is, the weaker its hold is on its electrons. This means if we rub wool and amber together, electrons will be transferred from the wool to the amber. This results in the wool being positively charged and the amber being negatively charged.

Hold electrons tightly

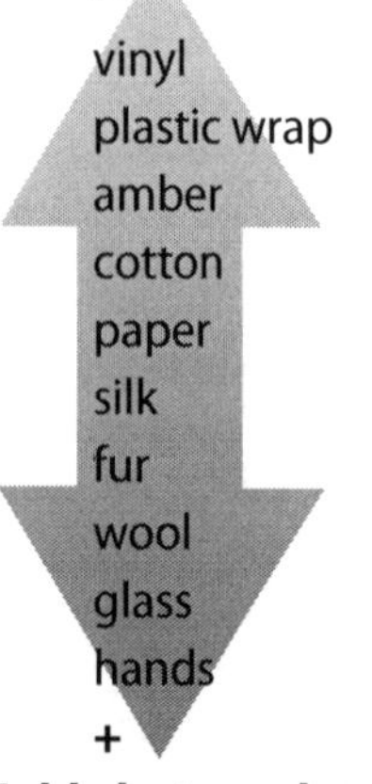

Hold electrons loosely

Figure 7.1.4 *The electrostatic or triboelectric series*

Conductors and Insulators

Conductors are materials that allow charged particles to pass through them easily. Metals such as silver, copper, and aluminum are excellent conductors of electricity, but all metals conduct to some extent. Atoms of metals have one or more outer electrons that are very loosely bound to their nuclei — so loosely attached that they are called "free" electrons.

In Figure 7.1.5, a metal rod is supported by a plastic cup. Plastic does not conduct electricity. A negatively charged vinyl strip is allowed to touch one end of the metal rod. When the vinyl touches the metal, a few excess electrons are conducted to the rod, so it becomes negatively charged as well. The negatively charged strip repels excess electrons to the far end of the metal rod. An initially neutral metal sphere, hanging from a silk string, is attracted to the charged rod. When the sphere touches the negatively charged rod, some of the excess electrons are conducted onto the sphere. Since the sphere is now the same charge as the rod, it is repelled from the rod.

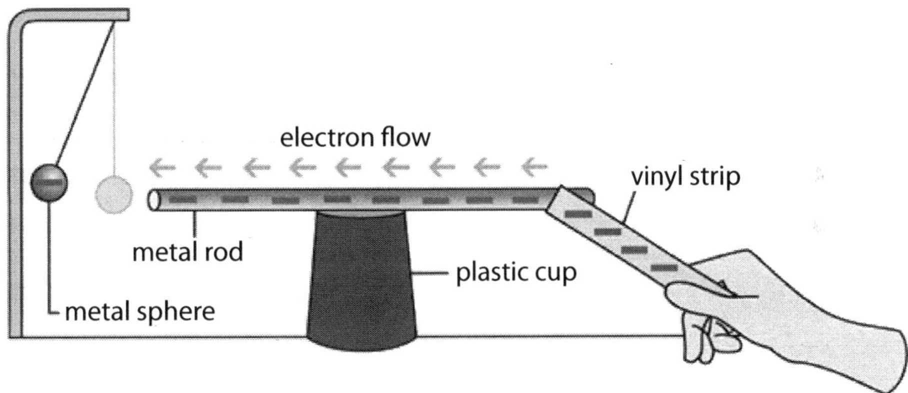

Figure 7.1.5 *Electrons transfer from the vinyl strip to the metal rod and onto the sphere.*

Now both the rod and the sphere have an excess of electrons. If the vinyl strip is taken away, the rod and the sphere will retain their negative charge and the sphere will remain in its "repelled" position. On a dry day, it may stay there for many hours.

If the metal rod is replaced with a glass or plastic rod of similar dimensions, the metal sphere does not move. This is because glass and plastic are **insulators**. Insulators are materials that resist the flow of charged particles through them. Plastics, rubber, amber, porcelain, various textiles, mica, sulphur, and asbestos are examples of good insulators. Carbon in the form of diamond is an excellent but very expensive insulator. Carbon in the form of graphite is a good conductor.

Non-metals such as silicon and selenium find many uses in transistors and computer chips because of their "semiconductor" behavior.

It is easy to place a static charge on an insulator, because electrons are transferred only where the two objects come in contact. When an excess of charge builds up at a point on an insulator, the charge will not flow away — it remains static.

Charging by Conduction

An **electroscope** is a device designed to detect excess electric charge. In Figure 7.1.6, a positively charged acetate strip is brought close enough to touch the neutral, metal-coated sphere of an electroscope. When they touch, the free electrons on the surface of the conducting sphere will be attracted to the positively charged acetate plastic. The acetate will gain a few electrons, but its overall charge will remain overwhelmingly positive. The sphere, however, now has a positive charge, so it is repelled by the acetate strip. We say the sphere has been charged by contact or by **conduction**. You could just as easily charge the sphere negatively by touching it with a charged vinyl strip.

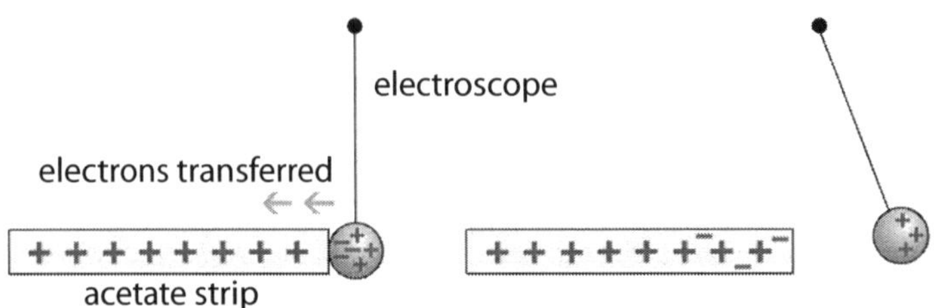

Figure 7.1.6 *Charging by conduction*

Charging by Induction

Objects can be charged without being touched at all, in which case we call it **charging by induction**. There are many ways to do this. Figure 7.1.7 shows one way. Two metal spheres are on insulated stands and are touching each other. A positively charged acetate strip is brought near the two spheres, but it does not touch them. Free electrons from the right sphere are attracted toward the left sphere by the positive acetate strip. Now the right sphere is pushed away using the insulated support stand. Tests with an electroscope will show that the right sphere has been charged **positively** by **induction**. The left sphere is charged **negatively** by **induction**.

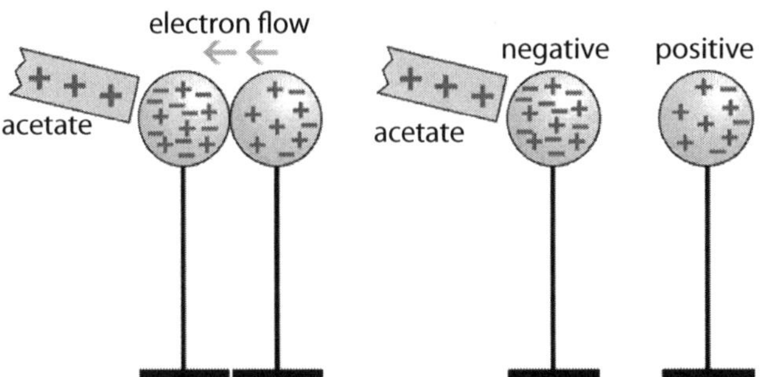

Figure 7.1.7 *Charging by induction*

Note that charge has not been "created" during this procedure. All that has happened is this: a few electrons have been transferred from the right sphere to the left sphere. The total charge is still the same as it was before the charging by induction was attempted. The net charge is still zero.

Investigation 7.1.1 Charging by Conduction and Induction

Purpose

To experiment with two different ways of placing a charge on an object

Part 1 Charging by Conduction

When you charge an object by touching it with another charged object, the electrons are conducted directly to it. In this process, you are charging by conduction.

Styrofoam acts as an insulator.

Procedure

1. Set two aluminum pop cans on or in Styrofoam cups as shown in the Figure. Styrofoam is an excellent insulator, so it will keep any static charge you place on the cans from escaping to the bench.
2. Place a negative charge on one of the cans as follows:
   (a) Rub a vinyl strip with wool or fur. You may hear a crackling sound when the vinyl is being charged. The vinyl will have a negative charge on it.
   (b) Rub the charged vinyl strip over one of the insulated pop cans. Excess electrons from the vinyl will flow onto the can, giving the can a negative charge.
   (c) Repeat the process several times to make sure there is a lot of excess negative charge on the can.
3. Place a positive charge on the other can as follows:
   (a) Rub an acetate strip with cotton or paper. This will make the acetate positively charged, since electrons flow from the acetate to the cotton.
   (b) Rub the acetate strip onto the second can. The positively charged acetate strip will attract electrons from the second metal pop can, making the can positively charged.
   (c) Repeat this process several times to make sure the second can has lots of positive charge.
4. Do not touch the metal cans. Touching only their insulated Styrofoam bases, move the cans toward each other until they are about 3 cm apart.
5. Lower a graphite or pith ball between the two oppositely charged cans. Write down what you see happening.

Concluding Questions

1. What charge was on
   (a) the first can at the start?
   (b) the second can at the start?
   (c) the graphite ball before it was lowered between the cans?
2. Explain what happened to the graphite or pith ball during the experiment. Describe what happened to the electrons going to and from the three objects involved
3. Why does the action eventually stop?

Part 2 Charging by Induction

Imagine you have only a negatively charged strip, but you wish to place a positive charge on another object. If you touch the other object with a negatively charged strip, you will charge it negatively by conduction. However, if you use the induction method, you can give it a charge that is opposite to the charge on the charging body.

Procedure

1. Place a pop can on or in a Styrofoam cup.
2. Charge a vinyl strip negatively.
3. Bring the charged vinyl strip near and parallel to the pop can but do not let the vinyl strip touch the can.
4. Briefly touch the can with your finger, and then remove it and the vinyl strip completely. What do you think the charge is on the can? Repeat steps 2 to 4 until you can produce the same result three times in a row.
5. Work out a procedure to test for yourself whether the charge on the can is positive, negative, or neutral.

Concluding Questions

1. Before you brought your finger near the can,
   (a) what charge was on the vinyl strip?
   (b) what charge was on the side of the can near the vinyl strip?
   (c) what charge was on the other side of the can?
2. Your finger can conduct electrons to or from your body. In this experiment, were electrons conducted to the can from your body or from the can to your body?
3. (a) What was the final charge on the can?
   (b) Was this charge "conducted" from the vinyl strip?
   (c) How did the can obtain this charge?

7.1 Review Questions

1. What are the similarities and differences between the properties of an electron and a proton?

2. Describe the difference between a positive charge and a negative charge in terms of electrons.

3. Why do clothes sometimes have static on them as soon as they come out of the clothes dryer?

4. What will be the charge on a silk scarf if it is rubbed with glass? With plastic wrap?

5. A charged rod is brought near a pile of tiny plastic spheres. The spheres are attracted to the charged rod and are then fly off the rod. Why does this happen?

6. What would happen if the vinyl strip in Figure 7.1.5 was replaced with a positively charged acetate strip? Why?

7. Outline a method by which you could determine, with certainty, whether the charge on your comb after you comb your hair is positive or negative.

7.2 Current Events in History

Warm Up

Your teacher will give you a light source, energy source, and wire. How many different ways can you arrange these three items so that the light source goes on? Draw each circuit.

Galvani's and Volta's Experiments

Until 200 years ago, the idea of producing a steady current of electricity and putting it to use was nonexistent. The discovery of a way to produce a flow of electric charges was, in fact, accidental. In the year 1780, at the University of Bologna, Italian professor of anatomy Luigi Galvani (1737–1798) was dissecting a frog. First, he noticed that when a nearby static electricity generator made a spark while a metal knife was touching the frog's nerves, the frog's legs would jump as its muscles contracted! Galvani proceeded to look for the conditions that caused this behaviour. In the course of his investigations, Galvani discovered that if two different metal objects (such as a brass hook and an iron support) touched each other, while also touching the frog's exposed flesh, the same contractions of the frog's legs occurred. Galvani thought that the source of the electricity was in the frog itself, and he called the phenomenon "animal electricity."

Another Italian scientist, physics professor Alessandro Volta (1745–1827), of the University of Pavia, set about to test Galvani's "animal electricity" theory for himself. Before long, Volta discovered that the source of the electricity was in the contact of two different metals. The animal (frog) was incidental. If any two different metals are immersed in a conducting solution of acid, base, or salt, they will produce an electric current. Volta was able to show that some pairs of metals worked better than other pairs. Of course, no ammeters or voltmeters were available in those days to compare currents and voltages. One way that Volta compared currents was to observe the response of the muscle tissue of dead frogs.

Neither Galvani nor Volta could explain their observations. (There is no truth to the rumour that the frog's leg jumped because 1780 was a leap year.) Many years later, it was learned that radio waves generated by the sparking generator induced a current in the metal scalpel that was penetrating the frog, even though the scalpel was some distance from the generator!

Volta eventually invented the first practical electric battery. Zinc and silver disks, separated by paper pads soaked with salt water, acted as electric cells. Stacked one on top of another, these cells became a "battery" that yielded more current than a single cell.

Cells and Batteries

There are many types of electric cells in existence today. Usually when you purchase a "battery" in a store, you are actually buying a single **cell.** Strictly speaking, a battery consists of two or more cells connected together. Nine-volt batteries used in portable radios, tape recorders, calculators, and smoke alarms are true batteries. If you open up a discarded 9 V battery, you will see six small 1.5 V cells connected together, one after the other in what is called "a series."

Figure 7.2.1 shows one type of **voltaic cell** (named after Volta). The two rods, called **electrodes**, are made of carbon and zinc, as in the traditional **dry cell**, but they are immersed in a solution of ammonium chloride (NH_4Cl). In a real dry cell, a paste containing NH_4Cl, sawdust, and other ingredients is used. The chemistry of voltaic cells will be left to your chemistry courses. The reaction that occurs, however, has the effect of *removing electrons* from the carbon electrode (making it *positive*) and adding them to the zinc (making the zinc *negative*). In a real dry cell, the outer casing of the cell is made of zinc. The zinc is dissolved away as the cell is used, and may eventually leak its contents.

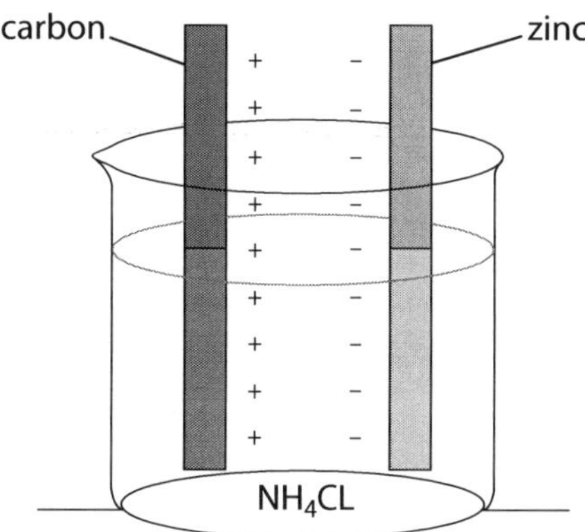

Figure 7.2.1 *A voltaic cell*

There are many kinds of cells and batteries. Rechargeable "batteries" may use nickel and cadmium, or molybdenum and lithium, or lead and lead oxide (as in the standard car battery). There are many kinds of cells on the market today, but they all produce electric current when connected to a conducting path.

Electromotive Force

In a carbon-zinc dry cell, forces resulting from the chemical reaction within the cell drive charges to the terminals, doing work to overcome the repulsive forces. The work done on the charges increases their potential energy. The difference in potential energy between the terminals amounts to 1.5 J for every coulomb of charge separated. We say the **potential difference** is 1.5 J/C, or 1.5 V. For a cell or battery that is not supplying current, the potential difference is at its peak value, which is called the **electromotive force (emf)**. It is given the symbol $\mathcal{E}$.

For a dry cell, the emf is 1.5 V. A nickel-cadmium cell is usually labelled 1.2 V or 1.25 V, but a freshly charged nickel-cadmium battery will have an even higher emf than its labelled rating. The cells in a lead storage battery have emfs of 2 V each. Six of these cells connected in series within the battery give a total emf of 12 V.

Electric Current

When electric charges *flow*, we say a current exists. A current will exist as long as a continuous conducting path is created for charges to flow from and back to a source of emf, as shown in Figure 7.2.2.

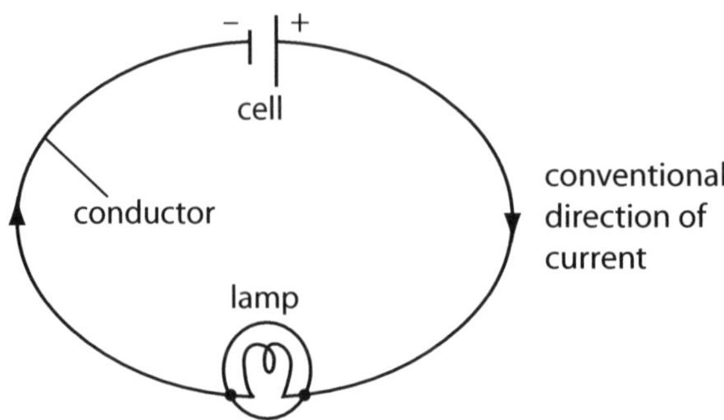

Figure 7.2.2 *Electric charges flow as a current through a conductor as long as there is no break in the path.*

Electric current is defined as the amount of electric charge that passes a point in a circuit in one second. If an amount of charge Q passes a point in a circuit in a time t, then the average current I through that point is $I = \frac{Q}{t}$.

Current could quite logically be measured in coulombs per second (C/s), but this unit is called the **ampere (A)** after André Ampère (1775–1836), a French physicist.

1 A = 1 C/s

One ampere is the sort of current that exists in a 100 W light bulb in a lamp in your home. (A 100 W lamp in a 110 V circuit would draw approximately 0.9 A.) In terms of electrons,

$$1\ \text{A} = 6.24 \times 10^{18}\ \text{electrons/s}$$

Current Direction

The direction of current was defined arbitrarily by André Ampère to be the direction that positive charges would move between two points where there is a difference of potential energy. In many simple circuits, we now know it is negative charges (electrons) that actually move. In solid conductors, the positive charges are locked in the nuclei of atoms, which are fixed in their location in the crystal. Loosely attached electrons can move through the conductor from atom to atom. In liquids and gases, however, the flow of charges may consist of positively charged ions as well as negatively charged ions and electrons.

Throughout this book, we shall use conventional current direction: the direction that positive charges would move between two points where there is a potential difference between the points.

Drift Velocity

How fast do electrons move in a wire carrying a current of, for example, 1 A? When a switch is closed in a circuit, the effect of the current can be detected immediately throughout the entire circuit. This might lead you to conclude that the electric charges (usually electrons) travel at very high velocity through the circuit. In fact, this is not so! The average **drift velocity** of electrons in a given set of circumstances can be calculated.

Within a length of metal wire, there are many, many loosely attached electrons (sometimes called "free electrons"). These electrons move about much like the molecules in a container of gas might move.

Let's consider the movement of electrons in a silver wire. Silver is an excellent conductor. Let's assume there is one free electron for every silver atom in a piece of wire. When the wire is connected to a source of emf, the potential difference (voltage) will cause electrons to move from the negative terminal of the source of emf toward the positive terminal. This movement is *superimposed* on the random motion of the electrons that is going on all the time with or without a source of emf.

The trip the electrons make from the negative to the positive terminal is not a smooth one (as it is, for example, in the vacuum of a CRT). Electrons in the metal wire collide with positive silver ions on the way, and transfer some of their kinetic energy to the silver ions. The increased thermal energy of the silver ions will show up as an increase in temperature of the silver conductor.

Assume the current in the silver wire in Figure 7.2.3 is 1.0 A. Then there are 6.24×10^{18} electrons passing the observer each second. This is because

$$\mathbf{1.0\ A = 1.0\ C/s = 6.24 \times 10^{18}\ e/s}$$

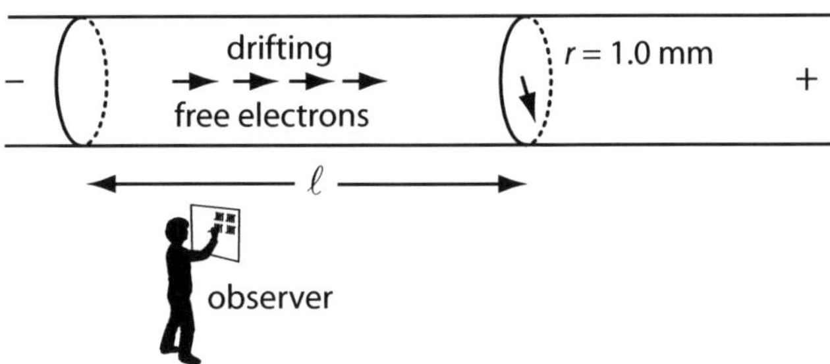

Figure 7.2.3 *Calculating the average drift velocity of electrons through a silver wire*

To calculate the average drift velocity of the electrons, we start by again assuming that there is *one free electron for every silver atom,* a reasonable assumption, since chemists tell us that silver usually forms ions with a charge of +1.

All we need to know is what length of the silver wire in Figure 7.2.3 would contain 6.24×10^{18} silver atoms (and therefore 6.24×10^{18} free electrons). We can find this out in three steps, as follows:

1. The mass of silver needed to have 6.24×10^{18} free electrons is

$$\text{mass} = \frac{6.24\quad 10^{18}\ \text{atoms}}{6.02\quad 10^{23}\ \text{atoms/mole}}\quad 108\ \text{g/mole} = 1.12\quad 10^{\ 3}\ \text{g}$$

2. The volume of silver wire needed to have 6.24×10^{18} free electrons is

$$\text{volume} = \frac{\text{mass}}{\text{density}} = \frac{1.12\quad 10^{\ 3}\ \text{g}}{10.5\ \text{g/cm}^3} = 1.07\quad 10^{\ 4}\,\text{cm}$$

3. The radius of the silver wire in Figure 7.2.3 is 1.0 mm, or 1.0 x 10^{-1} cm. Its cross-sectional area is πr^2, so the length, ℓ, can be found as follows:

$$\text{length}, \ell = \frac{\text{volume}}{\text{area}} = \frac{1.07 \quad 10^{-4}\ \text{cm}^3}{(1.0 \quad 10^{-1}\ \text{cm})^2} = 3.4 \quad 10^{-3}\ \text{cm}$$

Since a length of 3.4×10^{-3} cm contains 6.24×10^{18} electrons, and this many electrons pass the observer in 1 s, the average drift velocity of the conducting electrons is 3.4×10^{-3} cm/s, or 0.034 mm/s! This is true only for the stated conditions, of course. If the amount of current, the nature of the material in the conductor, or the dimensions of the conductor change, then the drift velocity will also change.

When you turn on a switch to light a lamp using a battery, the change in the electric field may travel at the speed of light, but the electrons themselves drift ever so slowly through the wire, under the influence of the electric field.

Representing Electric Circuits

Figure 7.2.4 shows a simple electric circuit. There is an energy source or battery, a device to use the electrical energy (such as a lamp), a switch or control, and wires to carry the energy.

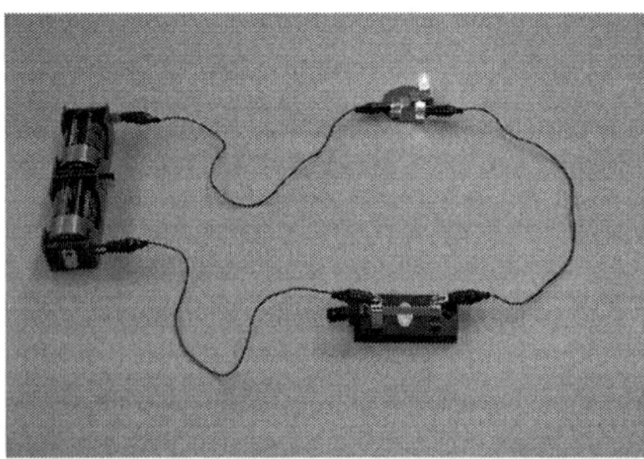

Figure 7.2.4 *A simple electric circuit*

Any circuit can be represented with a schematic diagram using a set of common symbols. Table 7.2.1 lists some of the more common symbols used for drawing electrical circuits. You will need to know each of these symbols so you can draw electrical circuits.

Table 7.2.1 *Common Symbols Used in Circuit Diagrams*

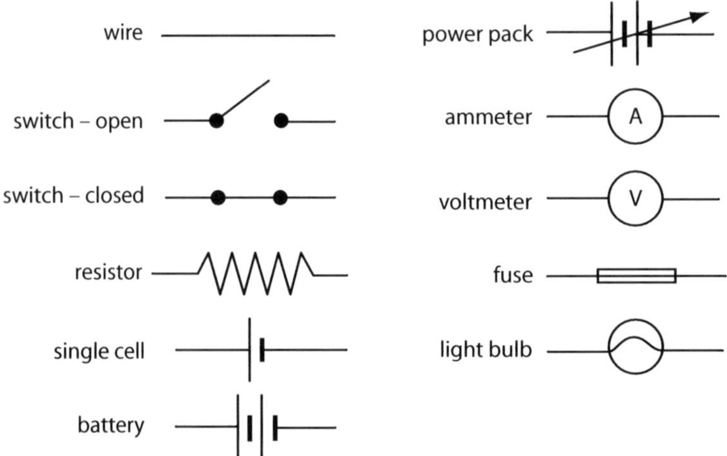

The circuit in Figure 7.2.4 can be represented as shown in Figure 7.2.5.

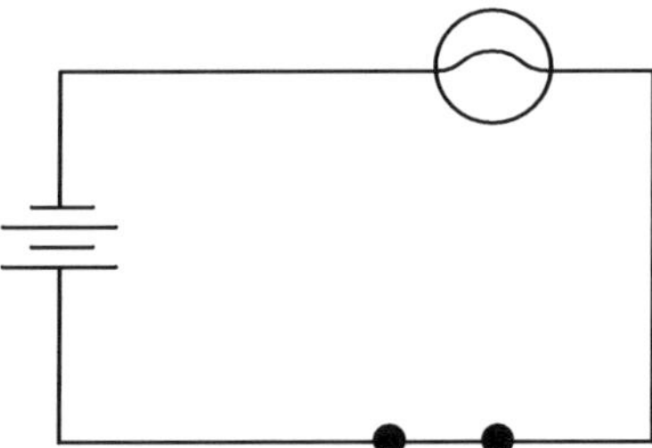

Figure 7.2.5 *A schematic drawing of the circuit shown in Figure 7.2.4*

Quick Check

1. Draw a circuit that has two light bulbs, a battery, a fuse, and closed switch.

2. Design a circuit that has a switch that can turn off two light bulbs at the same time.

3. Design a circuit that has two light bulbs and one switch that can turn one light bulb on and off while keeping the other light bulb on.

How to Read the Scale on an Ammeter

Figure 7.2.5 shows the face of a typical milliammeter. There are three scales printed on the face, but there are eight different ranges for this meter. When you connect the meter into a circuit, the terminal post labeled "C" is always connected to the negative terminal of the power source or to a part of the circuit that eventually leads to the negative terminal.

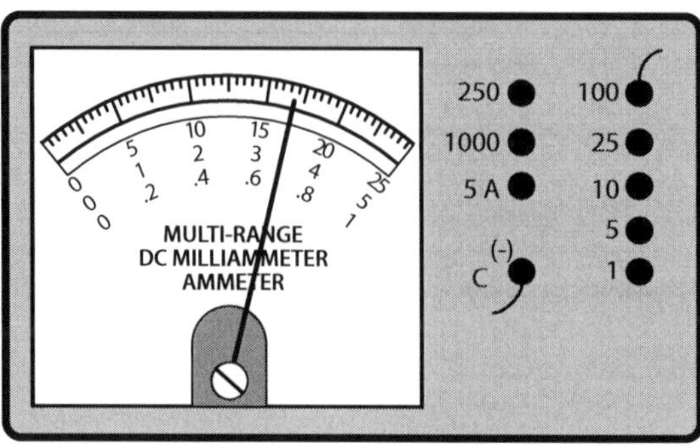

Figure 7.2.6 *An ammeter*

You must choose a suitable range for the current you have to measure. If you are not sure what range to use, try the red 5A terminal post first. This is the least sensitive range for the meter, so it can handle the most current safely. On this range, the milliammeter can handle up to 5 A.

What do the numbers on the terminal posts mean?

If you connect to the 5 A range, the meter reads anywhere from 0 A up to a maximum of 5 A. Read the middle scale of your meter. The markings mean exactly what they say: 0 A, 1 A, 2 A, 3 A, 4 A, and 5 A. On this range, the needle in Figure 7.2.6 is at 3.3 A.

If you connect to the 1000 range, the meter reads anywhere between 0 mA and 1000 mA. Read the bottom scale, but read the 1 on the scale as 1000 mA. Read 0.2 as 200 mA, 0.4 as 400 mA, 0.6 as 600 mA, and 0.8 as 800 mA. On this range, the needle in Figure 7.2.6 reads 660 mA.

If you connect to the 250 range, the meter reads anywhere from 0 mA up to 250 mA. Use the top scale but 25 reads as 250 mA. Read 5 as 50 mA, 10 as 100 mA, 15 as 150 mA, and 20 as 200 mA. On this range, the needle in Figure 7.2.6 reads 170 mA.

Quick Check

1. Look at the 100 scale on the meter in Figure 7.2.6.
   (a) What is the highest reading the scale will measure?

   (b) What is the needle reading in Figure 7.2.6?

2. What is the needle reading in Figure 7.2.6 for each of the following scales?

   (a) the 25 mA scale

   (b) the 10 mA scale

   (c) the 5 mA scale

   (d) the 1 mA scale

Investigation 7.2.1 Measuring Current Using Electroplating

Purpose

To measure current by counting copper atoms deposited on a carbon rod in a measured amount of time

Introduction

A solution of copper II sulfate contains two kinds of ions: Cu^{2+} ions, which give the solution its blue colour, and SO_4^{2-} ions, which are colourless (Figure 7.2.7). Two electrodes are immersed in the copper II sulfate solution and connected to a source of emf. The electrode connected to the positive terminal of the cell will attract SO_4^{2-} ions, and the electrode connected to the negative terminal of the cell will attract Cu^{2+} ions.

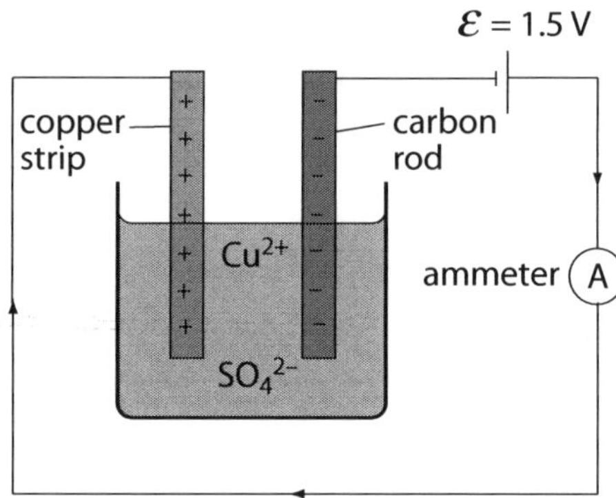

Figure 7.2.7

Cu^{2+} ions attracted to the negative electrode pick up two electrons, and deposit themselves on the negative electrode as copper atoms, Cu^0.

$$Cu^{2+} + 2e^- \rightarrow Cu^0$$

Meanwhile, at the positive electrode, which is made of copper, copper atoms *lose* two electrons and become copper ions, thus replenishing the Cu^{2+} ions in the solution.

$$Cu^0 \rightarrow Cu^{2+} + 2e^-$$

The two electrons return to the source of emf, the cell.

In this experiment, you allow the copper atoms to plate onto a negatively charged carbon electrode. If you measure the increase in mass of the carbon electrode after, say, 20 min of copper plating, you can calculate the mass of copper plated. This will give you the number of copper atoms plated, and from this, the number of electrons that were transferred in the 20 min. Finally you can calculate the current in amperes. You can also compare your calculated current with the current measured with an ammeter placed in the same circuit.

Procedure

1. Measure the mass of a dry, clean carbon rod as precisely as you can.
2. Set up the circuit shown in Figure 7.2.7. Make sure the carbon rod is connected to the negative terminal of the dry cell or other DC power source. The red binding post of the ammeter should be connected to the positive terminal of the cell, and an appropriate current range chosen as quickly as possible when the current is turned on. *Let the current run for a carefully measured time, such as 20 min.* Record current frequently, and *average* it.
3. As soon as the current is turned off, carefully remove the carbon electrode. Dip it in a beaker of methyl hydrate, and allow it time to dry. A heat lamp can be used to speed drying.

Caution! Methyl hydrate is both highly toxic and flammable!

4. Measure the mass of the plated carbon rod precisely, and calculate the amount of copper that has plated on its surface. Record the mass of copper.
5. To remove the copper, set up the circuit once more, but *reverse the connections* to the cell so that the copper plates back onto the copper strip.

Concluding Questions

1. One mole of copper atoms (63.5 g) contains 6.02×10^{23} atoms. Using this information and the mass of copper plated on the carbon rod, calculate
   (a) the number of copper atoms plated
   (b) the number of electrons transferred
   (c) the number of coulombs transferred in 20 min
2. If 1 A = 1 C/s, what was the current in amperes?
3. Compare your calculated current with the measured current by calculating the percent difference between the two currents.

7.2 Review Questions

1. If the current in a wire is 5.0 A, how many coulombs of charge pass a point in the wire in 1 min?

2. What is the current if 6.0×10^3 C pass a point in a circuit in 10.0 min?

3. If the current in a circuit is 12 A, how many electrons pass a point in 1 h?

4. The drift speed of electrons in a copper wire running from a battery to a light bulb and back is approximately 0.020 mm/s. The battery is at the front of a classroom and wires run around the perimeter of the room to the light bulb. The total length of wire is 40.0 m. How long would it take a single electron to drift from the negative terminal of the battery back to the positive terminal? Express your answer in days.

5. How much copper would be plated by a current of 1.5 A in a time of 1.0 h?

6. How much silver is deposited by a current of 1.000 A in 1.000 h? The mass of one mole of silver atoms is 107.9 g.

$$Ag^+ + 1e^- \rightarrow Ag^0$$

7. Draw a circuit with three light bulbs and two switches, and show the different combinations where one, two, and three light bulbs are lit.

8. What is the reading of the milliammeter below?

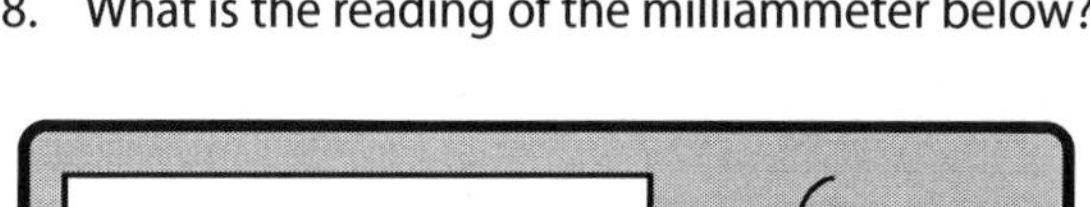

7.3 Ohm's Law

Warm Up

If you draw a line with a graphite pencil, it will conduct electricity. Why does more current go through a 5.0 cm line of graphite than a 10.0 cm line?

____

____

____

Resistance

Georg Simon Ohm (1787–1854) experimented with current in wires using variations in voltage to produce different currents. He found that for metal conductors at a given temperature, the current was directly proportional to the voltage between the ends of the wire.

$$I \propto V$$

$$\text{Therefore, } \frac{V}{I} = \text{constant.}$$

For example, the potential difference (voltage) between the ends of a wire is 1.50 V and the current is 2.00 A. If the potential difference is increased to 3.00 V, the current will also double to 4.00 A.

The constant of proportionality is called the **resistance (*R*)** of the length of wire. The relationship among current, voltage, and resistance is written:

$$\frac{V}{I} = R$$

where *R* is the resistance, in **ohms** (Ω)**.** This is called **Ohm's law.** Ohm's law can be written in two other forms, but all three forms are equivalent.

$$\frac{V}{I} = R \qquad V = IR \qquad \frac{V}{R} = I$$

Sample Problem — Ohm's Law

The current in a portable stove's heating element is 12.0 A when the potential difference between the ends of the element is 120 V. What is the resistance of the stove element?

What to Think About	How to Do It
1. Determine what you know from the problem.	$I = 12.0\ A$ $V = 120\ V$
2. Determine the appropriate formula.	$R = \frac{V}{I}$
3. Solve.	$R = \frac{120\ V}{12.0\ A} = 1.0 \quad 10^1\ \Omega$

Practice Problems — Ohm's Law

1. A resistor allows 1.0 mA to exist within it when a potential difference of 1.5 V is applied to its ends. What is the resistance of the resistor, in kilohms? ($1 \text{k}\Omega = 10^3 \ \Omega$)

2. If a 10.0 Ω kettle element is plugged into a 120 V outlet, how much current will it draw?

3. A current of 1.25 mA exists in a 20.0 kΩ resistor. What is the potential difference between the ends of the resistor?

Resistors

Under normal circumstances, every conductor of electricity offers some resistance to the flow of electric charges and is therefore a **resistor**. However, when we use the term "resistors," we are usually referring to devices manufactured specifically to control the amount of current in a circuit.

There are two main kinds of resistor: (1) wire-wound resistors, made of a coil of insulated, tightly wound fine wire and (2) carbon resistor (Figure 7.3.1). Carbon resistors consist of a cylinder of carbon, with impurities added to control the amount of resistance. Metal wire leads are attached to each end of the carbon cylinder, and the whole assembly is enclosed in an insulating capsule.

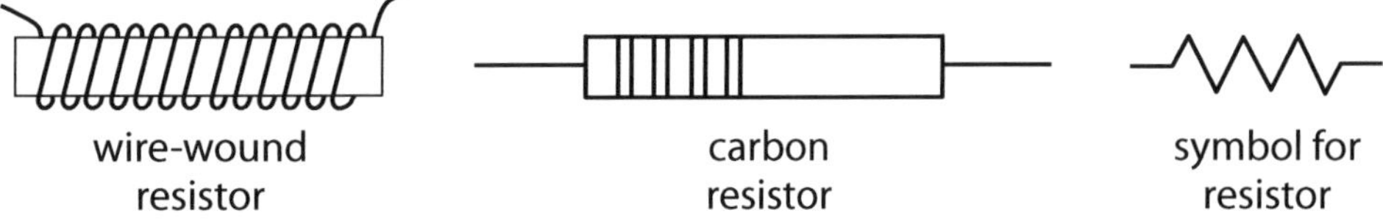

Figure 7.3.1 *Types of resistors and the symbol for resistors used in circuit diagrams*

In any resistor, electrical energy is transformed into thermal energy. There are some materials which, if cooled to temperatures approaching 0 K, offer no resistance to the flow of charges. These materials are called **superconductors**.

Resistor Colour Code

Resistors are either labelled with their resistance or colour-coded with four coloured bands, each of which has significance. The first coloured band gives the *first digit*. The second coloured band gives the *second digit*. The third coloured band gives the *power-of-10 multiplier (the number of zeros following the first two digits)*. Table 7.3.1 lists the colours and their codes. If there is no fourth coloured band, the manufacturer's tolerance is 20%. If the fourth band is gold, the tolerance is 5%. If the fourth band is silver, the tolerance is 10%. Think of tolerance as a range for the value of the resistor. No resistor is exactly the value indicated — the value is plus or minus the tolerance percentage given.

Table 7.3.1 *Resistor Colour Codes*

Band Colour	Number	Multiplier	Tolerance
black	0	10^0	
brown	1	10^1	
red	2	10^2	
orange	3	10^3	
yellow	4	10^4	
green	5	10^5	
blue	6	10^6	
violet	7	10^7	
gray	8	10^8	
white	9	10^9	
gold			5%
silver			10%
(no colour)			20%

Sample Problem — Resistor Colour Codes

What is the value of a resistor that has the colours gray, blue, red, and silver?

What to Think About	How to Do It
1. Use Table 7.3.1 to interpret the colour code.	First colour: gray = 8 Second colour: blue = 6 Third colour: red = 2 Resistor rating: 8600 Ω
2. Determine the tolerance of the resistor.	Tolerance: silver (10%) 10% of 8600 Ω ± 860 Ω
3. Summarize the result.	Resistor's value is 8600 Ω ± 860 Ω.

Practice Problems — Resistor Colour Codes

Use Table 7.3.1 to figure out the resistance rating of the following colour-coded resistors:

1. Red, red, red, silver

2. Brown, black, orange, gold

3. Brown, green, green, silver

4. Yellow, violet, yellow

Limitations of Ohm's Law

Ohm's law applies to metal resistors and metal-like resistors such as those made of compressed carbon. The ratio of potential difference to current, which is resistance, is constant for this class of material, providing that the temperature of the material remains constant.

Ohm's law only applies to metallic or metal-like conductors at a specific temperature. It does *not* apply to just any conductor in a circuit. For example, Ohm's law would not apply to a conducting solution or to a gas discharge tube.

Joule's Law

The English physicist James Prescott Joule (1818–1889) did experiments to measure the amount of heat released by various resistors under different conditions. He found that, for a particular resistor, the amount of thermal energy released in a unit of time by a resistor is proportional to the square of the current. The rate at which energy is released with respect to time is called **power**, so Joule's results can be expressed as follows:

$$P \propto I^2$$

$$\text{or } P = \text{constant} \cdot I^2$$

The constant in this equation will have units with the dimensions W/A^2, since constant = P/I^2. Consider the following simplification of these measuring units (W/A^2):

$$1\frac{\text{W}}{\text{A}^2} = 1\frac{\frac{\text{J}}{\text{s}}}{\frac{\text{C}^2}{\text{s}^2}} = 1\frac{\frac{\text{J}}{\text{C}}}{\frac{\text{C}}{\text{s}}} = 1\frac{\text{V}}{\text{A}} = 1$$

The ohm (Ω) is the unit for resistance. In fact, the constant of proportionality in the relationship discovered by Joule is the same constant of proportionality that is in Ohm's law. The ratio P/I^2 is the resistance of the resistor.

Joule's law can be written as follows: $P = RI^2$. By combining Joule's law with Ohm's law for resistors, other expressions for electrical power can be derived:

$$P = RI^2 = \frac{V}{I}I^2 = VI$$

And $$P = VI = V\;\frac{V}{R} = \frac{V^2}{R}$$

In summary, $$P \quad RI^2 \quad VI \quad \frac{V^2}{R}$$

Quick Check

1. What is the resistance of a 60.0 W lamp, if the current in it is 0.50 A?

2. A 600 W coffee percolator is operated at 120 V.
   (a) What is the resistance of the heating element of the percolator?

   (b) How much thermal energy does it produce in 6.0 min?

3. How much thermal energy is released by a 1500 W kettle in 5.0 min?

EMF, Terminal Voltage, and Internal Resistance

In Figure 7.3.2, the dry cell has a rated emf of 1.50 V. Assume you are using a high quality voltmeter to measure the potential difference between the terminals A and B of the cell, when essentially no current is being drawn from the cell other than a tiny amount going through the voltmeter itself. In that case, the voltage between the terminals will be nearly equal to the ideal value of the emf. That is, with no current, the terminal voltage of the battery, V_{AB}, will equal the emf, $\mathcal{E}$.

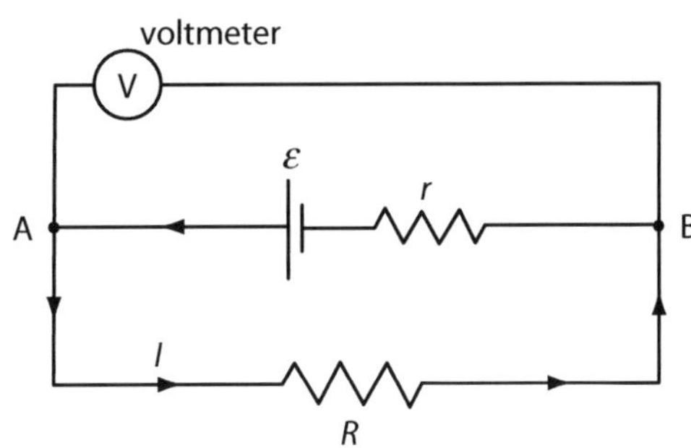

Figure 7.3.2 *The dry cell in this circuit has a rated emf of 1.50 V.*

If, however, the cell is connected to a resistor R so that a current I exists in the simple circuit including in the cell itself, then the terminal voltage is *less than* the cell emf.

$$V_{AB} < \mathcal{E}$$

This is because the cell itself has an internal resistance of its own, symbolized by r. According to Ohm's law, the loss of potential energy per coulomb between the terminals is Ir. The measured terminal voltage of the cell will be less than the ideal emf by an amount equal to Ir.

$$V_{AB} = \mathcal{E} - Ir$$

Sample Problem — Terminal Voltage and Internal Resistance

A dry cell with an emf of 1.50 V has an internal resistance of 0.050 Ω. What is the terminal voltage of the cell when it is connected to a 2.00 Ω resistor?

What to Think About	How to Do It
1. Determine what you know from the problem.	$\mathcal{E} = 1.50$ V $R = 2.00\ \Omega$ $r = 0.050\ \Omega$
2. To solve, apply Ohm's law to the circuit as a whole, and consider the internal resistance r to be in series with the external resistance R. This means you will solve for the current in the circuit.	$I = \dfrac{\mathcal{E}}{R + r} = \dfrac{1.50\text{ V}}{2.05\ \Omega} = 0.732$ A
3. Now find the terminal voltage.	$V_{AB} = \mathcal{E} - Ir$ $V_{AB} = 1.50\text{ V} - (0.732\text{ A})(0.050\ \Omega)$ $V_{AB} = 1.50\text{ V} - 0.037\text{ V}$ $V_{AB} = 1.46$ V

Practice Problems — Terminal Voltage and Internal Resistance

1. A dry cell with an emf of 1.50 V and an internal resistance of 0.050 Ω Is "shorted out" with a piece of wire with a resistance of only 0.20 Ω. What will a voltmeter read if it is connected to the terminals of the dry cell at this time?

2. A battery has an emf of 12.50 V. When a current of 35 A is drawn from it, its terminal voltage is 11.45 V. What is the internal resistance of the battery?

Investigation 7.3.1 Ohm's Law

Purpose

To investigate the relationship between the voltage applied to a resistor and the current in the resistor

Procedure

1. Set up the circuit shown in Figure 7.3.3. Start with one cell, an ammeter, and a carbon resistor. These are all in series as they form one path. A voltmeter is connected in parallel with the resistor, as there are two paths for the current to travel.

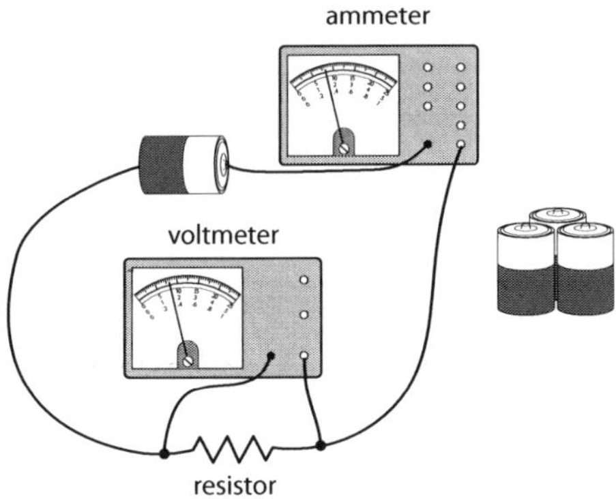

Figure 7.3.3

2. Prepare a copy of Table 7.3.2.

Table 7.3.2 Data Table

Number of Cells Used	Voltage across Resistor (V)	Current in Resistor (A)	Calculated Resistance (Ω)
1			
2			
3			
4			

Resistor rating: ______________________

3. With one cell in the circuit, measure the current in milliamperes (mA) and the voltage in volts (V). Convert the current from mA to A by dividing by 1000. (Move the decimal three places to the left. For example, 2.4 mA is equal to 0.0024 A.) Enter the current and voltage in your copy of Table 7.3.2.
4. Add a second cell in series with the first cell. Record the current and the voltage in your copy of Table 7.3.2.
5. Repeat with three cells, then with four cells. Enter your results in your copy of Table 7.3.2.
6. Complete the final column of your copy of Table 7.3.2. Divide voltage (V) by current (I) for each trial. This ratio, V/I, is the resistance (R) of the resistor, measured in ohms.
7. Replace the resistor with one of a different colour and repeat Procedure steps 1 to 6.

Concluding Questions

1. What happens to the voltage across a resistor when the number of cells in series with it is
   (a) doubled? (b) tripled? (c) quadrupled?
2. What happens to the current across a resistor when the number of cells in series with it is
   (a) doubled? (b) tripled? (c) quadrupled?
3. What happens to the resistance ($R = V/I$) across a resistor when the number of cells in series with it is
   (a) doubled? (b) tripled? (c) quadrupled?
4. What is the resistance in ohms (Ω) of (a) the first resistor you used? (b) the second resistor you used?
5. Consult Table 7.3.1 to see the manufacturer's rating of your resistors. Record these resistances in your notes. Why is the measured value different from the manufacturer's rating?

7.3 Review Questions

1. A current of 1.2 mA exists in a resistor when a potential difference of 4.8 V is applied to its ends. What is the resistance of the resistor? Express your answer in kilohms (1 kΩ = 1000 Ω).

2. A current of 3.0 mA exists in a 2.0 kΩ resistor. What is the voltage between the ends of the resistor?

3. What current will exist in a 30 Ω resistor if a 120 V voltage is applied to its ends?

4. A 3.0 V battery is connected to a carbon resistor.
   (a) If the current is 3.0 mA, what is the resistance of the resistor?

   (b) If a 6.0 V battery is connected to the same resistor, what will the current be?

   (c) What is the resistance of the resistor when the 6.0 V battery replaces the 3.0 V battery?

5. A 12 V battery sends a current of 2.0 A through a car's circuit to the headlights. What is the resistance of the filament in a headlight?

6. What voltage is needed to send 0.5 A through a 220 Ω light bulb filament?

7. What current exists in a 120 V coffee percolator, if the resistance of its heating element is 24 Ω?

8. A resistor has the following coloured bands: brown, black, red, gold. What is the manufacturer's rating of this resistor (see Table 7.3.1)?

9. Use Table 7.3.1 to figure out the resistance rating of the following colour-coded resistors:
   (a) Orange, red, brown, silver

   (b) Red, black, black, gold

   (c) Gray, green, blue, silver

   (d) White, violet, red

10. What colour code would you find on the following resistors?
    (a) 500 Ω ± 20%

    (b) 37 000 Ω ± 5%

    (c) 10 Ω ± 10%

    (d) 8600 Ω ± 20%

11. What is the resistance of the element of a 1500 W kettle if it draws 12.5 A?

12. A 1500 W kettle is connected to a 110 V source. What is the resistance of the kettle element?

13. When you pay your electricity bill, you are charged not for power but for the energy used. The unit for measuring the energy used is the kilowatt•hour (kW•h).
    (a) How many joules are there in one kW•h?

    (b) How much energy, in kW•h, does a 400-W TV set use in a month (30 days), if it is used an average of 6.0 h each day?

    (c) If electrical energy costs $0.06/kW•h, what will it cost you to operate the TV set for one month?

14. How many kW•h of energy does a 900 W toaster use in 3.0 min?

15. A 1.0 kΩ resistor is rated ½ W. This rating means the resistor will be destroyed if more than than ½ W passes through it. What is the maximum voltage you can apply to this resistor without risking damage to it?

16. A battery with an emf of 6.00 V has an internal resistance of 0.20 Ω. What current does the battery deliver when the terminal voltage reads only 5.00 V?

7.4 Kirchhoff's Laws

Warm Up

What will happen to the brightness of the remaining six light bulbs in a parallel circuit if the seventh bulb in the circuit is unhooked?

____

____

____

Resistors in Series

In Figure 7.4.1, four resistors are connected end-to-end so that there is one continuous conducting path for electrons coming from the source of emf, through the resistors, and back to the source. Electrons move through the resistors, one after the other. The same current exists in each resistor. Resistors arranged like this are said to be "in **series**" with each other. Figure 7.4.1 shows a typical series circuit.

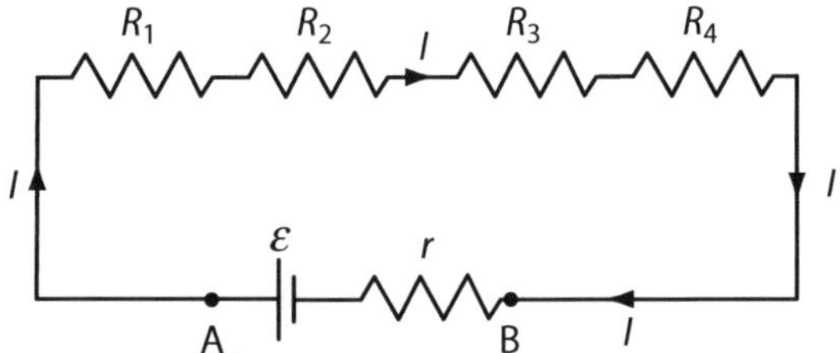

Figure 7.4.1 *A series circuit*

Within the cell, the gain in potential energy per unit charge is equal to the emf, ε. When a current I exists, energy will be lost in resistors R_1, R_2, R_3, R_4, and r. The loss of potential energy per unit charge in each resistor is the voltage V across that resistor. From Ohm's law, we know that $V = IR$. The law of conservation of energy requires that the total gain in energy in the cell(s) must equal the total loss of energy in the resistors in the circuit. It follows that the total gain in energy per unit charge (E) must equal the total loss of energy per unit charge in the circuit.

$$E = Ir + IR_1 + IR_2 + IR_3 + IR_4$$

$$\therefore\ E - Ir = IR_1 + IR_2 + IR_3 + IR_4$$

Recalling that terminal voltage $V_{AB} = E - Ir$,

$$V_{AB} = IR_1 + IR_2 + IR_3 + IR_4 = V_S$$

where V_S is the sum of voltages across the resistors in the external part of the circuit.

Another way of writing this is: $V_{AB} = V_1 + V_2 + V_3 + V_4 = V_S$

Equivalent Resistance

What is the total resistance of a series circuit like the one in Figure 7.4.1? In other words, what single resistance, called the **equivalent resistance** R_S, could be used to replace R_1, R_2, R_3, and R_4 without changing current I?

If $V_S = IR_S$ and $V_S = IR_1 + IR_2 + IR_3 + IR_4$, then

$$IR_S = IR_1 + IR_2 + IR_3 + IR_4$$

$$\therefore R_S = R_1 + R_2 + R_3 + R_4$$

Summary: For a Series Circuit

1. Current (I) is the same everywhere throughout the circuit.
2. The net gain in potential energy per coulomb in the circuit equals the net loss of potential energy per coulomb in the circuit. That is, for a circuit like the one in Figure 7.4.1, with a single source of emf,
$$V_{AB} = V_1 + V_2 + V_3 + V_4 + ... + V_n$$
3. The equivalent resistance of all the resistors in series with each other is equal to the sum of all their resistances.
$$R_S = R_1 + R_2 + R_3 + R_4 + ... + R_n$$

Resistors in Parallel

The resistors in Figure 7.4.2 are connected in **parallel**. The current divides into three branches. Electrons coming from the cell take one of three paths, which meet at a junction where the electrons all converge to one path again and return to the battery.

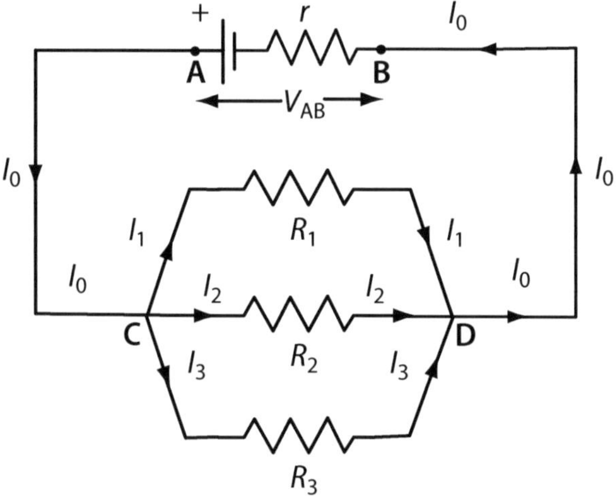

Figure 7.4.2 *Resistors R_1, R_2, and R_3 are placed in parallel in this circuit.*

Electric charge is a conserved quantity. The electrons are not "created" or "lost" during their journey through the parallel network of resistors. The number of electrons entering a junction (such as D) per second will equal the number of electrons leaving that junction per second. Likewise, the number of electrons entering junction C per second will equal the number of electrons leaving C per second. (The actual direction of electron flow is opposite to the conventional current direction shown in Figure 7.4.2.) If we express current in C/s or in A, as is normally the case,

$$I_0 = I_1 + I_2 + I_3$$

The net gain in potential energy per unit charge in the cell, which is V_{AB}, is equal to the loss in potential energy per unit charge between C and D. If you think of C as an extension of terminal A and D as an extension of terminal B of the cell, you can see that the difference in potential between C and D is the same no matter which of the three paths the electrons take to get from one terminal to the other. In fact,

$$V_{AB} = V_1 = V_2 = V_3$$

where V_{AB} is the terminal voltage of the cell, and V_1, V_2, and V_3 are the voltages across resistors R_1, R_2, and R_3 respectively.

Since the voltages are the same in each branch, we shall use the label V_p for the voltage in *any* branch of the parallel network.

Equivalent Resistance

What single resistance could be used in place of the parallel network of resistors, and draw the same total current? Call this the **equivalent resistance** R_p.

If the voltage across the parallel network is V_p, and the equivalent single resistance is R_p, we can apply Ohm's law as follows to find the total current I_0 entering the network:

$$I_0 = \frac{V_p}{R_p}$$

However, $I_0 = I_1 + I_2 + I_3$

Using Ohm's law again: $$\frac{V_p}{R_p} = \frac{V_p}{R_1} + \frac{V_p}{R_2} + \frac{V_p}{R_3}$$

Eliminating V_p: $$\frac{1}{R_p} = \frac{1}{R_1} + \frac{1}{R_2} + \frac{1}{R_3}$$

Summary: For a Parallel Circuit Network

1. Voltage is the same between the ends of each branch of a parallel network.
2. The total current entering a junction of a parallel network is equal to the total current leaving the same junction. As a result, the total current entering a parallel network of resistors or leaving the same network is equal to the sum of the currents in the branches.
3. The reciprocal of the single equivalent resistance that will replace all the resistance in a parallel network, and draw the same current, is equal to the sum of the reciprocals of the resistances in the branches.

$$\frac{1}{R_p} = \frac{1}{R_1} + \frac{1}{R_2} + \frac{1}{R_3} + \ldots + \frac{1}{R_n}$$

Combined Series and Parallel Circuits

Figure 7.4.3 shows a combined **series-parallel circuit**. The rules you have learned for series and parallel circuits can be applied to this problem. A logical approach for finding the equivalent resistance and current for the circuit in Figure 7.4.3 is to first reduce the parallel network to a single equivalent resistance, then treat the circuit as a series circuit.

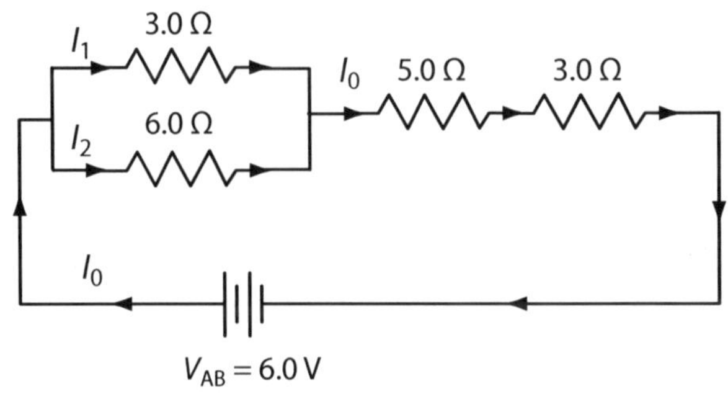

Figure 7.4.3 *A combined series-parallel circuit*

Sample Problem — Resistors in Parallel

(a) What is the equivalent resistance of the circuit in Figure 7.4.3?
(b) What is the voltage across the 6.0 Ω resistor?

What to Think About	How to Do It
(a)	
1. First, reduce the parallel network to an equivalent single resistance.	$\frac{1}{R_p} = \frac{1}{3.0\ \Omega} + \frac{1}{6.0\ \Omega} = \frac{2+1}{6.0\ \Omega} = \frac{3}{6.0\ \Omega} = \frac{1}{2.0\ \Omega}$ $R_p = 2.0\ \Omega$
2. Next, add the three resistances that are in series with one another.	$R_s = 2.0\ \Omega + 5.0\ \Omega + 3.0\ \Omega = 10.0\ \Omega$
3. Then, find the current using Ohm's law with the total equivalent resistance and the battery terminal voltage.	$I_0 = \frac{V_{AB}}{R_s} = \frac{6.0\ \text{V}}{10.0\ \Omega} = 0.60\ \text{A}$
(b)	
1. Find the voltage across the parallel network by using Ohm's law on the parallel network by itself.	$V_p = I_0 R_p = (0.60\ \text{A})(2.0\ \Omega) = 1.2\ \text{V}$

Practice Problems — Resistors in Parallel

1. (a) Draw a circuit showing a 6.0 V battery with an internal resistance of 0.50 Ω connected to a parallel network consisting of a 25.0 Ω resistor in parallel with a 6.25 Ω resistor.

   (b) Calculate the current in the battery.

2. Calculate the equivalent resistance of each of the networks of resistors in Figure 7.4.4.

   (a)

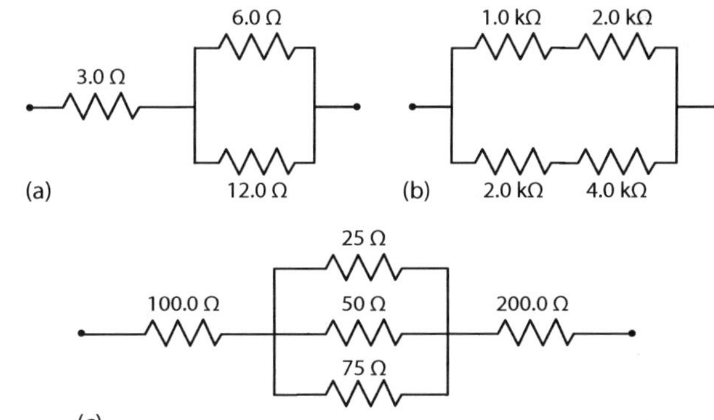

Figure 7.4.4

   (b)

   (c)

Kirchhoff's Laws for Electric Circuits

So far, we have looked at series and parallel circuits from the points of view of (a) conservation of energy, (b) conservation of charge, and (c) Ohm's law. Most simple circuits can be analyzed using the rules worked out for series and parallel circuits in this section. For more complicated circuits, a pair of rules called **Kirchhoff's rules** or **Kirchhoff's laws** can be applied.

> **Kirchhoff's Current Rule**
> At any junction in a circuit, the sum of all the currents entering that junction equals the sum of all the currents leaving that junction.

Kirchhoff's current rule follows from the law of conservation of electric charge. Charged particles are not "lost" or "created" in a circuit. The number of charged particles (usually electrons) that enter a junction point equals the number that leave that junction point.

> **Kirchhoff's Voltage Rule**
> The algebraic sum of all the changes in potential around a closed path in a circuit is zero.

Kirchhoff's voltage rule is really a restatement of the law of conservation of energy. In Investigation 7.4.1, you will examine several circuits from the point of view of Kirchhoff's laws.

Quick Check

1. Calculate the current in the cell in the circuit in Figure 7.4.5.

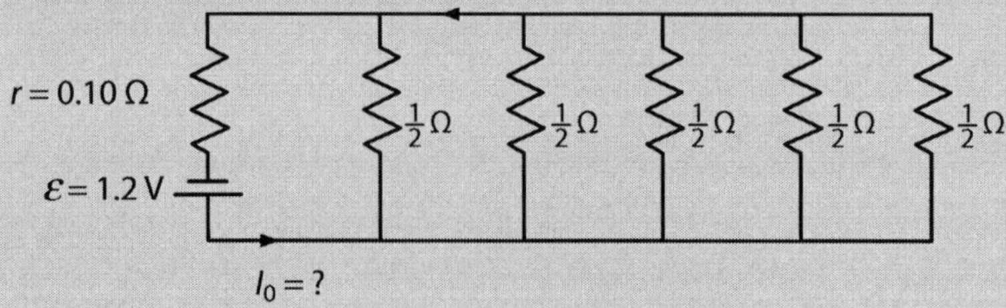

Figure 7.4.5

Quick Check continues

2. A wire has length ℓ and resistance R. It is cut into four identical pieces, and these pieces are arranged in parallel. What will be the resistance of this parallel network?

3. Four identical resistors are connected in parallel, as shown in Figure 7.4.6. The current is 2.0 A with all four resistors in the circuit. What will be the current if the wire at X is cut?

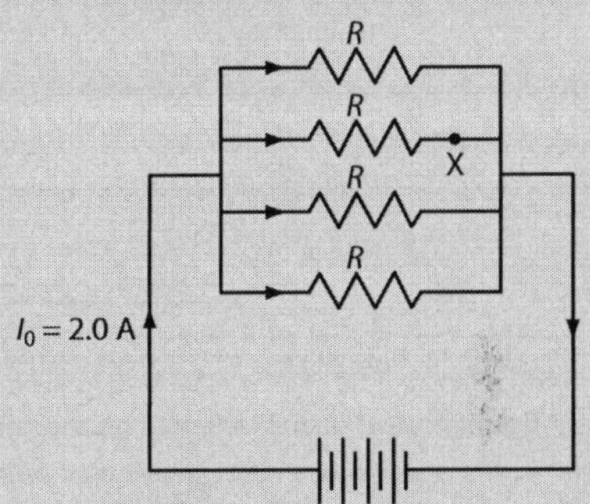

Figure 7.4.6

4. (a) What is the equivalent resistance of the network of resistors in Figure 7.4.7?

(b) What current exists in the 3.0 Ω resistor?

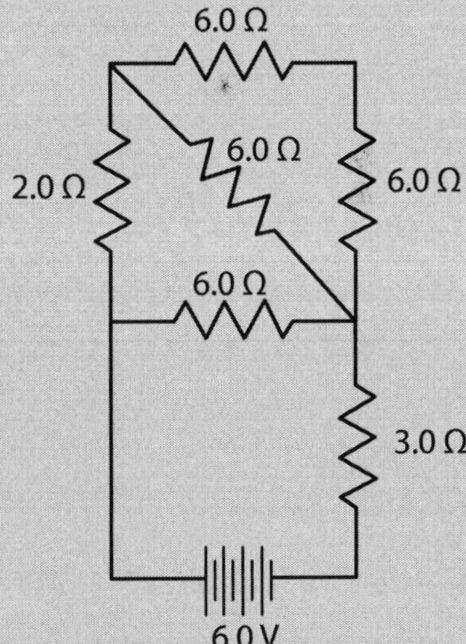

Figure 7.4.7

Investigation 7.4.1 Kirchhoff's Laws for Circuits

Purpose

To examine several circuits from the point of view of Kirchhoff's laws

Part 1 — A Series Circuit

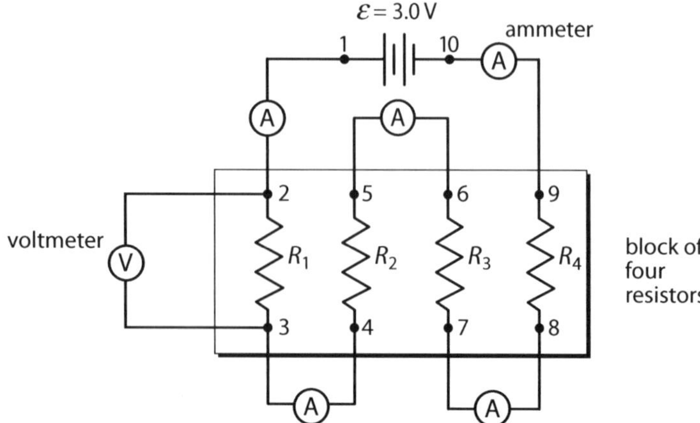

Figure 7.4.8

Procedure

1. To check Kirchhoff's current law, wire a series circuit like the one in Figure 7.4.8, and insert your ammeter in *each* of the locations, in turn, where the symbol A for ammeter is shown in the diagram. Record each current in your notebook (possibly on a diagram like Figure 7.4.8).

   I_{1-2} = ______ I_{3-4} = ______ I_{5-6} = ______ I_{7-8} = ______ I_{9-10} = ______

2. To check Kirchhoff's voltage law, measure the terminal voltage of the battery or power supply, V_{1-10}. Then measure the voltages between the ends of each resistor. Remember that the voltmeter is not in the same conducting path as the circuit. An example is shown in Figure 7.4.8, where the voltmeter is connected correctly across the ends of resistor R_1. The symbol for the voltmeter is V. Record all the voltages in your notebook.

   V_{1-10} = ______ V_{2-3} = ______ V_{4-5} = ______ V_{6-7} = ______ V_{8-9} = ______

Concluding Questions

1. Do your current readings support Kirchhoff's current law? How would you describe the current at various junctions in your series circuit?
2. Compare the potential gain in the battery (terminal voltage) with the potential drop in the resistors in the circuit. Do your results suggest that $\sum V = 0$?
3. What are some sources of error in this investigation? For example, how might the ammeter itself affect the results for current, and how might the voltmeter affect the results for voltage?
4. Calculate the resistance of each resistor using Ohm's law and the current and voltage readings for each individual resistor. Compare your calculated resistances with the manufacturer's ratings. (See Table 7.3.1 for resistor colour codes.) Organize your results in a table like Table 7.4.1 below.

Table 7.4.1 *Data Table*

	R_1	R_2	R_3	R_4
Measured Voltage, V	V	V	V	V
Measured Current, I	A	A	A	A
Calculated Resistance, R	Ω	Ω	Ω	Ω
Colour Code Rating, R	Ω	Ω	Ω	Ω

5. Calculate the equivalent resistance R_S of the whole series circuit by using Ohm's law and dividing the terminal voltage of the battery or power supply by the current in the battery. Compare this value with the sum of the individual calculated resistances.
6. What is the percent difference between R_S and $\sum [R_1 + R_2 + R_3 + R_4]$?

Part 2 — A Parallel Circuit

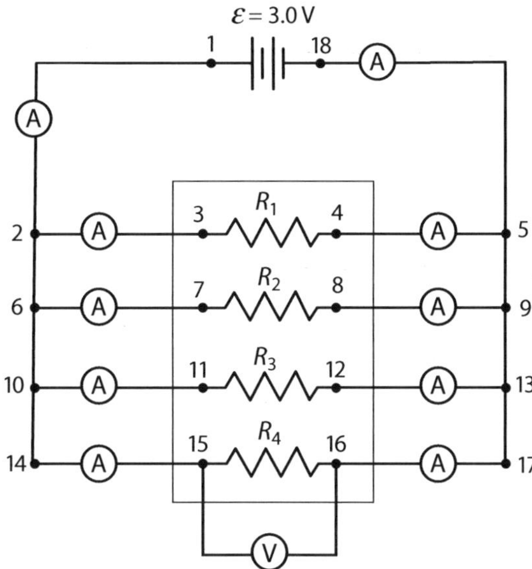

Figure 7.4.9

Procedure

1. Set up the circuit shown in Figure 7.4.9. To simplify recording your data, copy the diagram into your notebook. When you measure the current at each point labeled A, record the current right on the diagram in the ammeter circle.
2. Measure the voltage of the battery (V_{1-18}) and also the voltage across each resistor. Record the voltages in your notebook.

V_{1-18} = ______ V_{3-4} = ______ V_{7-8} = ______ V_{11-12} = ______ V_{15-16} = ______

Concluding Questions

1. Examine the currents at each of the eight junctions of the parallel network of resistors. Do your results confirm Kirchhoff's current law?
2. Compare the potential gain in the battery (terminal voltage) with the potential drop across each branch of the circuit, in turn. Do your measurements seem to confirm Kirchhoff's voltage law?

3. What are some sources of error in this experiment?
4. Use the measured voltage across each resistor, and the measured current in each resistor, to calculate R_1, R_2, R_3, and R_4. Calculate the resistance of the parallel network:

$$\frac{1}{R_p} = \frac{1}{R_1} + \frac{1}{R_2} + \frac{1}{R_3} + \frac{1}{R_4}$$

Organize your data in a table like Table 7.4.2 below.

Table 7.4.2 *Data Table*

	R_1	R_2	R_3	R_4
Measured Voltage, V	V	V	V	V
Measured Current, I	A	A	A	A
Calculated Resistance, R	Ω	Ω	Ω	Ω

(a) R_p calculated in Concluding Question 4 =	Ω
(b) R_p calculated from $\frac{V_{1-18}}{I_0}$ =	Ω
Percent difference between (a) and (b) =	%

5. Calculate the equivalent resistance of the parallel network by dividing the terminal voltage of the battery by the current in the battery. What is the percent difference between this R_p and the result from Procedure step 4?

Challenge

1. Set up a series-parallel circuit like the one in Figure 7.4.10. Test Kirchhoff's two laws for this circuit.

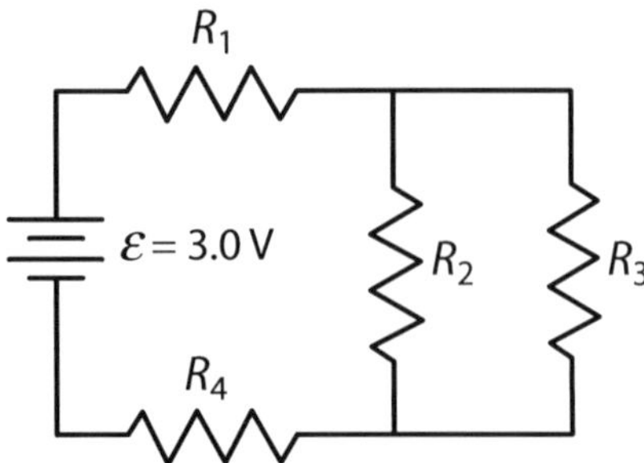

Figure 7.4.10

7.4 Review Questions

1. The current through A is 0.50 A when the switch S is open. What will the current be through A when the switch S is closed?

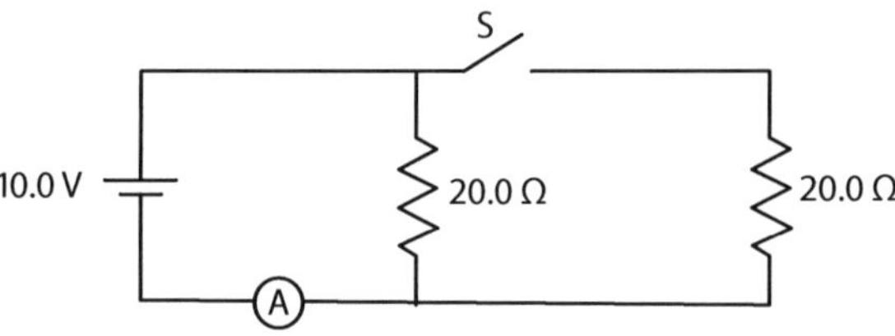

2. Which one of the following arrangements of four identical resistors will have the least resistance?

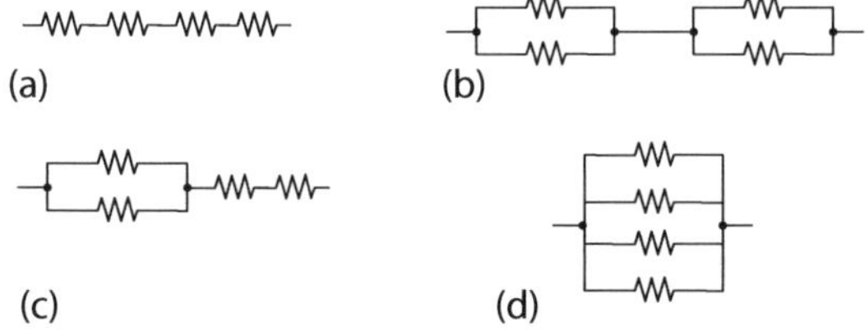

3. Use this circuit diagram to answer the questions below.

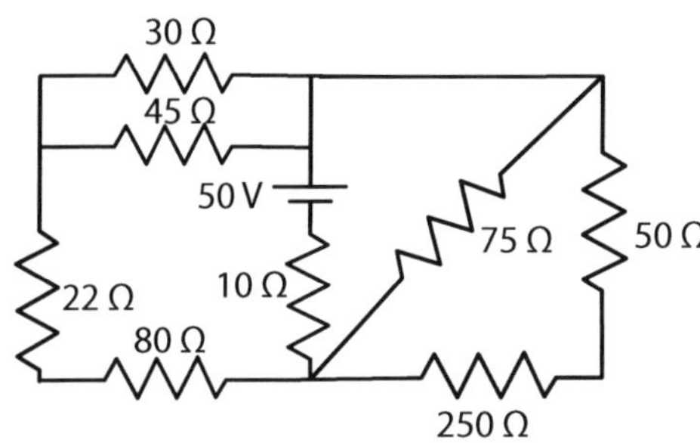

(a) What is the equivalent resistance of the entire circuit?

(b) What current is drawn from the battery?

(c) What is the current in the 50 Ω resistor?

(d) What is the voltage across the 22 Ω resistor?

4. What is the current in the ammeter A in this circuit?

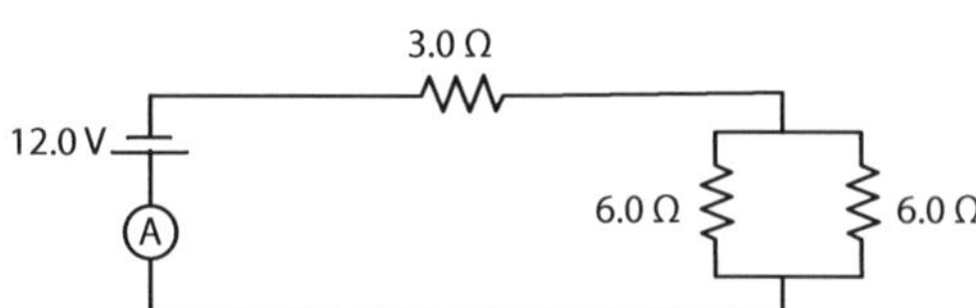

5. What is the emf of the battery if the current in A is 1.2 A and the internal resistance of the battery is 0.0833 Ω in this circuit?

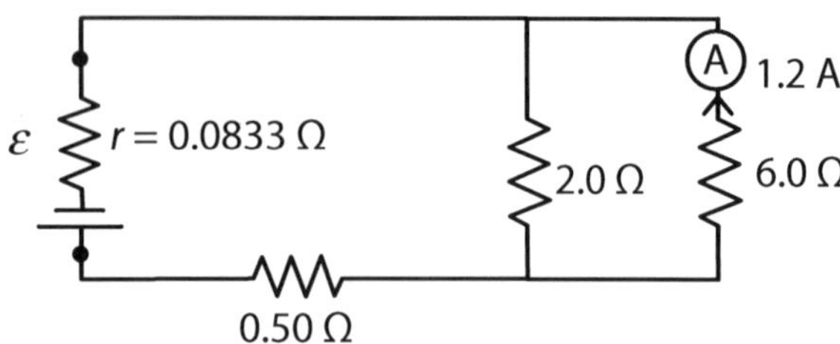

6. What is the voltage V of the power supply in the circuit below?

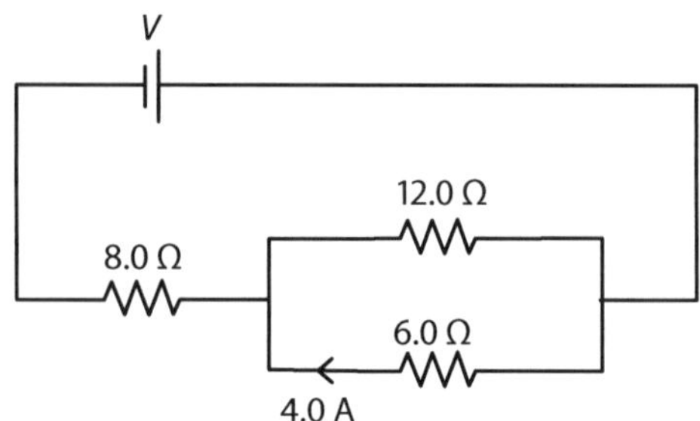

7. What is the internal resistance of the battery shown here?

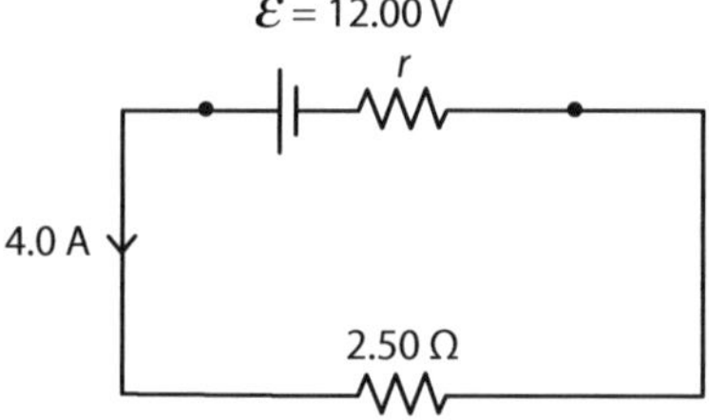

8. Use this circuit diagram to answer the questions below.

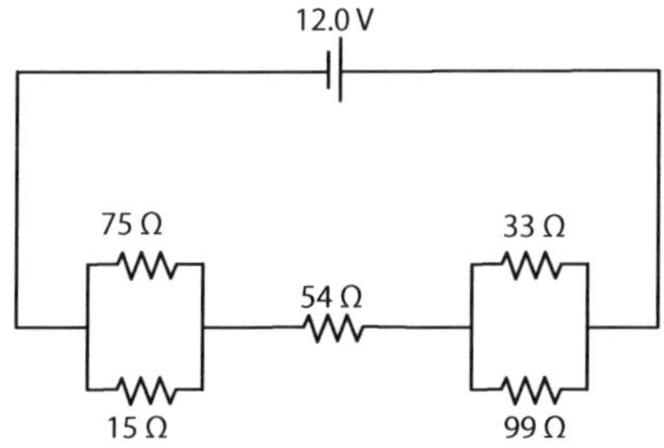

(a) What is the equivalent resistance of this circuit?

(b) What is the current through the 54 Ω resistor?

(c) How much power is dissipated in the 54 Ω resistor?

9. Use this circuit diagram to answer the questions below.

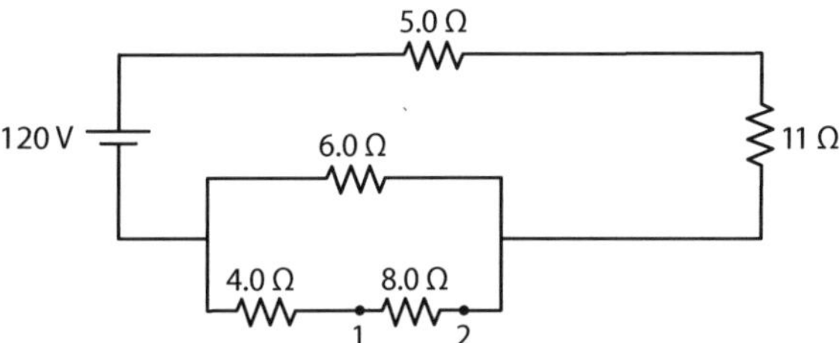

(a) What is the voltage across the 8.0 Ω resistor (between 1 and 2)?

(b) How much power is dissipated in the 5.0 Ω resistor?

Chapter 7 Conceptual Review Questions

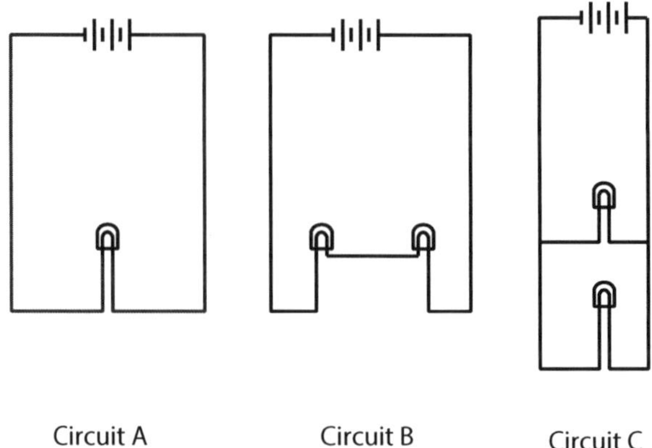

1a. In the image above similar batteries and light bulbs are used to arrange the three circuits. In which circuit will the light bulb(s) be the brightest? Explain your answer.

1b. Which circuit will the light bulbs burn out last? Explain your reasoning.

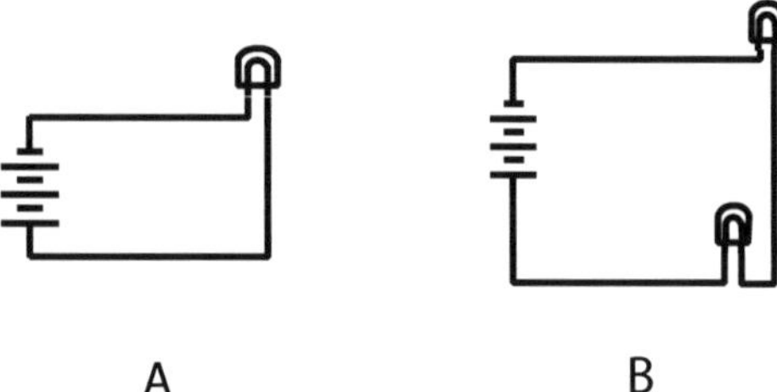

2. Assuming batteries and light bulbs are identical, which of the above circuits will carry less current? Explain.

Chapter 7 Review Questions

1. What is the difference between the terminal voltage of a battery and its emf?

2. What current exists in a wire if 2.4×10^3 C of charge pass through a point in the wire in a time of 6.0×10^1 s?

3. The current through an ammeter is 5.0 A. In one day, how many electrons will pass through the ammeter?

4. How much silver will be electroplated by a current of 0.255 A in one day?

5. A mercury cell has an emf of 1.35 V and an internal resistance of 0.041 Ω. If it is used in a circuit that draws 1.50 A, what will its terminal voltage be?

6. A set of eight decorative light bulbs is plugged into a 120 V wall receptacle. What is the potential difference across each light bulb filament, if the eight light bulbs are connected:

   (a) in series?

   (b) in parallel?

7. What is the resistance of a resistor if a potential difference of 36 V between its ends results in a current of 1.20 mA?

8. What is the potential difference (voltage) between the ends of a resistor if 24.0 J of work must be done to drive 0.30 C of charge through the resistor?

9. A resistor has the following coloured bands: brown, black, yellow, and gold. What is the manufacturer's rating of the resistance of this resistor?

10. You need a 4.7 MΩ resistor from a box of miscellaneous resistors. What coloured bands should you look for in your collection?

11. A 2.2 kΩ resistor is rated at ½ W. What is the highest voltage you could safely apply to the resistor without risking damage to it from overheating?

12. What current will a 1500 W kettle draw from a 120 V source?

13. A toaster draws 8.0 A on a 120 V circuit. What is its power rating?

14. A 60.0 W light bulb and a 40.0 W light bulb are connected in parallel in a 120 V circuit. What is the equivalent resistance of the two light bulbs?

15. A circuit in your house has the following appliances plugged into it: a 1500 W kettle, a 150 W light, and a 900 W toaster. The circuit is protected by a 20 A circuit breaker. If the house voltage is 120 V, will the circuit breaker be activated? Explain your answer.

16. How many kW•h of energy will a 400 W television set use in one month, if it is turned on for an average of 5.0 h per day? What will it cost you at \$0.06/kW•h?

17. The cell in the diagram below is short-circuited with a wire of resistance 0.10 Ω. What is the terminal voltage under these conditions?

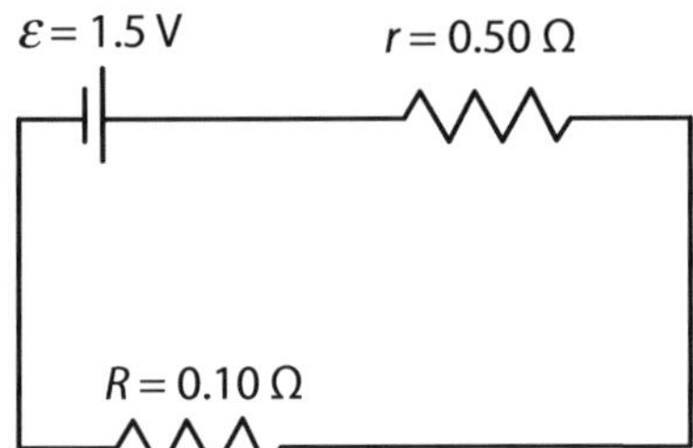

18. A storage battery has an emf of 12.0 V. What is the terminal voltage if a current of 150 A is drawn just as the starter motor is turned on? The internal resistance is 0.030 Ω.

19. What is the equivalent resistance of resistors of 8.0 Ω, 12.0 Ω, and 24.0 Ω if they are connected

(a) in series?

(b) in parallel?

20. A resistor is intended to have a resistance of 60.00 Ω, but when checked it is found to be 60.07 Ω. What resistance might you put in parallel with it to obtain an equivalent resistance of 60.00 Ω?

21. A 12.0 Ω resistor and a 6.0 Ω resistor are connected in series with a 9.0 V battery. What is the voltage across the 6.0 Ω resistor?

22. What is the resistance R in diagram below, if the current through the battery is 5.0 A?

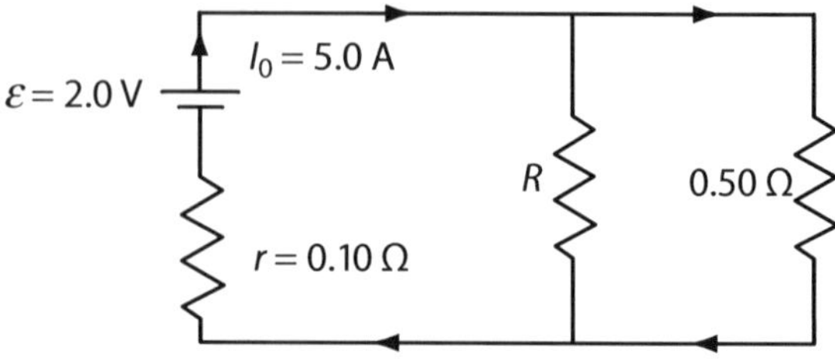

23. You have three 6.0 kΩ resistors. By combining these three resistors in different combinations, how many different equivalent resistances can you obtain with them? (All three must be used.)

24. For each circuit, find
(i) the equivalent resistance of the entire circuit, and
(ii) the current at the point marked I.

(a)

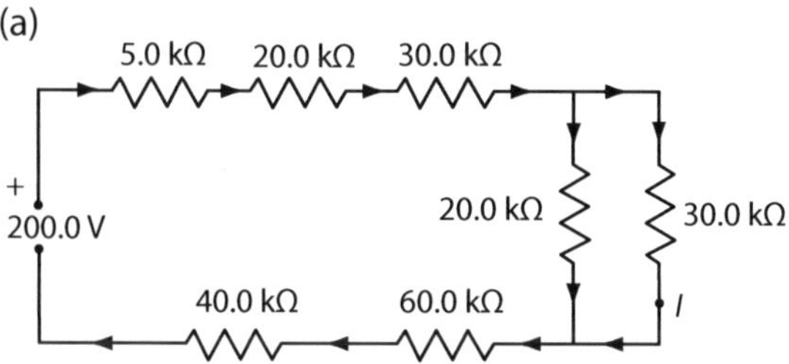

(b)

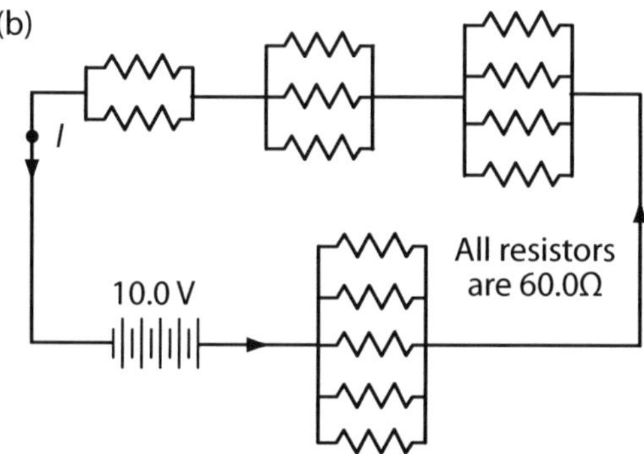

(c)

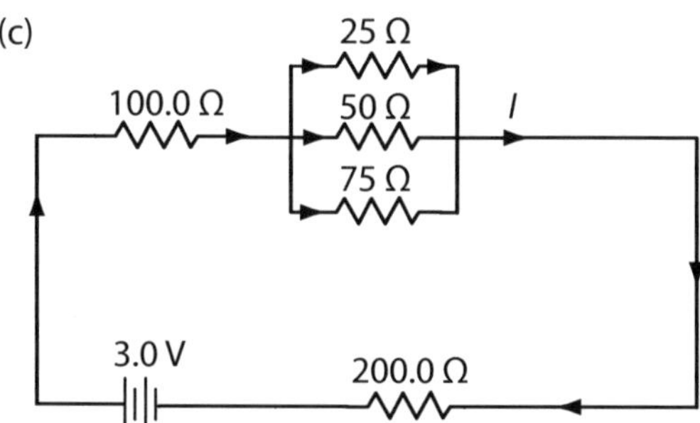

25. What is the voltage across the 6.0 Ω resistor in the diagram below?

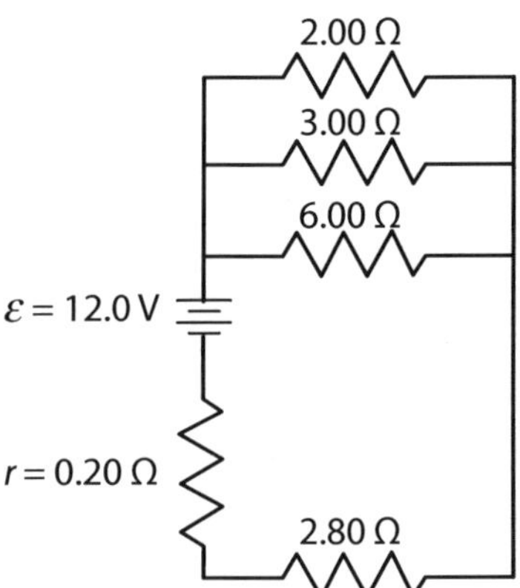

26. Twelve identical pieces of resistance wire, each of resistance 1.0 Ω, are formed into a cubical resistance network, shown in the diagram below. If a current of 12 A enters one corner of the cube and leaves at the other corner, what is the equivalent resistance of the cube between the opposite corners? Use Kirchhoff's laws.

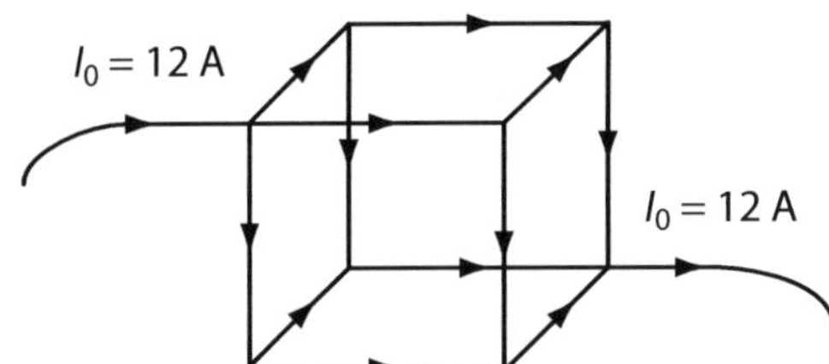

8 Wave Motion

In this chapter the focus will be on the Big Idea:

Mechanical waves transfer energy but not matter.

The content learning standards will include:

- Generation and propagation of waves
- Properties and behaviours of waves

By the end of this chapter, you should know the meaning of these **key terms**:

- amplitude
- constructive interference
- crests
- destructive interference
- diffraction
- Doppler effect
- frequency
- hertz
- longitudinal wave
- nodal lines
- period
- periodic wave
- pulse
- reflection
- refraction
- sonic boom
- sound barrier
- transverse wave
- troughs
- wavelength

By the end of this chapter, you should be able to use and know when to use the following formulae:

$T = \frac{1}{f}$ $v = f\lambda$

A tiny drop creates a pattern of circular waves.

8.1 Wave Properties

Warm Up

For this activity you will build a Gummi Bear wave machine. You'll need some duct tape, a couple dozen wooden skewers and a bag of Gummi Bears. Run about 4 m of duct tape between two desks. Make sure the sticky side is facing upwards. Then place skewers about 5 cm apart all the way down the duct tape. On the end of each skewer place a Gummi Bear. Scan the QR code to watch a short video on how to build this device.

1. Describe the motion in your Gummi Bear wave machine when you lift one Gummi Bear at one end.

____

____

____

____

Good Vibrations

There are many kinds of waves in nature. You have heard of light waves, sound waves, radio waves, earthquake waves, water waves, shock waves, brain waves and the familiar wave created by a cheering crowd at a sports event. Wave motion is an important phenomenon because it is so common and it is one of the major ways in which energy can be transmitted from one place to another.

There are two basic kinds of waves. First, there is the **pulse,** which is a non-repeating wave. A single disturbance sends a pulse from the source outward, but there is no repetition of the event. For example, you may give a garden hose a quick "yank" to one side, causing a pulse to travel the length of the hose.

Second, there is the **periodic wave.** Periodic waves are probably more familiar to you. You have watched water waves moving across a pond. The waves arrive at the shore of the pond at regularly repeated time intervals. Periodic means recurring at regular intervals. Water waves are caused by a disturbance of the water somewhere in the pond.

Whether the wave is a pulse or a periodic wave, a disturbance is spread by the wave, usually through a material substance. An exception is the medium for electromagnetic radiation (light, radio, X-rays, ultraviolet, infrared, gamma radiation, etc.). The medium for electromagnetic radiation is electric and magnetic fields created by charged particles.

To have a regularly repeating wave, there must be regularly repeating vibrations. For example, the regularly repeating sound waves from a tuning fork are caused by the vibrations of the two tines of the fork disturbing the air. Vibrating electrons disturb the electric field around them to create the microwaves that cook your supper or measure the speed of your car in a radar trap.

Describing Waves

Wavelength (λ)

Figure 8.1.1 depicts waves emanating from a vibrating source. They could be water waves. The highest points on the waves are called **crests** and the lowest points are called **troughs**. The distance between successive crests or between successive troughs is called the **wavelength** (λ) of the wave. The symbol λ is the Greek letter lambda. The **amplitude** or height of the wave is measured from its displacement from the horizontal line in the diagram to the crest or trough. The amplitude is shown on the diagram.

Wavelengths may be measured in metres, in the case of water waves, or in nanometres (1 nm = 10^{-9}), in the case of visible light. Microwaves may be measured in centimetres, while the waves produced by AC power lines may be kilometres long. Wavelengths of audible sounds range from millimetres up to metres.

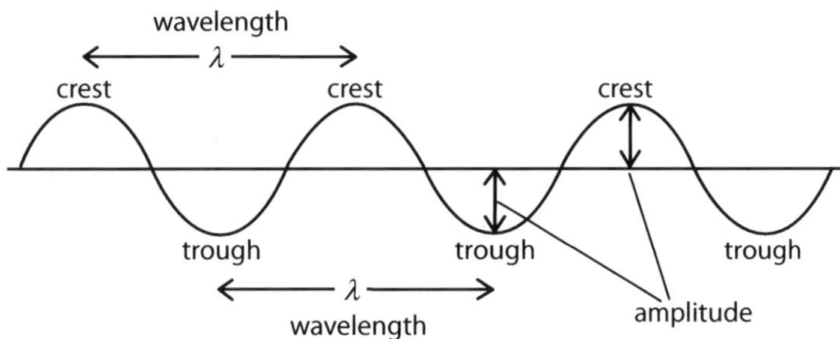

Figure 8.1.1 *Terms used for describing waves*

Frequency (*f*)

Another important aspect of waves is their **frequency**. The frequency of the waves tells you how often or frequently they and their source vibrate. If you are listening to a tuning fork, sound waves reach your ear with the same frequency as the vibrating fork. For example, the fork's tines vibrate back and forth 256 times in 1 s if the frequency of the fork is 256 vibrations per second. Frequency is measured in a unit called the **hertz (Hz)**. The unit is named after Heinrich Hertz (1857–1894), who was the first scientist to detect radio waves. One hertz is one vibration per second: 1 Hz $= 1\ s^{-1}$.

A pendulum 24.8 cm long has a frequency of 1 Hz. Electrons vibrating to and fro in an alternating current circuit have a frequency of 60 Hz. Radio waves may be several kilohertz (kHz), where 1 kHz = 1 000 Hz, or they may be in the megahertz (MHz) range, where 1 MHz is equal to 1 000 000 Hz.

Period (*T*)

Related to the frequency of a vibration is the **period** of the vibration. The period is the time interval between vibrations. For example, if the period of a vibration is 1/2 s, then the frequency must be 2 s^{-1} or 2 Hz. Consider a pendulum with a length of 24.8 cm. It will have a frequency of 1 Hz and a period of 1 s. A pendulum 99.2 cm long will have a frequency of 1/2 Hz and a period of 2 s. A pendulum 223 cm long will have a frequency of 1/3 Hz and a period of 3 s. As you can see, frequency and period are reciprocals of each other.

$$\text{frequency} = \frac{1}{\text{period}}$$

$$f = \frac{1}{T} \text{ or } \boldsymbol{T} = \frac{\mathbf{1}}{\boldsymbol{f}}$$

Quick Check

1. A dog's tail wags 50.0 times in 40.0 s.
   (a) What is the frequency of the tail?

   ____

   (b) What is the period of vibration of the tail?

   ____

2. A certain tuning fork makes 7680 vibrations in 30 s.
   (a) What is the frequency of the tuning fork?

   ____

   (b) What is the period of vibration of the tuning fork?

   ____

3. Tarzan is swinging back and forth on a vine. If each complete swing takes 4.0 s, what is the frequency of the swings?

   ____

Transverse and Longitudinal Waves

Figure 8.1.2 illustrates two ways to send a pulse through a long length of spring or a long Slinky. In method (a), the spring is pulled sideways, so that the disturbance is at right angles to the direction that the pulse will travel. This produces a **transverse wave.** In method (b), several turns of the spring are compressed and let go. The disturbance is in the same direction as the direction the pulse will travel. This produces a **longitudinal wave.** Transverse means *across* and longitudinal means *lengthwise*.

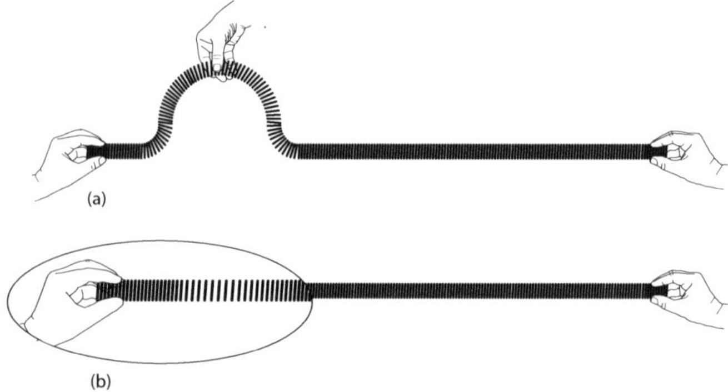

Figure 8.1.2 *(**a**) A transverse wave; (**b**) A longitudinal wave*

Wave Reflection and Refraction

When a wave encounters a boundary like a shoreline, wall or another medium, several things can happen. The two most common things are the wave will reflect or refract. **Reflection** occurs when a wave hits an object or another boundary and the wave is reflected back. If you attach or hold one end of a spring and send a wave down the spring, you will see it reflect off the end. Usually not all the wave is reflected back as some can be absorbed or refracted. **Refraction** is a bending of the wave and occurs when the wave hits an object at an angle or the wave enters a new medium. Refraction results from the change in the waves speed. The changing speed causes the wave to bend.

The Wave Equation

The wave shown in Figure 8.1.3 is moving through water in a wave tank. The waves in the wave tank are produced by a wave generator, which vibrates up and down with a frequency f and a period T where $T = 1/f$.

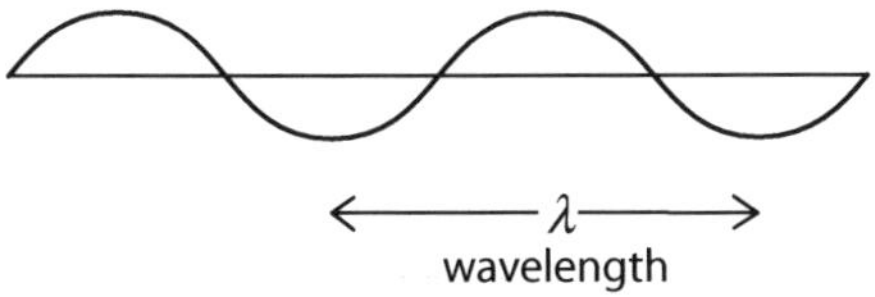

Figure 8.1.3 *A wave in a wave tank*

What is the speed of the wave? If you could see the wave tank, you could watch a wave travel its own length, or wavelength λ, and time exactly how long the wave takes to travel its own length. Since the waves are generated once every T seconds by the generator, then this T should be the period of the waves. To calculate the speed v of the waves, all you have to do is divide the wavelength by the period of the wave.

$$v = \lambda/T$$

Since $$T = 1/f \text{ or } f = 1/T$$

$$\mathbf{v = \lambda f}$$

This relationship is a very important one, because it is true for any kind of wave. This includes sound waves, earthquake waves, waves in the strings of musical instruments or any kind of electromagnetic wave (light, infrared, radio, X-radiation, ultraviolet, gamma radiation, etc.)! In words, the wave equation says

wave speed = wavelength × frequency

Sample Problem — Calculating Wave Speed

What is the speed of a sound wave if its frequency is 256 Hz and its wavelength is 1.29 m?

What to Think About	How to Do It
1. Determine what you need to find.	speed of sound
2. Select appropriate formula.	$v = \lambda f$
3. Find the speed of sound	$v = (1.29\ m)(256\ s^{-1}) = 330\ m/s$

Practice Problems — Calculating Wave Speed

1. If waves maintain a constant speed, what will happen to their wavelength if the frequency of the waves is
   (a) doubled?

   (b) halved?

2. What is the frequency of a sound wave if its speed is 340 m/s and its wavelength is 1.70 m?

3. Waves of frequency 2.0 Hz are generated at the end of a long steel spring. What is their wavelength if the waves travel along the spring with a speed of 3.0 m/s?

Investigation 8.1.1– Observing Transverse and Longitudinal Waves

Purpose

To observe pulses travelling in springs of different diameters

Procedure

1. With your partner's help, stretch a long spring about 2.5 cm in diameter to a length of 9 or 10 m. Hold on firmly as both you and the spring can be damaged if it is let go carelessly.
2. Create a transverse pulse by pulling a section of the spring to one side and letting it go suddenly. Observe the motion of the pulse and its reflection from your partner's hand.
3. Try increasing the amplitude of the pulse. Does this affect the speed of the wave through the spring?
4. Try tightening the spring. How does increasing the tension affect the speed of the pulse?
5. Observe the pulse as it reflects. Does a crest reflect as a crest or as a trough?
6. Have your partner create a pulse simultaneously with yours. Do the two pulses affect each other as they pass through each other?
7. Repeat Procedure steps 1 to 6 using a long Slinky, which is a spring with a much larger diameter.
8. Try sending a longitudinal pulse through each spring. To do this, bunch up a dozen or so turns of the spring, then let the compressed section go. Do longitudinal waves reflect at your partner's hand?

Concluding Questions

1. In which spring did the transverse waves travel faster — the small diameter spring or the Slinky?
2. In which spring did the longitudinal waves travel faster?
3. Does the amplitude of the waves affect their speed through the spring?
4. Does spring tension affect wave speed? Explain.
5. When a wave travels through the medium, like the spring, does the medium travel or just the disturbance in the medium?
6. When a wave reflects from a fixed end of the medium, does a crest reflect as a crest or is it reflected as a trough? In other words, is the wave inverted**?**

Investigation 8.1.2 – Wavelength, Frequency, and Speed of Water Waves

Purpose

To investigate the relationship among wavelength, frequency and wave speed

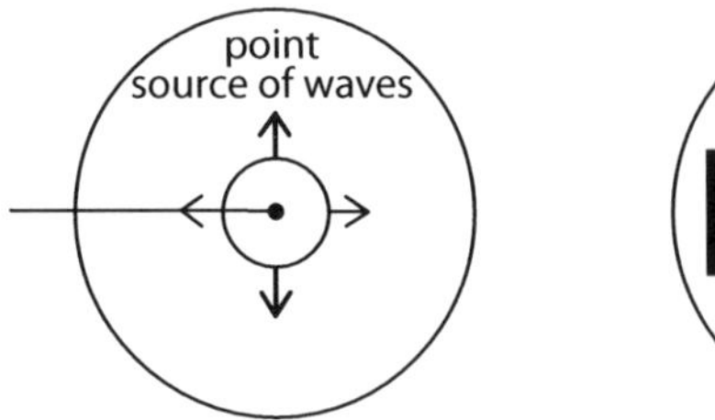

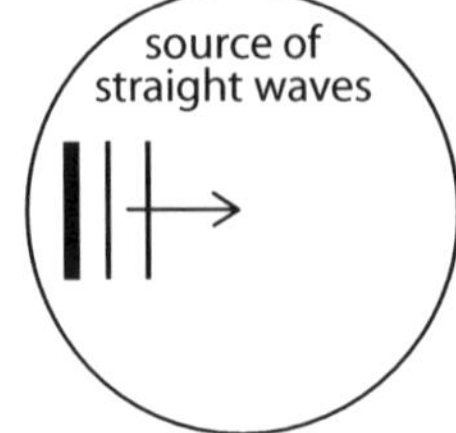

Figure 8.1.5 *Using different types of sources to observe water waves in a wave tank*

Procedure

1. Fill your wave tank with water to a depth of approximately 2 cm. If your tank requires them, make sure the screen dampers are in place.
2. To generate a circular wave, touch the surface of the water at the centre of the tank with the tip of your finger. Is there any evidence that the wave speeds up or slows down as it travels from the centre of the tank to its perimeter?
3. Imagine a single point on one of the crests that you see moving out from the centre of the tank. What path would this point on the crest take?
4. Set up your wave generator so that it generates circular waves at regular intervals. Start with a low frequency. Note the wavelength of the circular waves. This is the distance between successive crests. Increase the frequency of the wave generator and observe how the wavelength changes.
5. Set up your wave generator so that it produces straight waves instead of circular waves. Try different frequencies to see the effect of frequency on wavelength.

Concluding Questions

1. Does a circular wave travel out at the same speed in all directions? How do you know this?
2. Describe what happens to the wavelength of a water wave when the frequency of the wave increases.

8.1 Review Questions

1. What is the source of all wave motion?

2. What kind of wave has no amplitude and no frequency?

3. How many vibrations per second are there from a radio signal from 107.3 MHz?

4. What is the period of a wave that has a frequency of 25 Hz?

5. What is the frequency of a wave that has the period of 2.0 s?

6. When a salmon fishing boat captain describes waves as being 8 m high, what is the approximate amplitude of these waves? Explain your answer.

7. What is the frequency of one revolution of the second hand on a clock?

8. What is the frequency of one revolution of the hour hand on a clock?

9. If the frequency of a sound is tripled, what will happen to the period of the sound waves?

10. A student measures the speed of water waves in her tank to be 25 cm/s. If the wavelength is 2.5 cm, what is the frequency of the waves?

11. Some microwaves have a frequency of 3.0×10^{10} Hz. How long is a microwave of this frequency? (Microwave radiation travels at the speed of light.)

12. While fishing, a girl notices the wave crests passing her bob once every 6 s. She thinks the distance between crests is about 12 m. What is the speed of the water waves?

8.2 Wave Phenomena

Warm Up

You and a friend both throw rocks into a lake. The rocks enter the water 1.0 m apart. If you were looking down from above, draw what you think the wave pattern for each of the rocks will look like. Place the letter X at the point or points where the waves would be the highest.

Properties of Waves

You already know several properties of waves. Waves can be reflected and refracted. All waves conform to the wave equation. There are other important properties of waves, such as constructive and destructive interference, that lead to interesting natural phenomena.

Constructive and Destructive Interference

Figure 8.2.1 shows waves coming from two different sources — A and B. What happens if the two sets of waves arrive simultaneously at the same place? The result is shown in the third diagram. The amplitudes of the two sets of waves are additive. Since the waves from source A are in phase with the waves from source B, the resultant waves have twice the amplitude of the individual waves from A or B. This is an example of what is called **constructive interference.** Notice that crests are twice as high and troughs are twice as deep in the combined waves.

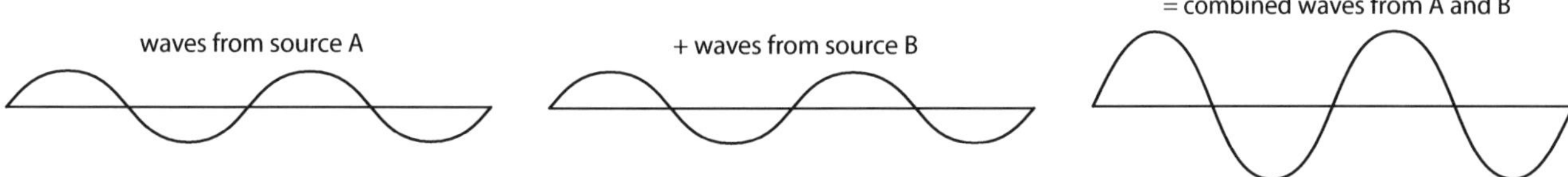

Figure 8.2.1 *Constructive interference*

In Figure 8.2.2, the waves from source A are exactly out of phase with the waves from source B. A crest from source A arrives simultaneously with a trough from source B. The two sets of waves exactly cancel each other. This is an example of **destructive interference.**

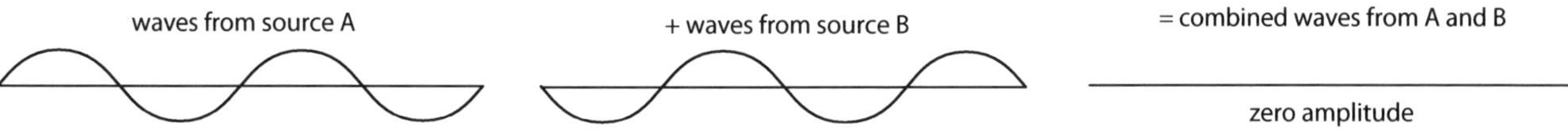

Figure 8.2.2 *Destructive interference*

Interference of waves occurs with all sorts of waves. You may have seen interference of water waves in the wave tank. You can hear interference of sound waves if you simply listen to a tuning fork as you rotate it slowly near your ear. Each tine of the fork produces a set of sound waves. Listen for constructive interference. It's the extra loud sound. Destructive interference is the minimum sound you hear as you slowly rotate the tuning fork.

Diffraction

You hear someone talking from around a corner. Light leaks through a crack in a closed door. These are both examples of another property of waves called diffraction. **Diffraction** is when a wave spreads out as it passes through narrow openings, around corners or small obstacles.

You have probably seen examples of diffraction many times, perhaps without knowing what it was. If you look out at streetlights through a window screen or a fine mesh curtain, the *starburst* effect you see is due to diffraction of light waves as they pass by the screen. Diffraction is often used in television programs to obtain starburst effects in musical productions. Diffraction is commonplace with sound. Figure 8.2.5 shows the diffraction of red laser light around a razor blade.

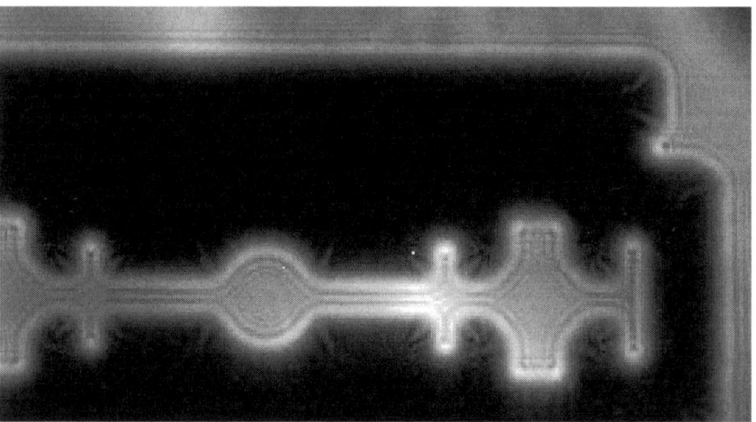

Figure 8.2.5 *Using the interference pattern to calculate the wavelength of light*

Investigation 8.2.1 – Properties of Waves

Purpose

To observe important properties of waves, using water waves in a wave tank as a model

Procedure

This investigation will require several periods to complete. There are six stations where you will observe different wave phenomena. Your teacher will point out any differences in equipment or procedures as required.

Station 1: Reflection of Circular Water Waves

1. Make a solid barrier of two paraffin wax blocks, standing on edge in the middle of the tank. Generate a circular wave by touching the surface of the water in the wave tank at a distance of approximately 10 cm in front of the barrier (Figure 8.2.8). Observe the curvature of the wave as it arrives at the barrier and as it leaves. Is the wave less curved, more curved, or does it have the same curvature after it reflects from the barriers? Sketch what you see.
2. From where does the reflected circular wave appear to come? Try generating a circular wave behind the barrier at the same time as you generate one in front of the barrier. Try different distances behind the barrier until you obtain a wave with the same curvature as the one that reflects from the other side of the barrier. The wave from the point behind the barrier will look just as if it is passing through the barrier and joining the reflected wave on the other side.

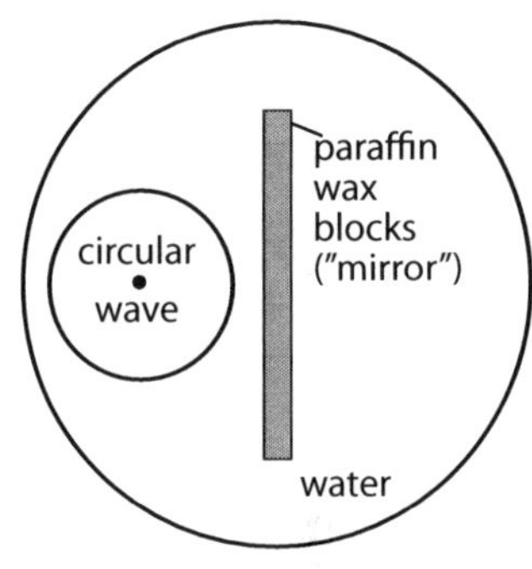

Figure 8.2.8 *Station 1*

Question

Can you reflect a wave completely? Explain your answer.

Station 2: Reflection of Straight Water Waves

1. Set up the straight-wave generator so that it sends parallel straight waves toward a barrier made of paraffin wax blocks. The angle formed where the incoming or incident waves strike the barrier is called the **angle of incidence** (labeled $\angle i$ in Figure 8.2.9). Measure both the angle of incidence and the **angle of reflection** ($\angle r$). Sketch what you see.
2. Adjust the barrier to change the angle of incidence. Measure the new angle of incidence and the new angle of reflection. Repeat for at least three other angles of incidence.
3. You will recall that wave speed, wavelength, and frequency are related by $v = \lambda f$. The frequency f is determined by the rate of vibration of the wave generator. It will not change during transmission of the waves. This means that the wave speed v is proportional to the wavelengthλ. If you observe the wavelength changing, this means the wave speed is changing proportionally. Is there a change in wavelength between the incident and reflected waves?

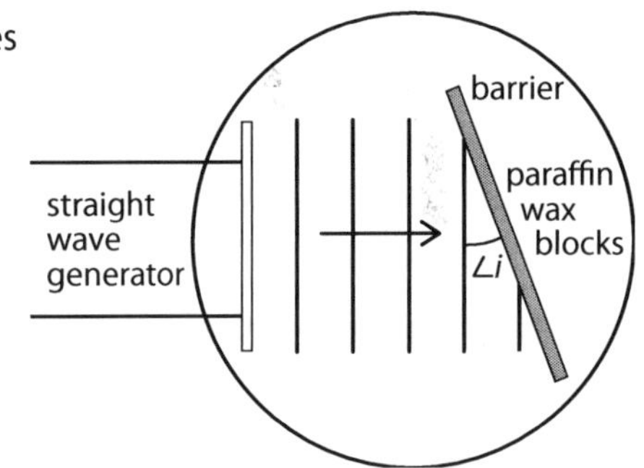

Figure 8.2.9 *Station 2*

Questions

1. When straight waves strike a straight barrier, how does the angle of incidence compare with the angle of reflection?
2. When the waves reflect from the barrier, does their speed change? Does their frequency change? Does their wavelength change?

Station 3: Reflection of Waves from a Curved "Mirror"

1. This time, instead of a straight barrier, you will use a piece of rubber tubing, which curls into a shape that is approximately parabolic. Set up the rubber tubing "mirror" so that it faces the straight-wave generator as in Figure 8.2.10(a).

2. Observe what happens when the incident straight waves reflect from the parabolic mirror. What shape do the waves have after the reflection? Locate the point to which the waves appear to converge. This point is called the **focus** or **focal point** of the mirror. Sketch what you see.

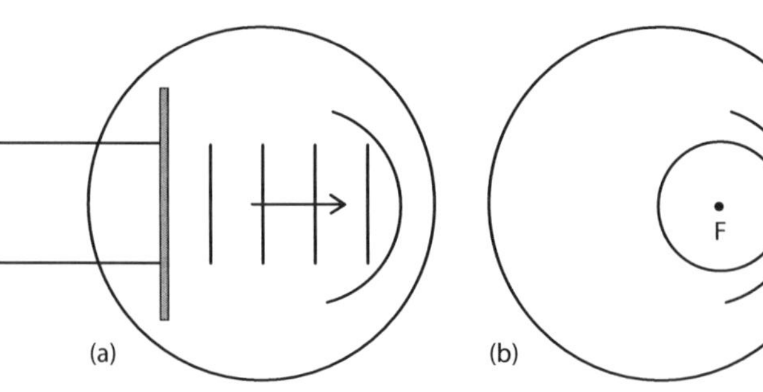

Figure 8.2.10 *Station 3*

3. Turn off the straight-wave generator. Use the tip of your finger to generate circular waves at the focus of the mirror as in Figure 8.2.10(b). What shape do the reflected waves have this time? Sketch what you see.

Questions

1. Describe what happens to straight waves when they reflect from a parabolic reflector. Are parabolic reflectors ever used to reflect (a) light? (b) sound? Give examples.
2. Describe what happens when circular waves originating at the focus of a parabolic mirror reflect from the mirror. Name a device that does this with light waves.

Station 4: Refraction of Water Waves

A. The Effect of Water Depth on Wave Speed

1. To observe the effect of water depth on wave speed, arrange the wave tank so that there is a region of deep water and a region of shallow water over which water waves can pass. To do this, mount a rectangular sheet of transparent plastic in the tank using coins or washers to prop it up. Add water to the tank until the level is approximately 1–2 mm above the top of the plastic sheet. Figure 8.2.11 illustrates side and top views. The straight wave generator is used to provide the waves.

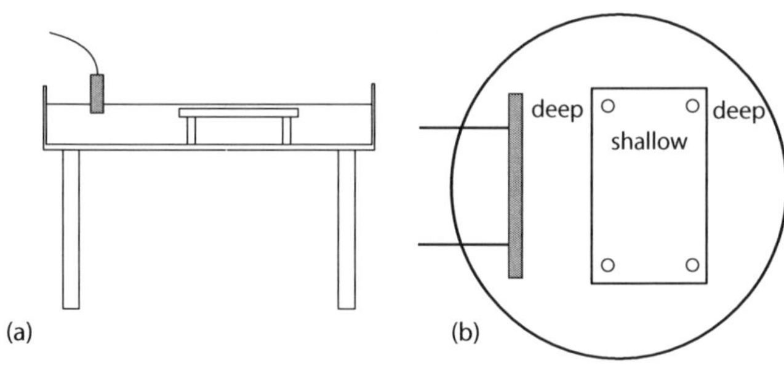

Figure 8.2.11 *Station 4A*

2. Generate continuous waves with the straight wave generator. Observe the wavelength of the waves in the deep water, and compare this with the wavelength in shallow water. Sketch what you observe. What happens when the waves re-enter the deep water? Measure the wavelengths in deep and shallow water and record them.

3. Calculate the ratio of the wavelength in shallow water to the wavelength in deep water. You can therefore calculate the ratio of the wave speed in shallow water to the wave speed in deep water.

B. Refraction of Water Waves

1. Arrange the shallow water region as in Figure 8.2.12, so that straight waves entering the shallow region meet its edge at an angle such as 30°. Adjust the generator frequency to obtain waves of long wavelength. Observe the waves as they pass into the shallow region.

2. Make the following measurements on the water waves, as seen on your "screen."
   (a) What is the wavelength in the deep water? In the shallow water?
   (b) What is the ratio of the wavelength in shallow water to the wavelength in deep water?
   (c) What is the ratio of the wave speed in shallow water to the wave speed in deep water? Where does the change in speed actually occur?
   (d) What angle does the incident wave make with the boundary between the deep water and the shallow water? This is the angle of incidence. What angle does the wave inside the shallow water make with the boundary? This is the angle of refraction.

Figure 8.2.12 *Station 4B*

3. Make a neat sketch illustrating what happens to water waves coming from deep water into shallow water. Show what happens to the waves when they again leave the shallow water.

4. Try different angles of incidence, such as 40° and 50°. Measure and record the angles at which the waves leave the boundary angles of refraction.

Questions

1. What happens to the speed of water waves when the waves pass from deeper water into shallower water?

2. You did not actually measure the wave speeds. How did you know the speeds had changed and by how much they had changed?

3. Why can you assume the wave frequency is constant as the waves proceed across the water in your wave tank?

4. When water waves enter shallow water in a direction such that the waves are parallel to the boundary, does the direction of the waves change?

5. When water waves enter shallow water from deep water in such a direction that the waves form an angle greater than 0° with the boundary, does their direction change? If so, in what way does it change? Is the angle of refraction greater than, equal to, or less than the angle of incidence?

6. When water waves leave shallow water and return to deep water, how does their direction change? For the water waves leaving the shallow water, how does the angle of refraction compare with the angle of incidence for the water waves that were coming into the shallow water in the first place?

Station 5: Diffraction of Water Waves

1. Set up a barrier (wall) near the middle of your wave tank using a block of paraffin wax or similar object. See Figure 8.2.13(a). Use the tip of your finger to generate waves on one side of the wall. Observe what happens to the waves as they spread past the edge of the barrier. Sketch what you observe. If these were sound waves, and you were standing at O, would you hear the sound?

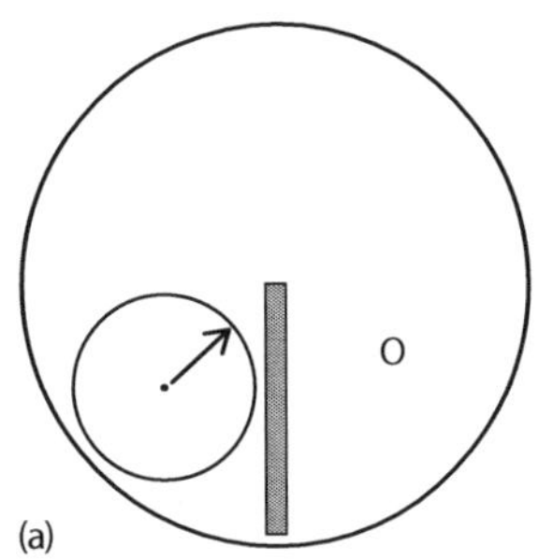

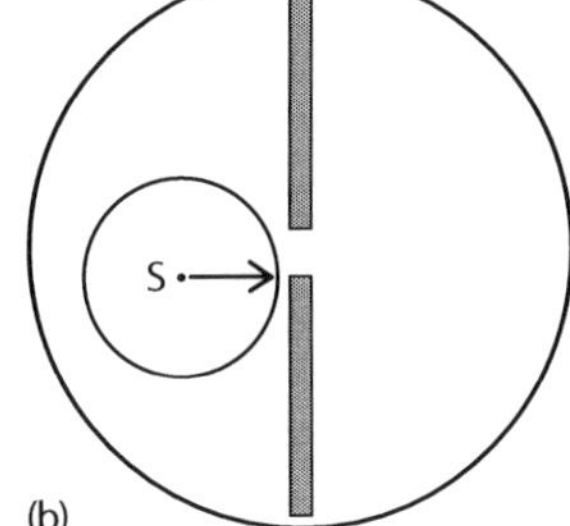

Figure 8.2.13 *Station 5*

2. Set up the arrangement in Figure 8.2.13(b) to simulate a doorway. Generate waves with the tip of your finger at S, and observe the waves as they pass through and beyond the door.
   Sketch what you observe. If these were sound waves, could you hear the sound in the adjacent room?

3. Change the width of the "doorway." Does this affect the amount of spreading of the waves as they pass through?

4. Remove the barriers from the tank and place a small object near the centre of the tank. Its shape is unimportant. A width of 2–3 cm would be appropriate. Generate waves on one side of the obstacle using the tip of your finger. Let the waves pass by the object. Sketch what you observe. Do they "cast a shadow" as they pass it, or do they seem to carry on unaffected by the obstacle? What happens if you use an obstacle that is (a) bigger? (b) smaller?

5. Set up your straight-wave generator and adjust the frequency so that the waves it produces have a wavelength of approximately 2 cm as seen on the screen on your table. By experimenting with different opening sizes and wavelengths, find out what the effect is of changing these two variables one at a time. Prepare a series of careful sketches showing how the waveforms look following diffraction.

6. Set up a small obstacle in the path of the straight waves. Experiment to see the effects of changing (a) wavelengths and (b) obstacle size. Sketch what you observe.

Questions

1. Is diffraction more noticeable with short wavelengths or long wavelengths?

2. Is diffraction more noticeable with small openings or large openings?

3. When straight waves pass through a small opening, what shape do the diffracted waves have? Sketch a diagram.

4. When straight waves pass by a small obstacle, what happens to the straight waves if the obstacle is (a) very small compared with the wavelength of the waves? (b) about the same size as the wavelength? (c) very large compared with the wavelength?

5. Describe at least three examples of situations you encounter daily that involve diffraction of waves of one sort or another. These might involve water waves, sound, or light.

Station 6: Interference

A. Interference in a Stretched Spring

1. To observe interference of waves in a Slinky, hold one end of the Slinky yourself and have your partner hold the other end of the stretched spring. Simultaneously, generate transverse disturbances in the same direction and with the same amplitude, as in Figure 8.2.14(a). Observe what happens when the two pulses pass through each other near the centre of the Slinky.

2. Repeat step 1, but this time, generate simultaneous disturbances that have the same magnitude but opposite amplitudes, as in Figure 8.2.14(b).

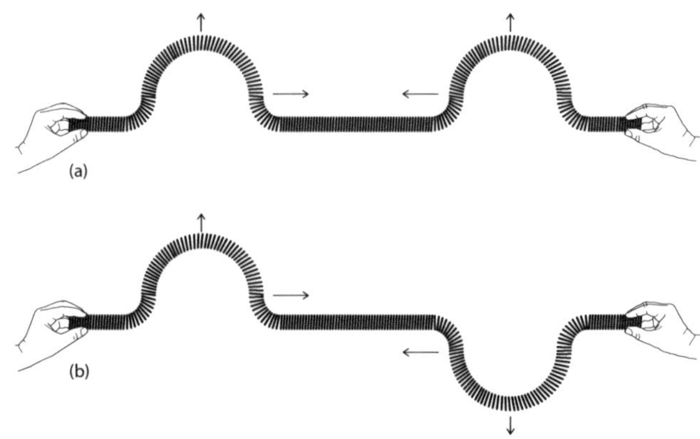

Figure 8.2.14 *Station 6A*

Questions

1. When the two pulses pass through each other such that a crest passes through a crest, as would happen in Figure 8.2.14(a), what happens to the amplitude of the combined waves?

2. When a crest arrives at the same point as a trough, as would happen in Figure 8.2.14(b), what happens to the amplitude of the combined waves?

B. Interference in Water Waves

1. Set up the arrangement in Figure 8.2.15. The generator generates straight waves, but as they pass through the twin slits, each slit causes diffraction and the two sets of circular waves are produced at the slits. Observe how the two sets of circular waves interfere with each other.

2. Each source of circular waves sends out successive crests and troughs, and the two sets of waves interfere with one another. Describe what you see on the screen where the troughs from one source of waves arrive simultaneously with the crests from the other source. What do you see in the areas where crests and troughs from one source arrive simultaneously with crests and troughs from the other source?

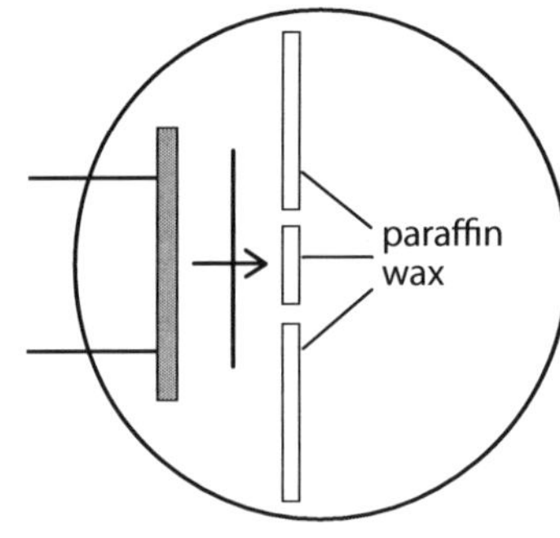

Figure 8.2.15 *Station 6B*

3. Replace the two-slit barrier with a twin point-source generator. Set up the twin point-source generator so that both vibrating point sources are in phase. This means that they both vibrate up and down in synchronization. If one point source vibrated upward while the other vibrated downward, they would be out of phase. This arrangement usually gives much better waves than the double slit arrangement.

Questions

1. When crests from one wave source arrive simultaneously with troughs from another wave source, what will you see on the screen at that point? Why?

2. When crests arrive with crests and troughs with troughs from two different wave sources, what will you see at that spot on the screen? Why?

3. Regions of zero disturbances on the screen appear as nearly straight lines called nodal lines. If a point on such a nodal line was a distance of $n\lambda$ from one point source of waves, where λ is the wavelength and n is an integer, how far would the same point be from the other point source? Is there more than one answer to this question?

4. Regions of maximum disturbance on the screen, sometimes called maxima, occur when the distance from one source is, for example, $m\lambda$, where m is an integer and λ is the wavelength. What is the distance to the other source? Is there more than one possible answer? Explain.

8.2 Review Questions

Complete these diagrams to show what happens to waves after they encounter the barrier or other obstacle. Name the phenomenon that occurs in each situation.

1.

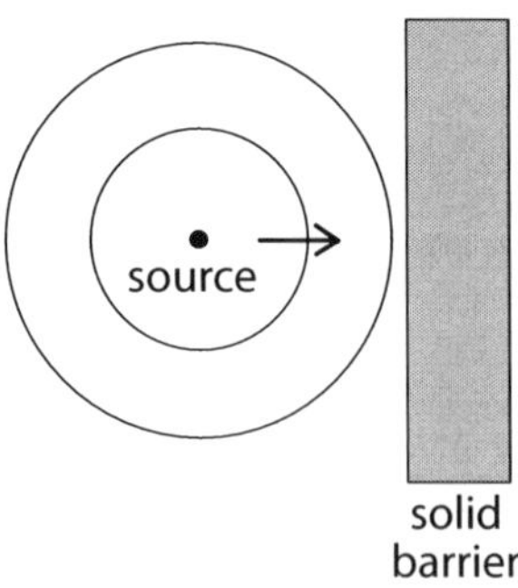

____
phenomenon

2.

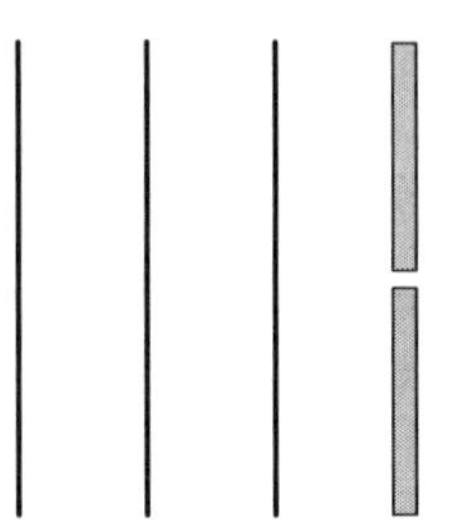

____
phenomenon

3. If you look at streetlights through a fine mesh curtain, you will see a "starburst" effect. What phenomenon is involved in this situation?

____
phenomenon

4. Use the following diagram to answer the questions below.

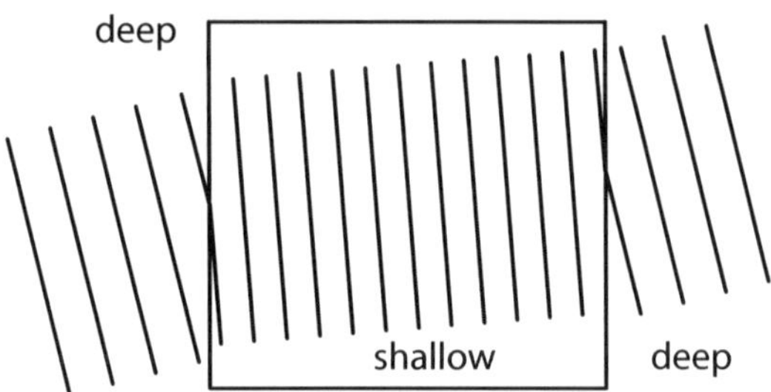

(a) The diagram shows water waves in a wave tank moving from deep water into shallow water and then back into deep water. What property of waves does this model illustrate?

(b) According to the diagram, what can you conclude happens to the waves when they enter the shallow water?

5. For the following situations, is there a point where the amplitude will be zero everywhere? If so, mark that point.

(a)

(b)

(c)

(d)

(e)

(f)

Chapter 8 Conceptual Review Questions

1. How do sound vibrations of atoms differ from thermal motion?

2. Six members of a synchronized swim team wear earplugs to protect themselves against water pressure at depths, but they can still hear the music and perform the combinations in the water perfectly. One day, they were asked to leave the pool so the dive team could practice a few dives, and they tried to practice on a mat, but seemed to have a lot more difficulty. Why might this be?

3. It is more difficult to obtain a high-resolution ultrasound image in the abdominal region of someone who is overweight than for someone who has a slight build. Explain why this statement is accurate.

Chapter 8 Review Questions

1. What is the difference between a pulse and periodic waves?

2. Explain, with the help of a sketch, what each of these terms means with respect to waves:
   (a) crest

   (b) trough

   (c) wavelength

   (d) frequency

   (e) amplitude

3. What is a hertz?

4. How are frequency and period related?

5. A dog wags its tail 50 times in 20 s. What are (a) the frequency and (b) the period of vibration of the tail?

6. What is the difference between a transverse wave and a longitudinal wave?

7. For any kind of wave motion, how are wave speed, wavelength, and frequency related to one another?

8. Alternating current in power lines produces electromagnetic waves of frequency 60 Hz that travel outward at the speed of light, which is 3.0×10^8 m/s. What is the wavelength of these waves?

9. If the speed of sound is 330 m/s, what wavelength does a sound of frequency 512 Hz have?

10. When waves slow down on entering a new medium, what happens to
   (a) their wavelength?

   (b) their frequency?

   (c) their direction?

   (d) Under what conditions will the direction *not* change?

11. (a) What is constructive interference?

   (b) What is destructive interference?

12. In a wave tank, what causes a nodal line? A maximum?

13. The following diagram shows two parabolic reflectors. A small source of infrared heat is placed at the focus of one of the mirrors. Soon after, a match at the focus of the other reflector lights on fire. Draw a diagram showing how the wave model explains this.

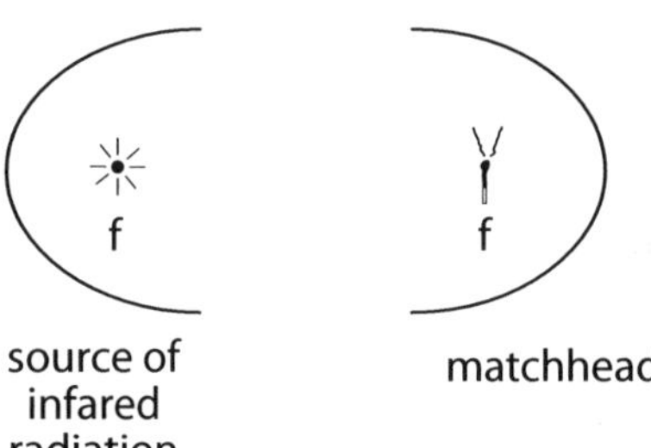

14. The sonar on a navy submarine produces ultrasonic waves at a frequency of 2.2 MHz and a wavelength of 5.10×10^{-4} m. If a sonar technician sends one wave pulse from underneath the submarine toward the bottom of the ocean floor and it takes 8.0 s to return, how deep is the ocean at this point?

9 Sound

In this chapter the focus will be on the Big Idea:

Mechanical waves transfer energy but not matter.

The content learning standards will include:

- Characteristics of sound
- Resonance and frequency of sound

By the end of this chapter, you should know the meaning of these **key terms**:

- beats
- compression
- decibel
- Doppler Effect
- frequency
- hertz
- infrasonic
- Intensity
- longitudinal
- oscilloscope
- overtones
- pitch
- rarefaction
- sonic boom
- sound barrier
- standing wave
- transverse
- ultrasonic

By the end of the chapter, you should be able to use and know when to use the following formula:

$v = 332\text{ m/s} + [0.6\text{ m/s }^{\circ}\text{C}^{-1}]\,T$

$$\text{Intensity} = \frac{\text{Energy}}{s \cdot m^2} = \frac{\text{Power}}{m^2}$$

$f_B = f_1 - f_2$

In this chapter you will be studying the properites of sound waves. An oscilloscope like the one above can measure a variety of signals, including sound waves. The screen shows the waveform for a given frequency.

9.1 Sound Properties

Warm Up

Take about 1 metre of string and attach it to the bottom of a styrofoam cup. Repeat with a second string and cup. Then attach the free ends of both strings to a metal coat hanger. Placing the cups over your ears, have a classmate gently strike the coat hanger with a pencil. Describe what do you hear?

____

____

____

Sound Waves

When a guitar string vibrates, it collides with air molecules around it. See Figure 9.1.1. Molecules near the string are alternately **compressed** together, and then **rarefied** (spread out). Regions of compression spread through the air, followed by regions of rarefied air. Compressions arrive at your ear with the same frequency as the frequency of vibration of the guitar string.

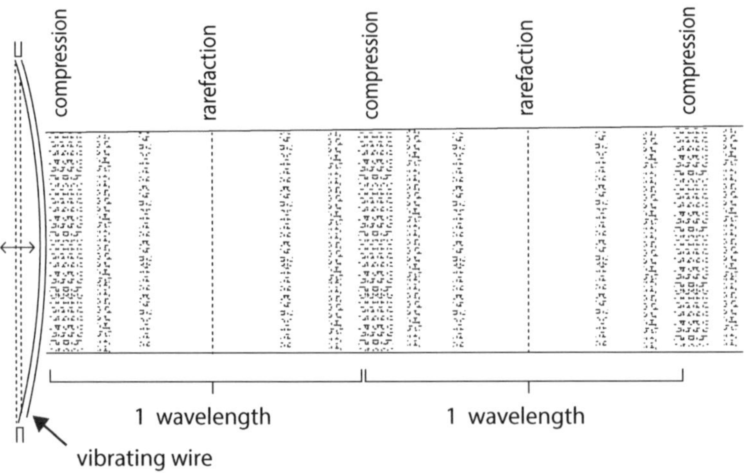

Figure 9.1.1 *A representation of the air molecules in the region around a vibrating guitar string*

Figure 9.1.1 shows a simplified model of what might be seen if one could 'see' the air molecules in the region around a vibrating guitar string. Of course, this is a two-dimensional picture, and sound travels in all directions away from the vibrating source.

Vibrations cause sound. However, not all vibrations produce sounds! The human ear cannot hear all frequencies. The range of frequencies that a person can hear, called the audible frequency range, is, approximately, from 20 Hz up to 20 000 Hz (or 20 kHz). One hertz is the same as one vibration per second.

This is the range of hearing for a healthy young person with good hearing. Sounds with frequencies below 20 Hz are called as infrasonic sounds, and sounds with frequencies above 20 000 Hz are ultrasonic sounds.

There are many ways that sound vibrations can be produced. Your vocal chords vibrate to produce the sound of your voice. Vibrating wires (strings) produce the sounds of guitars, pianos, harps and violins. Vibrating reeds make the sound in a saxophone, while vibrating columns of air make the sounds of instruments such as the organ and the flute.

The Speed of Sound

At a temperature of 20 °C, which is normal room temperature, sound will travel about 340 m/s in air, which is the same as 1220 km/h. The speed limit for vehicles on a modern highway might be 100 km/h, so the speed of sound in air is 12 times this highway speed limit!

Although the usual medium for sound is the air around us, air is not a good conductor of sound. Many materials conduct sound much better than air. The best sound conductors are made of elastic materials such as steel, glass or aluminum. Inelastic materials do not transmit sound energy as effectively.

The speed of sound in air depends on the temperature of the air and on atmospheric pressure. For air at sea level air pressure, the speed of sound at 0 °C is 332 m/s. The speed increases by about 0.6 m/s for every Celsius degree above 0 °C.

$$v = 332 \text{ m/s} + [0.6 \text{ m/s } ^{\circ}\text{C}^{-1}]\, T$$

For example, the speed of sound at 40 °C (a very hot day!) would be:

$$v = 332 \text{ m/s} + [(0.6 \text{ m/s } ^{\circ}\text{C}^{-1})(40\ ^{\circ}\text{C})]$$
$$v = 332 \text{ m/s} + 24 \text{ m/s}$$
$$v = 356 \text{ m/s.}$$

Table 9.1.1 *Speed of Sound in Various Materials*

Medium	Speed (m/s)	Temperature (C)
aluminum	5000	25
copper	3560	20
iron (steel)	5200	25
cork	500	
rubber	54	0
maple wood	4110	
granite rock	6000	
water	1500	25
air*	332	0
air	344	20
hydrogen	1270	0
carbon dioxide	258	0

** For many questions in this book the speed of sound is assumed to be 330 m/s. This is done to make calculations easier.*

Quick Check

1. What is speed of sound in a vacuum?

2. What frequencies are infrasonic and ultrasonic?

3. What is the speed of sound in air with a temperature of 35 °C?

Properties of Sound-Pitch

The pitch of a sound is our subjective impression of the frequency of the sound. The very low pitch of the piano note from the far left of the keyboard has a frequency of 27.5 Hz, while the very high pitch from the far right of the keyboard has a frequency of over 4 000 Hz!

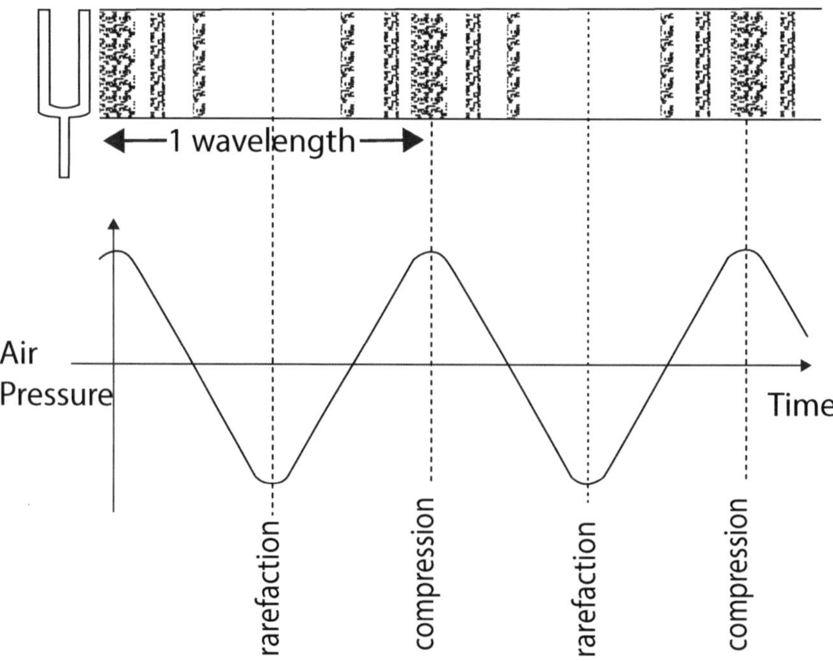

Figure 9.1.2 *Compression is a region of low press air pressure that registers as a peak in the pressure -time graph. A rarefaction appears as a dip on the graph.*

It is an interesting exercise to observe the waveforms of sounds of different pitches on the screen of an **oscilloscope**. Sound waves are **longitudinal** waves. (The air molecules vibrate to-and-fro in the direction of travel of the sound.) But the oscilloscope displays sound waves as if they were **transverse** waves. (In transverse waves, the vibration is in a direction perpendicular to the direction of travel of the wave. Water waves are a good example of transverse waves.)

What you see on the oscilloscope screen is actually a graph of air pressure vs time. A **compression** represents a region of unusually high air pressure, whereas a **rarefaction** is a region of low air pressure. Figure 9.1.2 shows that a compression will register as a 'peak' in the pressure-time graph that you see on the oscilloscope screen. A rarefaction appears as a 'dip' in the graph.

Imagine you are listening to a high-pitched tone of frequency 3 000 Hz. This means that there are 3 000 compressions and 3 000 rarefactions arriving at your ear every second. If you were looking at this sound on the oscilloscope screen, you would see peaks for the compressions, and dips for the rarefactions. On the horizontal time scale, the peaks would be spaced 1/3 000 s apart, or 0.00033 s.

Properties of Sound-Loudness

The frequency of sound vibrations is what determines the pitch of a sound. On the oscilloscope screen, the number of waves you see on the screen in a unit of time provides an indicator of the frequency, and therefore the pitch.

If you have used an oscilloscope to display sound waves you mauy have noticed that if the sound was louder, the height of the waves was greater. In fact, the **amplitude** is a measure of the loudness of a sound. The greater the wave amplitude is, the louder the sound will be.

The loudness of a sound depends on its intensity, a variable that can be measured. The **intensity** of a sound is the amount of sound energy arriving per second on a square metre of area.

$$\text{Intensity} = \frac{\text{Energy}}{s \cdot m^2} = \frac{\text{Power}}{m^2}$$

Intensity is measured in watts per square metre (W/m^2). A sound at the threshold of your hearing has an intensity of one millionth of one millionth of a watt per square metre, or 10^{-12} W/m^2!

A quiet conversation between two people involves an intensity of sound of the order of 10^{-6} W/m^2. The ratio of these two intensities is $10^{-6}/10^{-12} = 10^6$. In other words, the intensity of sound in a normal conversation is one million times the intensity of sound at the threshold of your hearing!

The ratio of a sound intensity to the intensity of sound at the threshold of hearing is often used to compare loudnesses. If a sound is 106 times as intense as sound at the threshold, we say its intensity is 6 bels.

The **bel** is named after Alexander Graham Bell (1847-1922), Canadian inventor of the telephone. Since the bel is a large unit, the **decibel** (dB) is used instead, and the intensity of normal conversation is expressed as 60 decibels.

The intensity of sound at a music concert might easily be 1 W/m^2. What is this intensity in decibels? The ratio of this intensity to the intensity at your threshold of hearing would be

$$\frac{1}{10^{-12}}=\frac{10^{0}}{10^{-12}}=10^{12}$$

Since the power of ten in the ratio is 12, the intensity of sound is 12 bels, which is the same as 120 decibels! This is a very loud sound!

Table 9.1.2 lists the intensities of various sounds both in W/m^2 and in decibels.

Table 9.1.2 *Speed of Sound in Various Materials*

Source	Intensity (W/m^2)	Intensity (dB)
Jet taking off	10^{2}	140
Pain threshold	10^{1}	130
Loud band	10^{0}	120
Pneumatic chisel	10^{-1}	110
Metalwork shop	10^{-2}	100
Heavy traffic	10^{-3}	90
Vacuum cleaner	10^{-4}	80
Loud conversation	10^{-5}	70
Normal conversation	10^{-6}	60
Office noise	10^{-7}	50
Library	10^{-8}	40
Quiet country scene	10^{-9}	30
Whisper	10^{-10}	20
Rustling leaf	10^{-11}	10
Threshold of hearing	10^{-12}	0

Sound Quality

Even if two different musical instruments play tones of equal pitch, you can tell one instrument from another. This is because each instrument has a characteristic **timbre** or **quality**. While both instruments produce the same fundamental frequency, the overtones they produce are different.

Overtones are frequencies that are twice, three times or even more times the fundamental frequency. The quality of a sound an instrument produces depends on the number of overtones and their relative loudness.

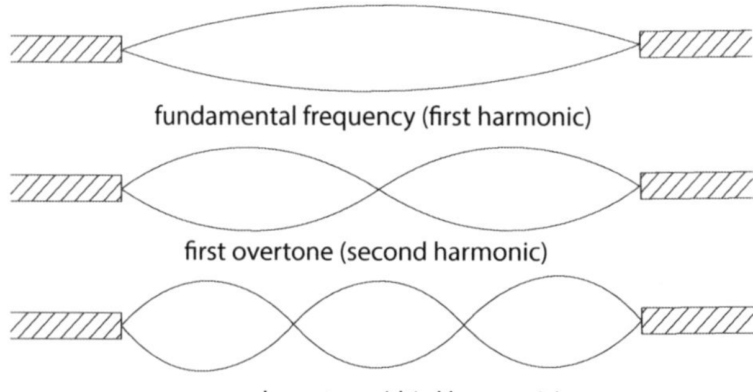

Figure 9.1.3 *Some vibration modes for a stringed musical instrument.*

Figure 9.1.3 shows some of the vibration modes for a stringed musical instrument. The strings can be made to vibrate in several ways. A bow made of long strands of tightly stretched horsehair is used to make a violin or cello string vibrate. Fingers or picks make guitar or harp strings vibrate, while felt mallets initiate the vibrations in piano strings.

The fundamental frequency of a string depends on its thickness, its length and the tension on the string. A skilled musician can control which overtones (harmonics) the strings of his or her instrument produces.

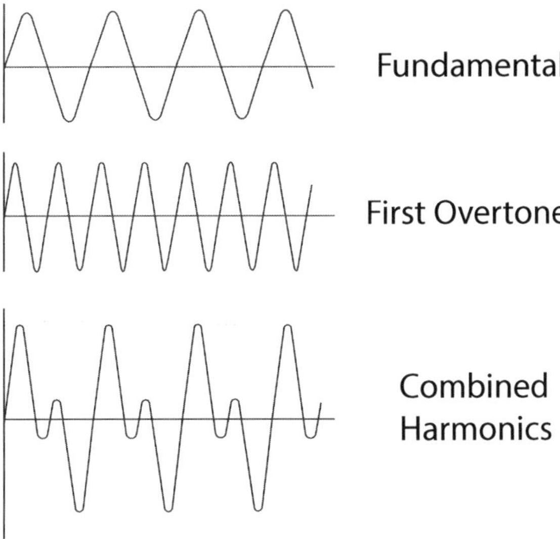

Figure 9.1.4 *Sound waves from a musical instrument*

Figure 9.1.4 shows the sound waves emitted by an instrument if the fundamental frequency and the first overtone (second harmonic) are produced (a) alone and (b) simultaneously. Notice that the combined frequency has a 'regularity' to it. The sound you hear when the two harmonics are produced simultaneously is richer and more interesting than either of the pure tones. Waveforms produced by different musical instruments playing the same note have different shapes because of the differing numbers and intensities of overtones, but the fundamental frequency will be the same for each one.

Investigation 9.1.1– Investigating Sounds Waves

Purpose

To examine wave patterns due to sounds of different pitch and from different musical instruments using an oscilloscope.

Procedure

Part 1: Seeing Sound Waves

1. Your teacher will have an oscilloscope set up to display sound waves. In the simplest set-up, a piezoelectric 'tweeter' speaker is used as a microphone, which is connected to the input jacks of the oscilloscope. (Improved results can be obtained using an amplifier in the set-up.)
2. Start by listening to sounds from sources of known frequency. Try tuning forks with frequencies such as 256 Hz, 512 Hz, and whatever other frequencies are available. Try speaking, whistling or singing at different frequencies. Sketch a typical waveform as seen on the screen for (a) low-pitched sound and (b) high-pitched sound.
3. Invite musicians to class to play notes of different pitch into the microphone, or play a recording of some complex music. Rarely will you see simple waveforms like those you obtained from a tuning fork, but the waveforms will be regularly repeated if the sounds are truly musical

Part 2: Visualizing Sound Quality

1. Have music students play a given note using different instruments (a clarinet, guitar, violin, or whatever is available). Sketch or take a picture of the waveforms obtained from each instrument.
2. Make some 'white noise', and examine its wave pattern on the screen. You might try rubbing some sandpaper on wood, near the microphone.

Concluding Questions

1. How does the waveform of a low-pitched sound differ from that of a high-pitched sound?
2. How does the waveform of a musical sound differ from the waveform of a noisy sound?

9.1 Review Questions

1. Are sound waves transverse or longitudinal?

2. A dynamite explosion occurs at one end of a ridge of granite rock that is 3.0 km long. If you are at the other end of the ridge, how long will it take

   (a) before you see the explosion?

   (b) before you hear the sound travelling through the rock?

   (c) before you hear the sound coming through the air?

3. Two rocks are banged together under water at the far side of a small lake 750 m away. If you are swimming in the water, how long will it take the sound to reach you? How much longer will it be before the sound reaches you through the air?

4. If the sound of thunder arrives at your ear 0.50 s after the flash of lightning arrives at your eyes, how far away from you did the lightning strike occur?

9.2 Sound Phenomena

Warm Up

Fill a wine glass with water. Dip your finger in the water and run your wet finger around the edge of the glass until the glass starts to emit a high-pitched sound. While you are doing this, watch the surface of the water near where your finger is making the glass vibrate. Try the same activity with varying depths of water.

1. What effect does adding water to the glass have on the pitch of the sound you hear?

   ____

2. Will the glass vibrate when it is empty? Why or why not?

   ____

   ____

Forced Vibrations

If you strike a tuning fork with a rubber hammer and just hold it in your hand, the sound from the fork will be quite faint and difficult to hear, even if you are a short distance away. Hold the base of the tuning fork on a tabletop and the sound will be much louder. The top of the table is now forced to vibrate in tune with the fork. The tabletop is acting as a sounding board.

Various musical instruments use sounding boards. Can you think of at least four stringed instruments that use sounding boards to amplify their sound? When a sounding board is used to amplify a sound (make it louder), the phenomenon is called **forced vibrations**.

Natural Frequency and Resonance

Any object, if it is reasonably elastic and can vibrate, has its own special natural frequency (or frequencies). Tuning forks, bells, stretched strings, and air columns in wind instruments all have natural frequencies. Even a child's swing has a natural frequency. A short tuning fork has a higher natural frequency than a long one. A tightly stretched violin string has a higher natural frequency than a loose one. A short pendulum has a higher natural frequency than a long pendulum.

Imagine you have a rather large friend sitting on a park swing. You can get even a massive person swinging with large amplitude if you time your pushes on the swing just right. If the frequency of your pushes, no matter how weak they are, is the same as the natural frequency of the swing (which is just a special pendulum), eventually the amplitude of the swing will become quite large. Whenever the frequency of the forced vibrations (in this case your pushing frequency) matches the natural frequency of an object, a large increase in amplitude will result.

A pair of identical (matched frequency) tuning forks can be used to illustrate resonance. Fork A (Figure 9.2.5) is struck and made to vibrate at its own natural frequency (typically 256 Hz). This fork produces quite a loud sound due to: (a) its sounding board and (b) its air column, both of which resonate with the fork itself. Vibrations of the fork and air column send sound waves toward fork B. Fork B begins to vibrate at the same frequency as A, due to resonance. Each passing sound wave from A gives B a nudge, eventually making it vibrate with high amplitude, just like the child on a swing being made to vibrate by a series of successive nudges from a friend.

Beats

If two sources of sound are made to produce sounds of slightly different frequencies simultaneously, you will hear **beats**. You can produce beats using the two identical mounted tuning forks. Attach a wad of Plasticine® to one tine of one of the forks. Strike both tuning forks with a rubber hammer. The extra mass will change the natural frequency of one of the forks just slightly, and you should hear beats. Try varying the amount of Plasticine® by taking a pinch off each time you strike the two forks. What happens to the **beat frequency**, as the forks become closer and closer to being the same frequency? How could a piano tuner use a tuning fork to tune a piano?

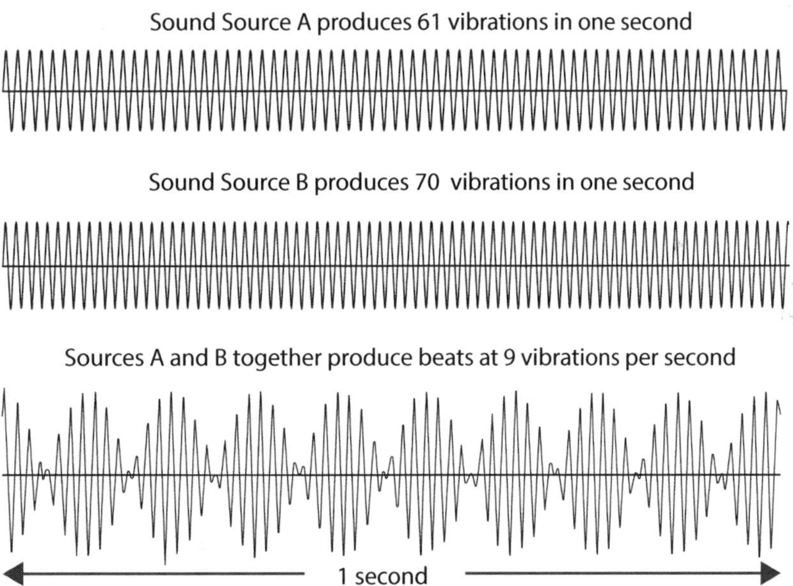

Figure 9.2.1 shows how the amplitudes of two sets of sound waves, from sources of frequencies 61 Hz and 70 Hz, combine when they pass a point at the same time. To your ear, the combined sound would be a throbbing sensation due to the regular rise and fall of the combined intensities of the sources. Notice that the beat frequency is 9 Hz, which is the arithmetic difference between the two individual source frequencies. You can calculate the beat frequency f_B by finding the difference between the two frequencies being heard.

$$f_B = f_1 - f_2$$

Standing Waves

Tie one end of a long, stretched spring to a wall, or have a partner hold it tightly so that his/her end cannot move. (See Figure 9.2.2.) Shake your end of the spring so that a pulse travels down the length of the spring, and reflects back to you. Notice that upon reflection from the fixed end, the wave is inverted

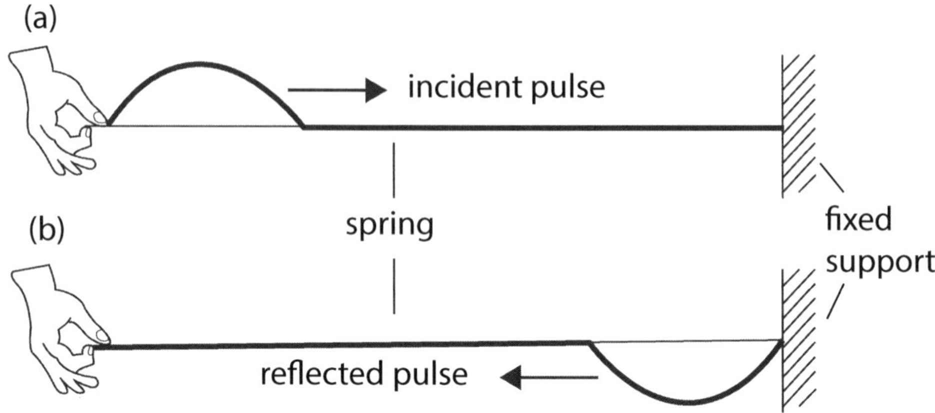

Figure 9.2.2 *Creating a standing wave with a stretched spring attached to a wall.*

If you shake the spring with just the right frequency, the reflected waves will interfere with the incident waves, and you will observe a standing wave. Figure 9.1.3 the overtones show possible standing wave patterns. Notice that parts of the wave are stationary. These parts are called nodes. At the nodes, the reflected waves are interfering destructively with the incident waves, thus producing a point of zero disturbance. The points on the standing wave where there is maximum amplitude result from constructive interference between the incident waves and reflected waves. These points of maximum disturbance are called antinodes. Notice that the distance between successive nodes, or between successive antinodes, is equal to one-half the wavelength of the waves in the spring.

You cannot obtain standing waves at all frequencies. If you can find out the lowest frequency at which you can obtain a standing wave (the fundamental frequency for the spring), you will be able to create other standing wave patterns using twice the fundamental frequency, three times the fundamental frequency, etc.

Standing waves occur in all musical instruments. In string musical instruments, the standing waves (Figure 9.1.3) are transverse waves. In wind instruments, the standing waves are longitudinal waves. When you hold a vibrating tuning fork over a glass cylinder full of air, you may create standing waves in the air column

The Doppler Effect

When a fast car or motorbike approaches you, the pitch of its sound rises. As the vehicle goes by, the pitch lowers. The effect is quite noticeable if you watch a high-speed automobile race on television. What causes this change in pitch? Austrian physicist C. J. Doppler (1803–1853) was the first to explain the effect in terms of waves, and therefore the effect is called the **Doppler effect**.

Figure 9.2.3 illustrates sound waves coming from a moving source. The vehicle is moving to the left. Sound waves coming from the vehicle are bunched in front of the vehicle, which tends to catch up with its own sound. (This diagram exaggerates the effect.) The wave fronts or compressions are closer together in front of the vehicle and farther apart behind the vehicle.

The observer at A hears a higher pitch than normal, since more compressions and rarefactions pass his ear per second than pass the observer at B. Observer B hears the normal pitch of the vehicle's sound. Behind the vehicle, compressions are spaced out, since the vehicle is travelling away from the sound it sends in that direction. The observer at C hears a lower pitch than normal. Fewer compressions and rarefactions pass his ear per second than if he was at A or B. As the vehicle passes observer A, he will hear the pitch go from high to normal to low in a very short time interval. He will hear the Doppler effect.

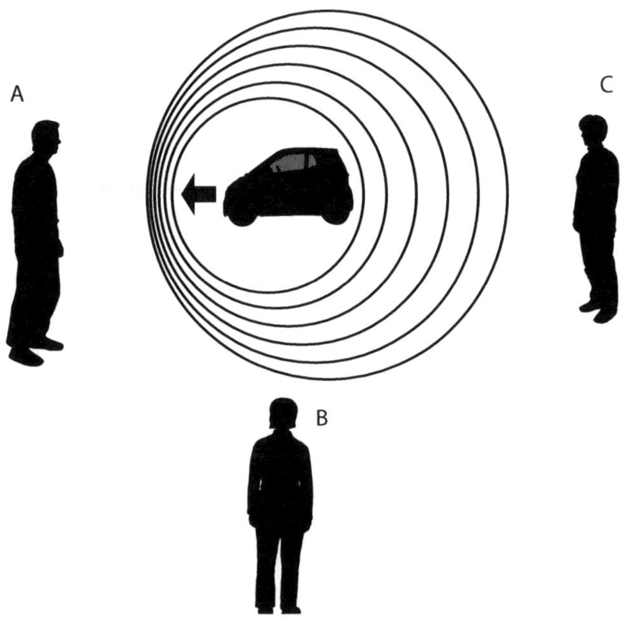

Figure 9.2.3 *The wave fronts are closer together at the front of the moving vehicle as it moves forward and more spread out behind.*

The Sound Barrier

An extreme case of the Doppler effect occurs when an aircraft or bullet travels at the same speed as the sound it is producing. At the leading edges of the aircraft, the compressions it creates tend to bunch up and superimpose on each other (Figure 9.2.4(a)). This creates a wall or barrier of compressed air called the **sound barrier**. Great thrust is needed from the plane's engines to enable the plane to penetrate the sound barrier. Once through the barrier, the plane experiences much less resistance to its movement through the air. The plane, once through the sound barrier, is then supersonic. Its speed is now greater than Mach 1!

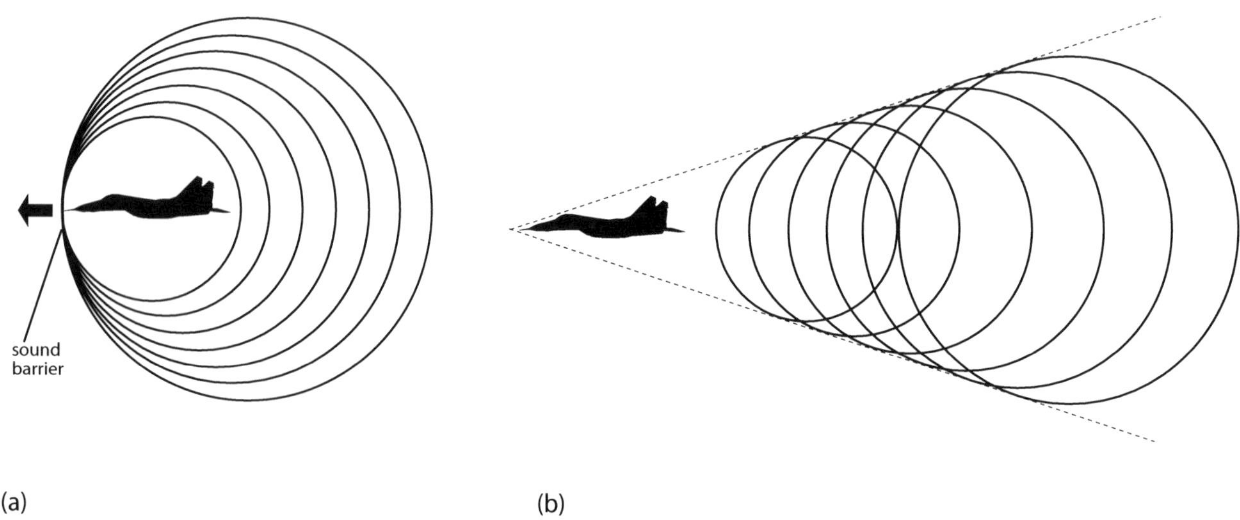

Figure 9.2.4 (**a**) *The airplane travelling at the speed of sound creates a wall of compressed called the sound barrier;* (**b**) *An airplane travelling faster than the speed of sound creates a shock wave that you hear as a sonic boom.*

Shock Waves and the Sonic Boom

If a plane travels *faster* than sound, it gets ahead of the compressions and rarefactions it produces. In two dimensions (Figure 9.2.4(b)), overlapping circular waves form a V-shaped bow wave, somewhat like what you see from the air looking down at a speedboat travelling through still water. In three dimensions, there is a cone of compressed air trailing the aircraft. This cone is called a shock wave. When the shock wave passes you, you hear a loud, sharp crack called the **sonic boom.** Aircraft are not the only producers of sonic booms. Cracking whips and rifle bullets causes miniature sonic booms!

Investigation 9.2.1– Exploring Resonance

Purpose

To observe several examples of a phenomenon called resonance.

Procedure

In this Investigation your teacher will have set up a series of stations for you to explore the properties of resonance.

Station 1: Tuning Forks

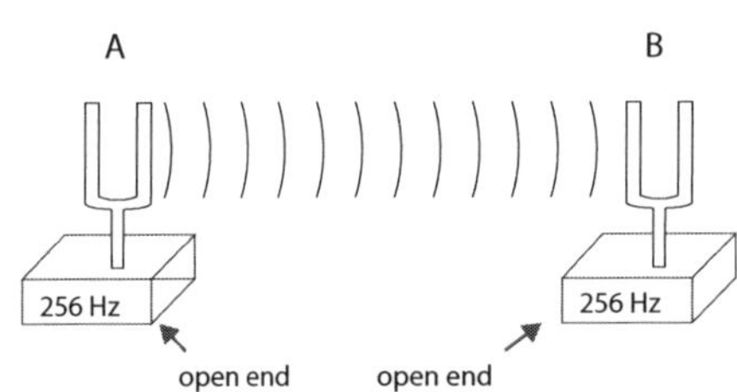

1. Using the equipment at this station, set up the materials as illustrated in Figure 9.2.5.
2. Strike fork A with a rubber hammer.
3. Stop fork A with your hand. Listen to fork B.
4. Over how great a distance can you make fork B resonate with fork A?

Station 2: Pendulums

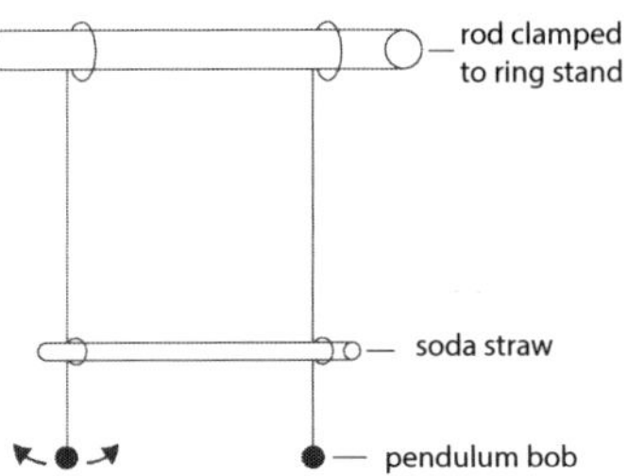

1. Set up a pair of identical pendulums, about 75 cm long, side by side and 25 cm apart. See Figure 9.2.6. Loop each string around a soda straw or thin wooden rod joining the two pendulums.
2. Set one of the pendulums vibrating gently, then watch carefully for an interesting example of resonance!
3. Try varying the position of the soda straw. Describe what you observe.

Station 3: Air Columns

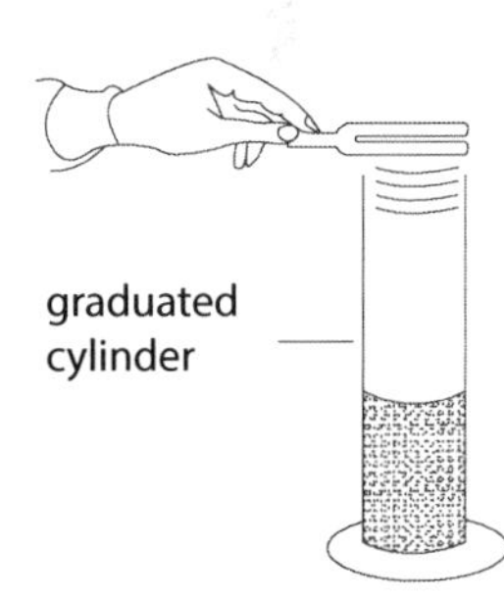

1. Use a rubber hammer to excite a tuning fork of known frequency. Hold the fork about 2 cm above a tall graduated cylinder (500 mL or larger) and direct the sound down into the graduate. Add water to the cylinder, thus changing the length of the air column, until the air column resonates at the frequency of the tuning fork. Record the tuning fork frequency and the length of the air column. Keep adding water to the graduate and find any other lengths of air column that produce resonance. Record these lengths. Is there any pattern to the lengths?

Concluding Questions

1. What conditions are needed for resonance to occur?
2. Could a musical note from one musical instrument cause resonance in a different musical instrument? (Ask your music teacher or a musician if you are in doubt.)
3. Tuning your radio is actually an example of resonance. What kind of vibrations is involved when your radio is resonating?
4. Why does a group of soldiers 'break step' when the soldiers walk across a rope suspension bridge?.
5. Investigate a method to determine the speed of sound using the apparatus from Station 3.

9.2 Review Questions

1. One tuning fork has a frequency of 440 Hz, while another has a frequency of 435 Hz. What will the frequency of the beats be?

2. One tuning fork is known to be accurate at 256 Hz. When it is struck at the same time as another fork, beats are heard every 0.20 s. What might the frequency of the second fork be?

3. For which of the following waves can the Doppler effect occur?

   ______ sound

   ______ light

   ______ water

4.. Does the Doppler effect occur if you are moving and the object making the noise is stationary? Explain your answer.

5. What property of sound determines its pitch?

6. Why does a note played by a violin sound different than the same note played by a cello?

7. How does noise differ from musical sound?

8.. A top-secret aircraft travels at a speed of Mach 2.8. How fast is this in km/h?

9. Explain what these terms mean:
   (a) forced vibrations;

   (b) natural frequency; and

   (c) resonance

Chapter 9 Conceptual Review Questions

1. How might two astronauts communicate with each other on the moon where there is no atmosphere? Explain.

2. In a space movie, an attacking space vehicle fires a weapon and hits an enemy craft. A loud explosion is heard. What is wrong with this scene?

3. Imagine a parade where there is only one band at the head of the parade, followed by soldiers stretching a distance of over 300 m along the road. Would the last row of soldiers be in step with the front row? Discuss.

4. If you hold a tuning fork near your ear while it is vibrating, and then rotate the fork slowly, what will its sound be like? Make a prediction, and then try it! What phenomenon is involved here?

5. Is the Doppler shift real or just a sensory illusion?

6. A drum in the school music room starts to vibrate on its own when a certain note is played on another instrument nearby. What phenomenon is involved here?

7. When you hear a sonic boom, you often cannot see the plane that made it. Why is that?

Chapter 9 Review Questions

1. A lightning strike occurs 1.0 km away from you. How many seconds will it be before you hear the sound of the thunder?

2. The speeds of high performance aircraft are often expressed as multiples of the speed of sound. If an aircraft travels at the speed of sound, its speed is said to have a Mach number of 1.

   (a) How fast is a jet interceptor travelling, in km/h, if its speed is Mach 2.2?

   (b) What is the Mach number of a space shuttle travelling 7.5 km/s?

3. What is the difference between a sonic boom and the sound barrier?

4. In 5.0 s, how far would sound travel through
   (a) air?

   (b) a steel railway track?

   (c) water?

   (d) granite?

10. Sound waves can be displayed on an oscilloscope screen as transverse waves. What do the transverse waves on the screen really measure?

6. What can you conclude about the speed of an airplane overhead if you hear a sonic boom?

7. Sketch a sound wave, as seen on the oscilloscope screen, to represent a sound of frequency f. Now sketch what the sound wave will look like
(a) if you make the same sound but louder, then

(b) if you double the frequency of the sound.

8. Calculate the ratio of the intensity of sound from a loud rock band to the intensity of sound from a whisper. See Table 9.1.2, Sound Intensities of Common Sources.

9. One organ pipe produces a sound of frequency 512 Hz. Another simultaneously produces sound of frequency 510 Hz. What beat frequency will be produced?

10. A piano tuner hears beats of frequency 0.50 Hz when he simultaneously strikes a tuning fork of frequency 264 Hz and a piano key. What is the frequency of the sound created by striking that key?

11. On a calm, quiet day, you watch a golfer swing a golf club on a tee 520 m away. There is a delay of 1.55 s before you hear the sound of the club hitting the ball. What is the speed of sound according to this data?

Answer Key

For the most current version of the answer key, scan the appropriate QR code with your mobile device. Or go to edvantagescience.com, login and select BC Science Physics 11. If you cannot login, please see your teacher for the enrollment code.

Chapter 1

Chapter 2

Chapter 3

Chapter 4

Chapter 5

Chapter 6

Chapter 7

Chapter 8

Chapter 9

Made in the USA
Monee, IL
17 August 2021

75929344R00153